AI WEIWEI
YOURS TRULY

AI WEIWEI
YOURS TRULY

Art, Human Rights, and the Power of Writing a Letter

Edited by David Spalding / With essays by Ai Weiwei, Cheryl Haines, Jasmine Heiss, and David Spalding

AI WEIWEI YOURS TRULY

CHRONICLE BOOKS
San Francisco

Library of Congress Cataloging-in-Publication Data

Names: Spalding, David, editor.
Title: Ai Weiwei: Yours truly: art, human rights, and the power of writing a letter / edited by David Spalding; with essays by Ai Weiwei, Cheryl Haines, Jasmine Heiss, and David Spalding.
Other titles: Ai Weiwei (Chronicle Books (Firm))
Description: San Francisco, CA: Chronicle Books, 2018.
Identifiers: LCCN 2017046633 | ISBN 9781452159294 (pbk. : alk. paper)
Subjects: LCSH: Ai, Weiwei. Yours truly. | Political prisoners in art. | Letter writing in art.
Classification: LCC N7349.A5 A79 2018 | DDC 700/.45--dc23 LC record available at https://lccn.loc.gov/2017046633

Manufactured in Hong Kong.

Designed by Alice Chau
Typesetting by Kevin Wong

10 9 8 7 6 5 4 3 2 1

Chronicle Books LLC
680 Second Street
San Francisco, CA 94107
www.chroniclebooks.com

Following pages:

Page 6: Alcatraz Island seen from the San Francisco Bay

Page 8: Main cellhouse, Alcatraz Island

Pages 10 and 12: Ai Weiwei, *Yours Truly*, 2014 (detail); interactive installation: custom-designed postcards, racks, tables, chairs; part of *@Large: Ai Weiwei on Alcatraz*, Alcatraz Island, 2014–2015

Page 14: Ai Weiwei, *Trace*, 2014; installation: LEGO plastic bricks; part of *@Large: Ai Weiwei on Alcatraz*, Alcatraz Island, 2014–2015

Page 16: Ai Weiwei, *Refraction*, 2014 (detail); installation: Tibetan solar panels, steel; part of *@Large: Ai Weiwei on Alcatraz*, Alcatraz Island, 2014–2015

Page 18: Ai Weiwei, *With Wind*, 2014 (detail); installation: handmade kites (paper, silk and bamboo); part of *@Large: Ai Weiwei on Alcatraz*, Alcatraz Island, 2014–2015

Page 20: Ai Weiwei, *Stay Tuned*, 2014 (detail); sound installation: custom-made furniture, audio files, speakers; part of *@Large: Ai Weiwei on Alcatraz*, Alcatraz Island, 2014–2015

Page 22: Ai Weiwei, *Illumination*, 2014 (detail); sound installation: audio files, speakers; part of *@Large: Ai Weiwei on Alcatraz*, Alcatraz Island, 2014–2015

Page 24: Ai Weiwei, *Blossom*, 2014 (detail); installation: porcelain, hospital fixtures (sinks, toilets, bathtubs); part of *@Large: Ai Weiwei on Alcatraz*, Alcatraz Island, 2014–2015

CONTENTS

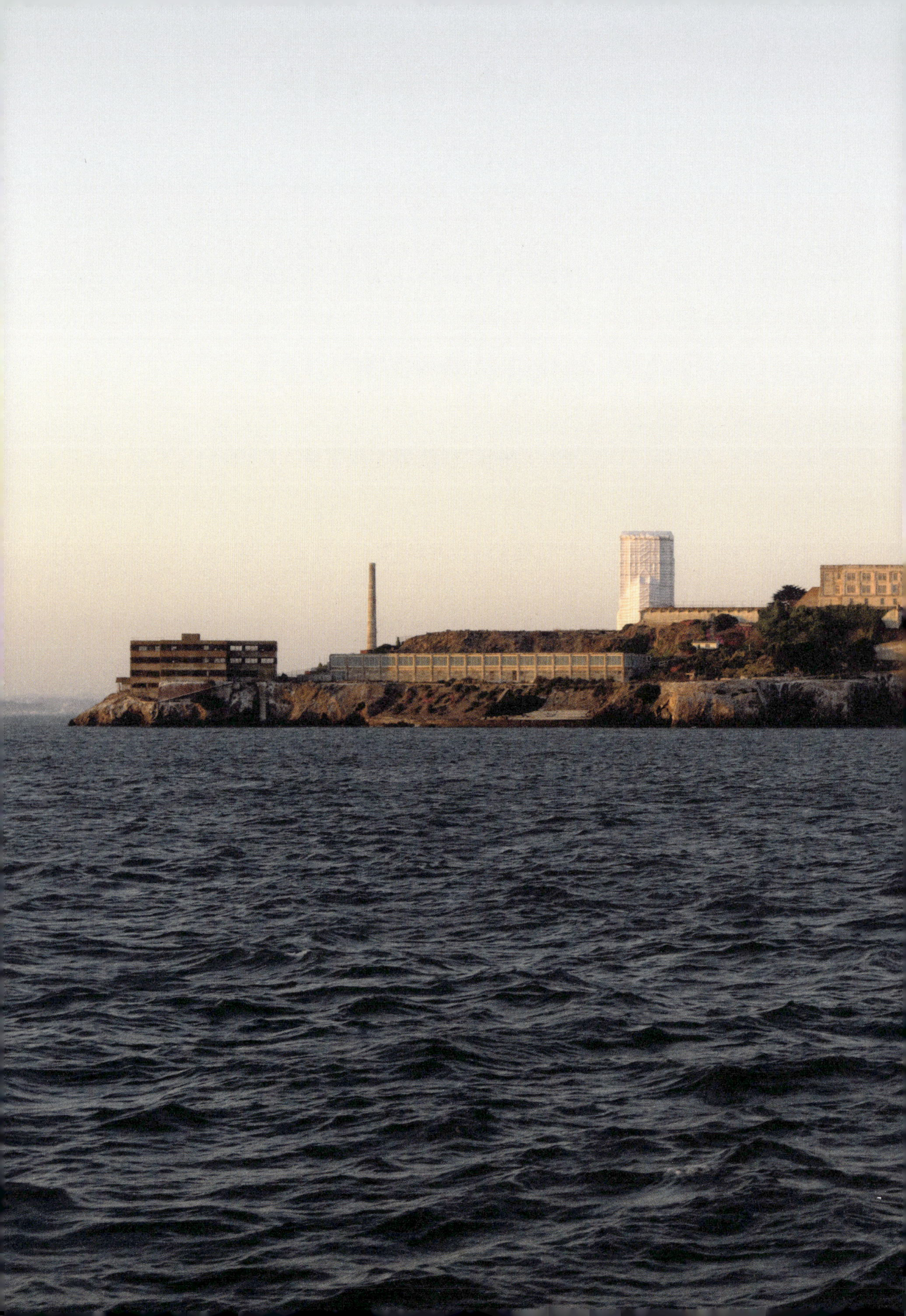

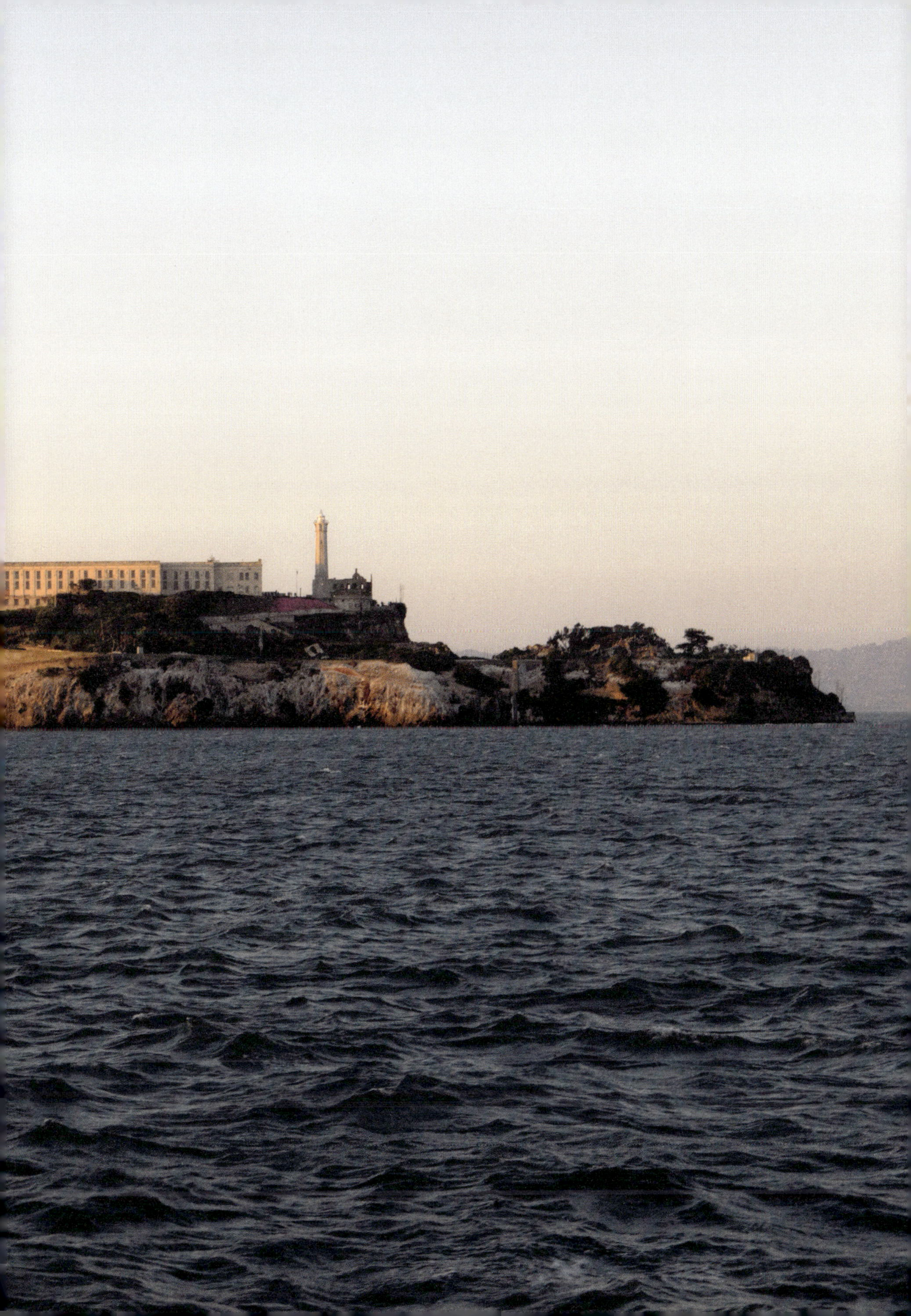

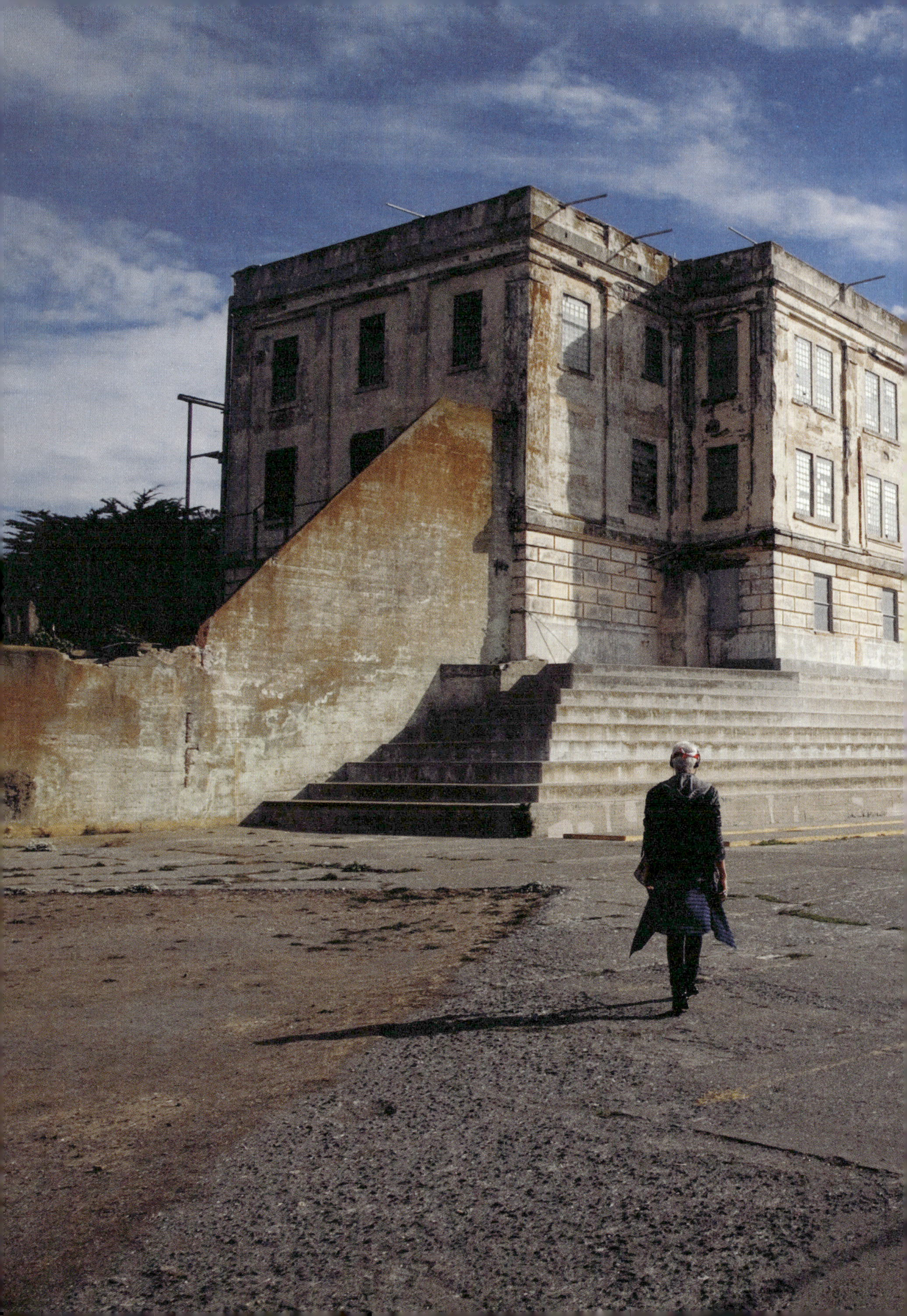

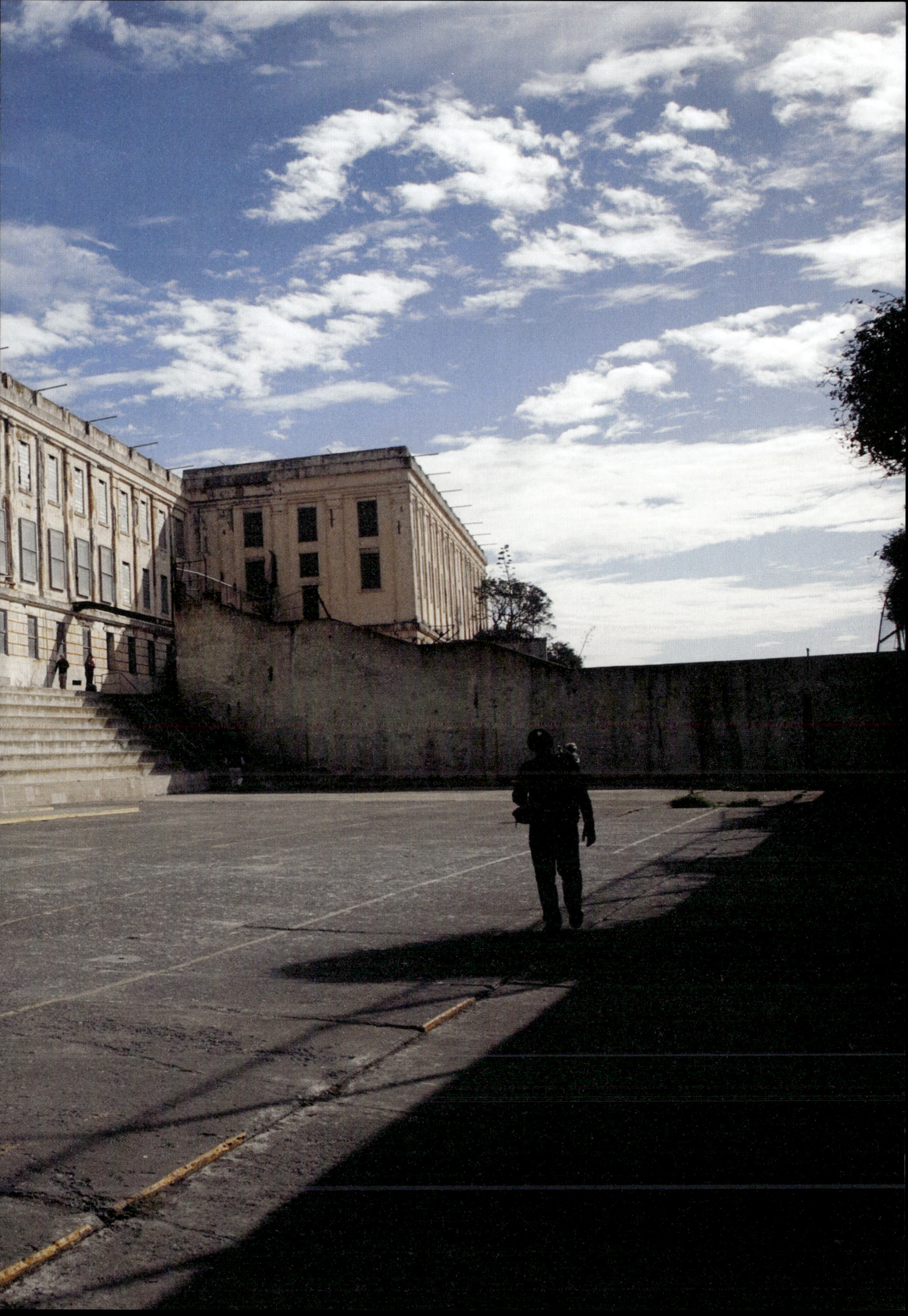

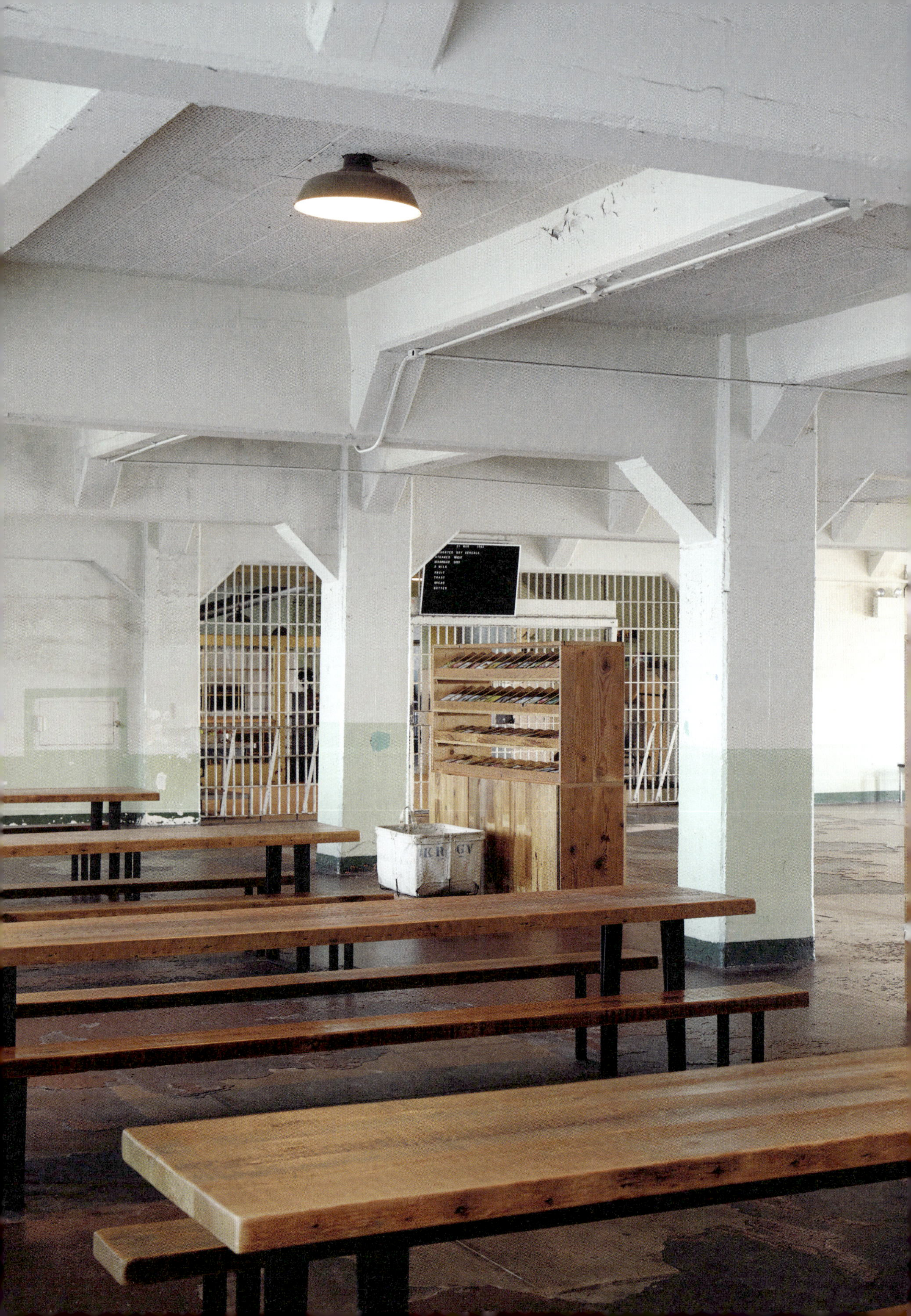

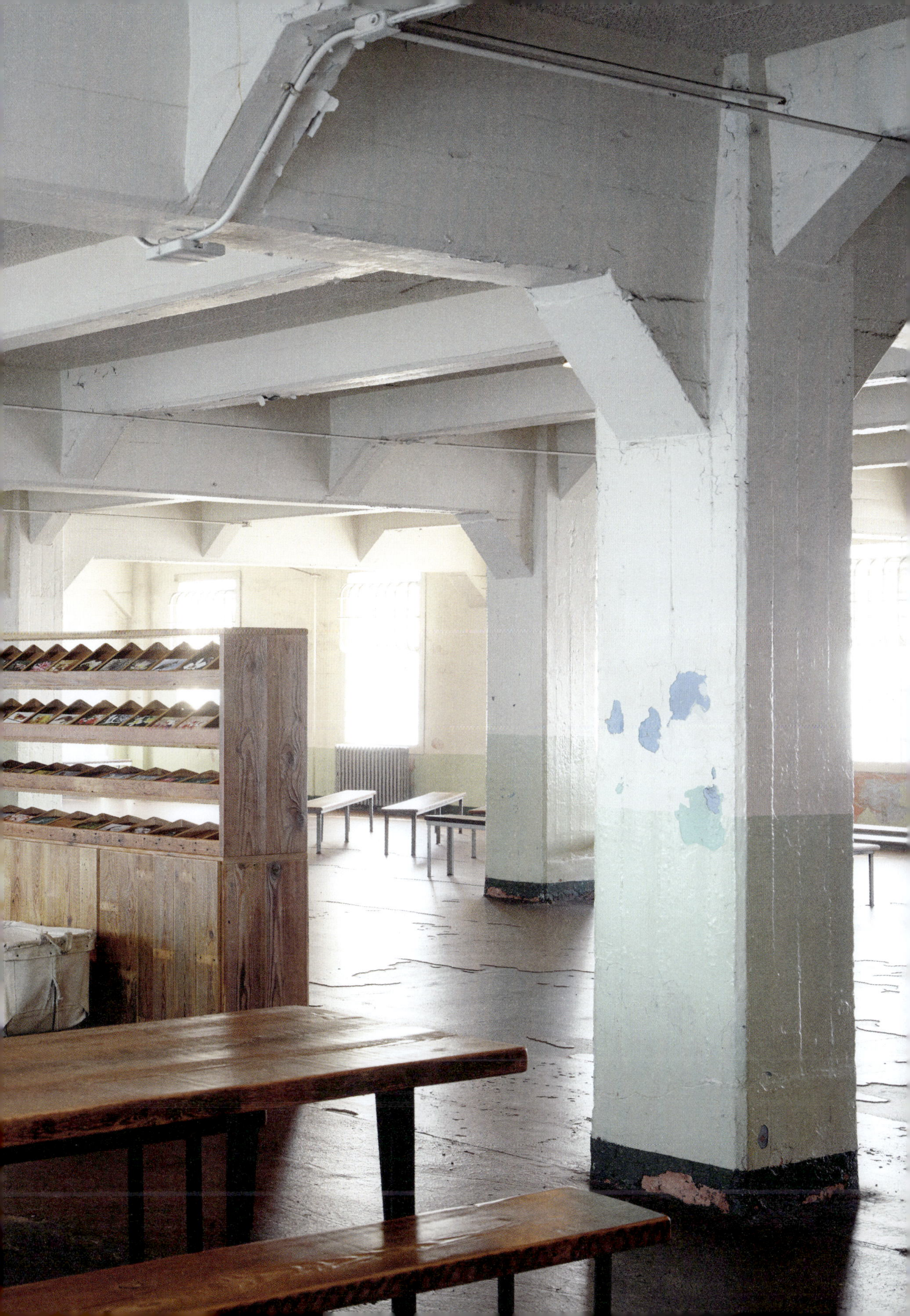

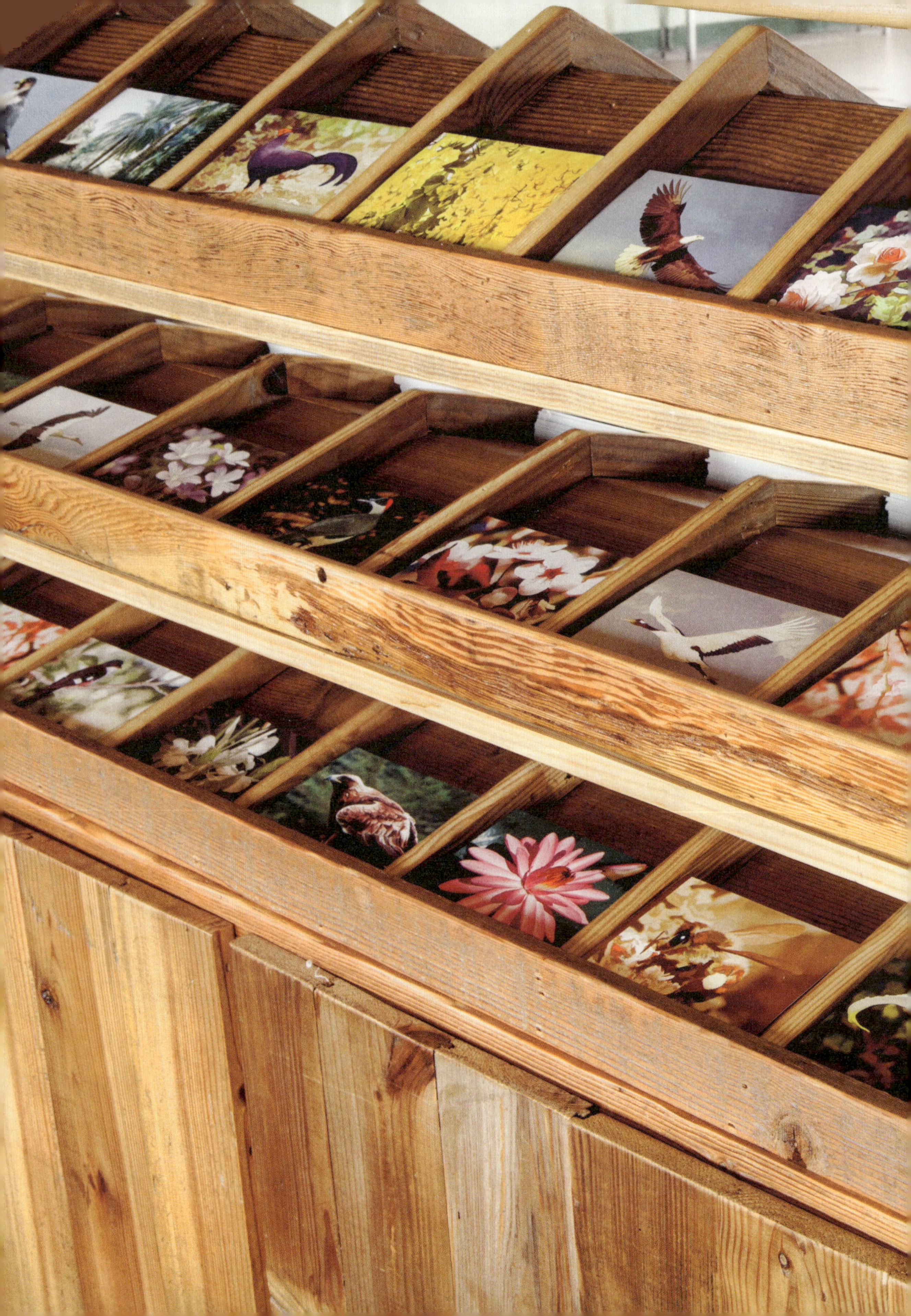

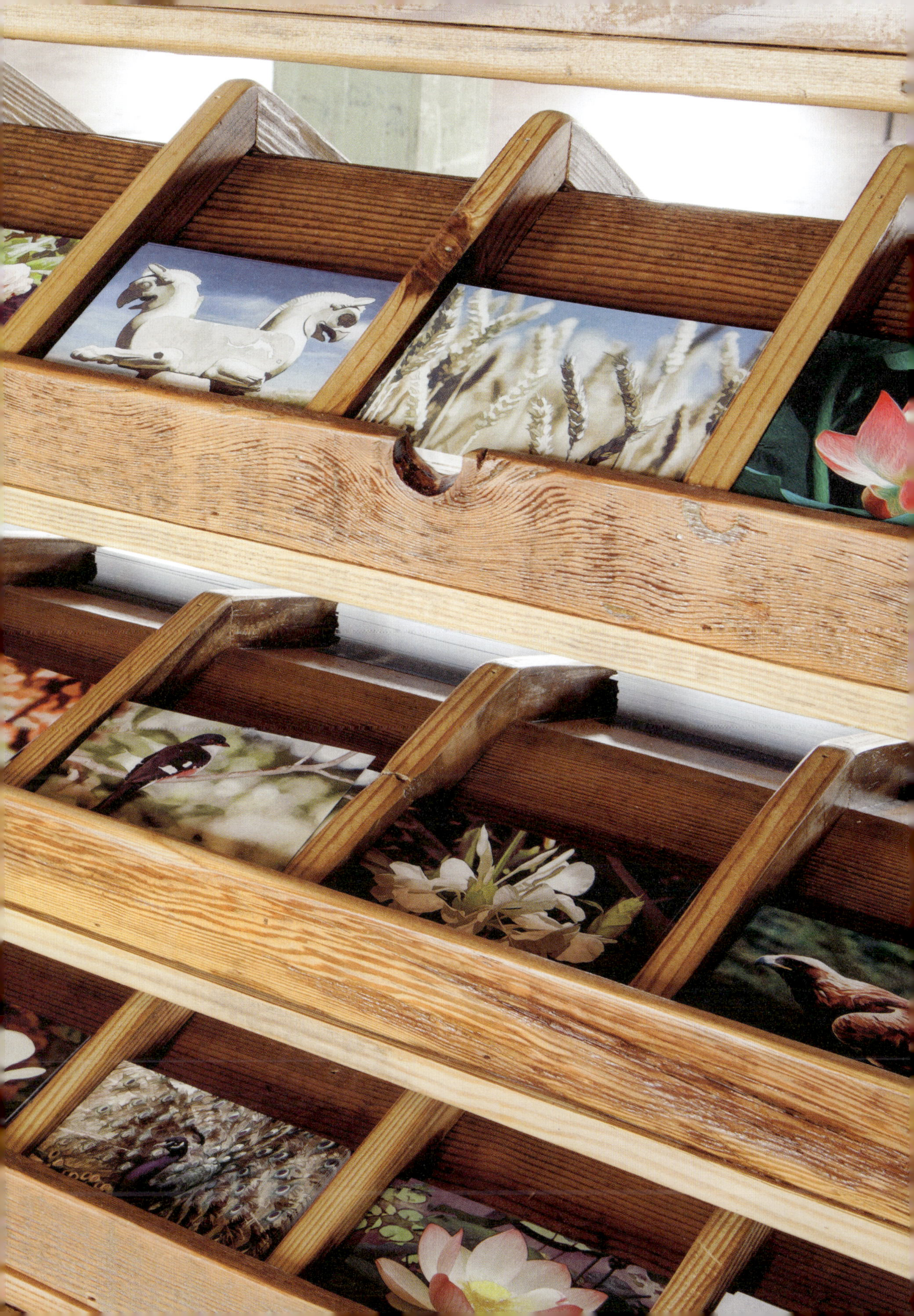

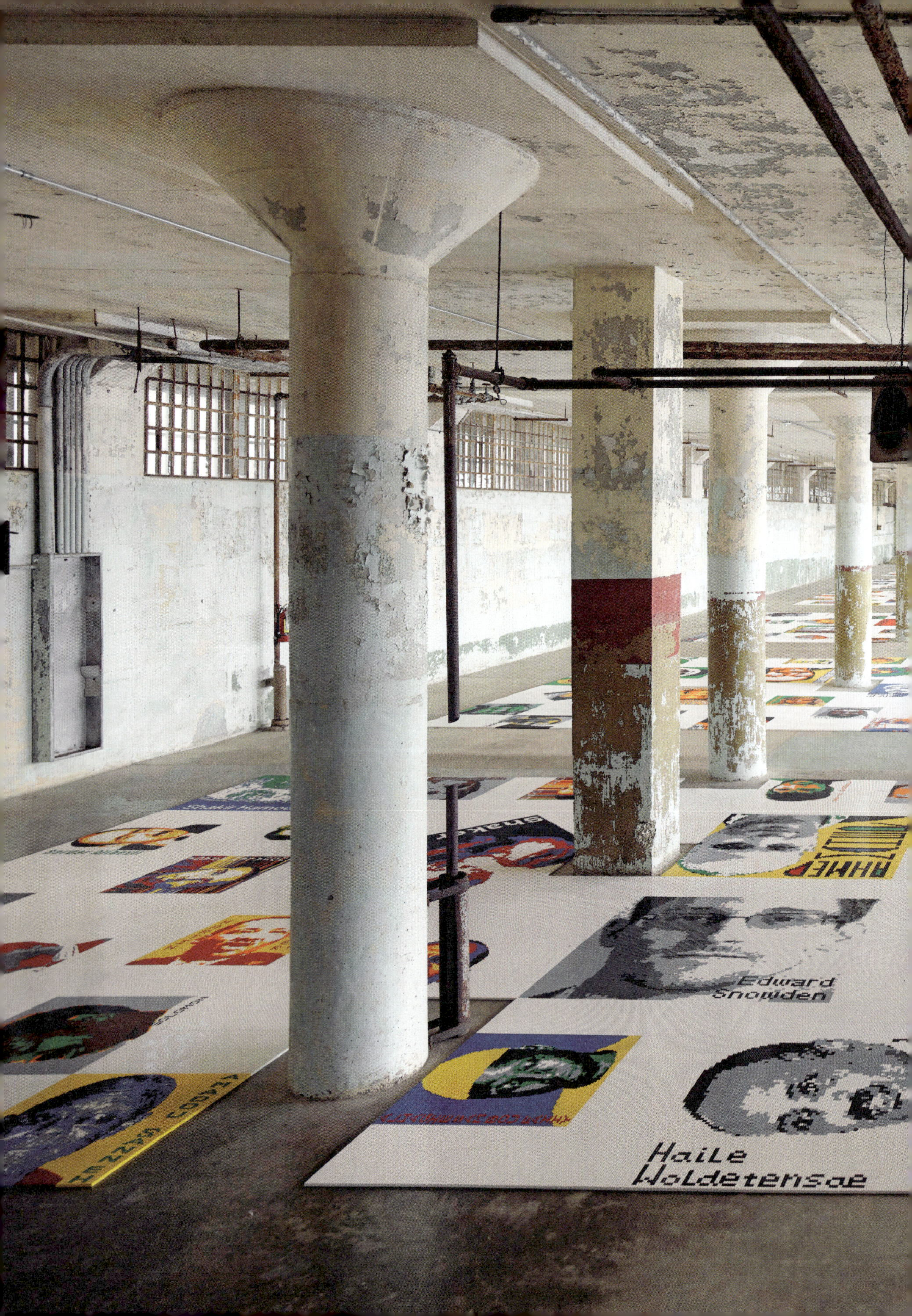
Edward
Snowden
Haile
Woldetensae

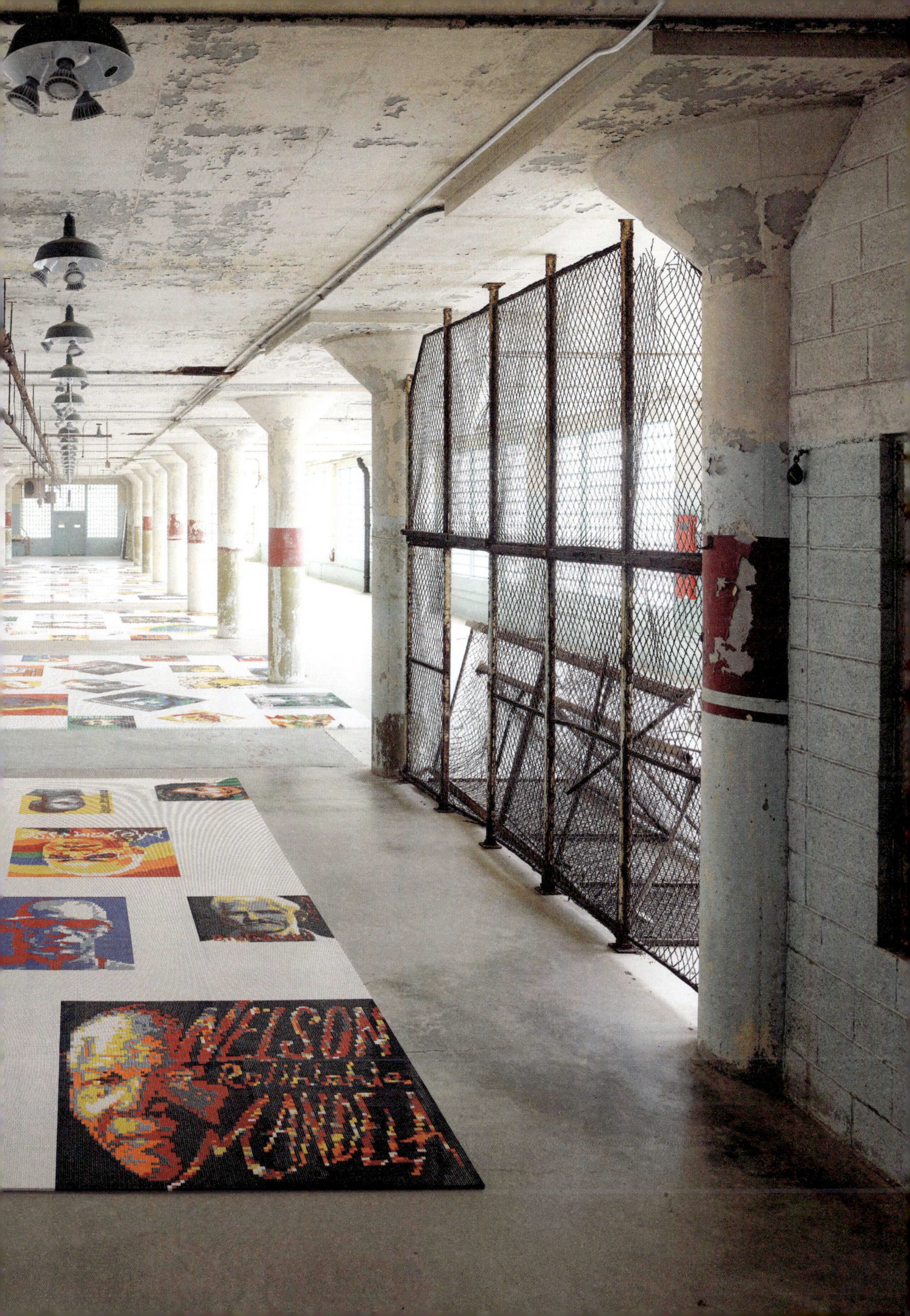
NELSON
MANDELA

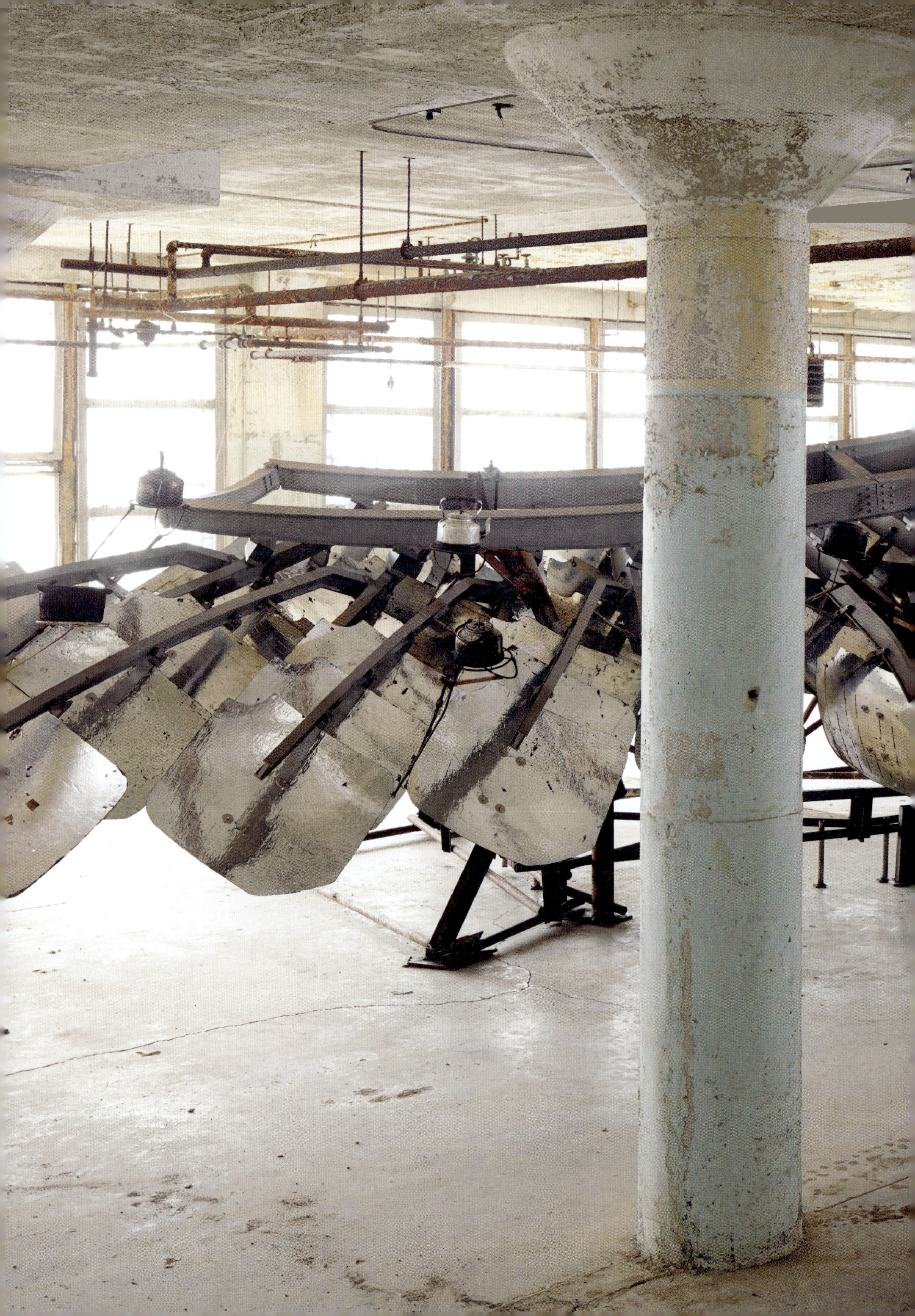

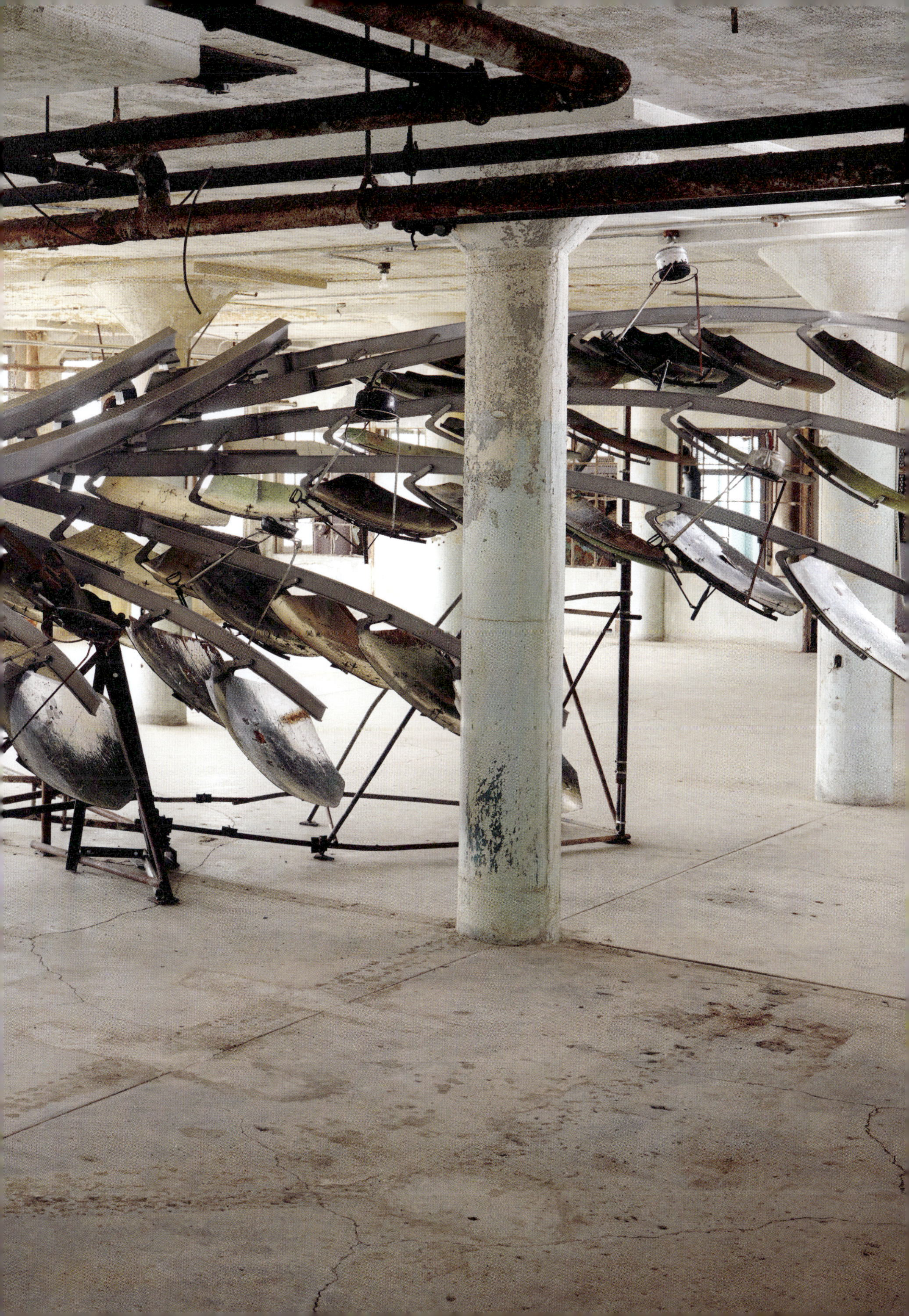

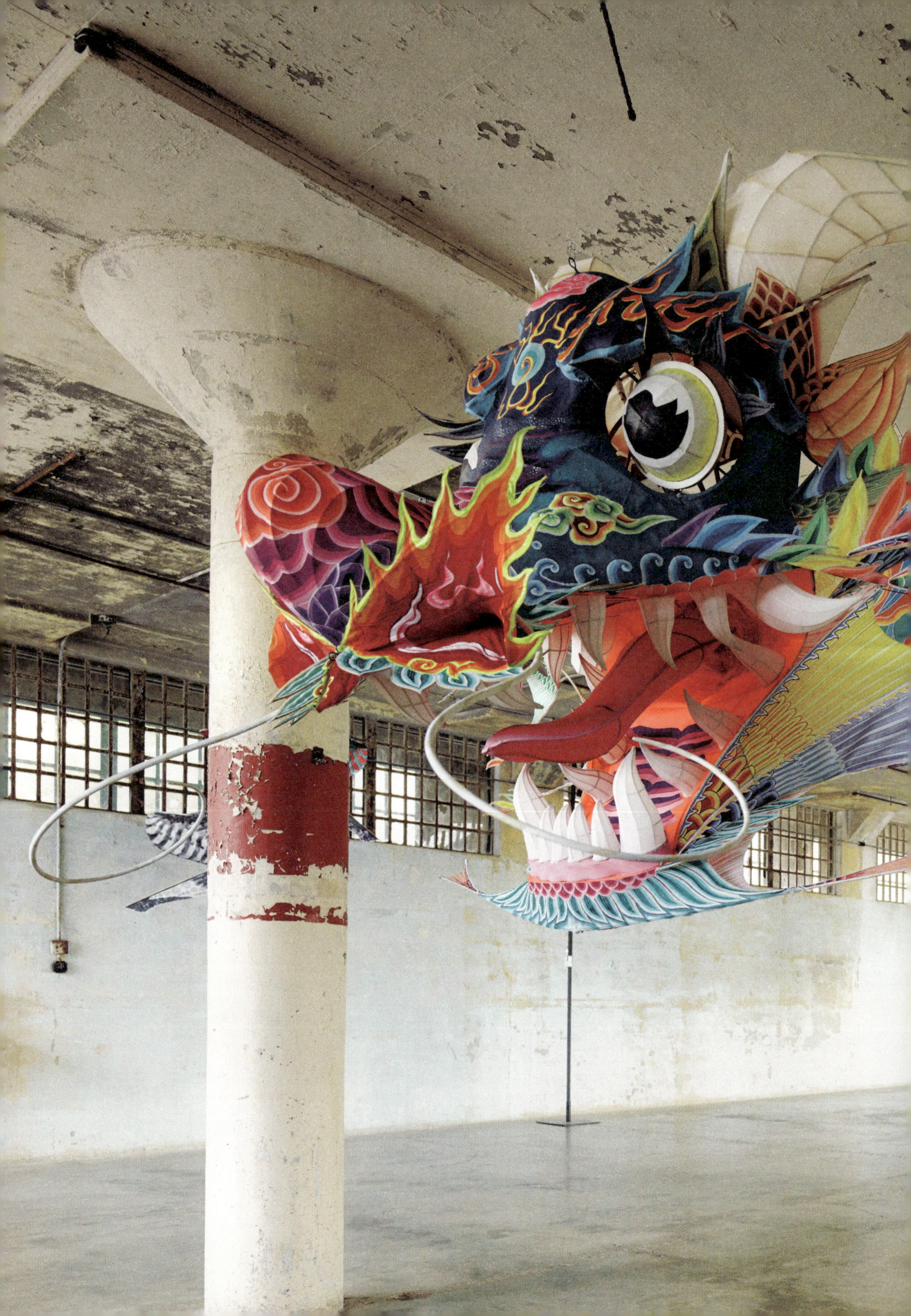

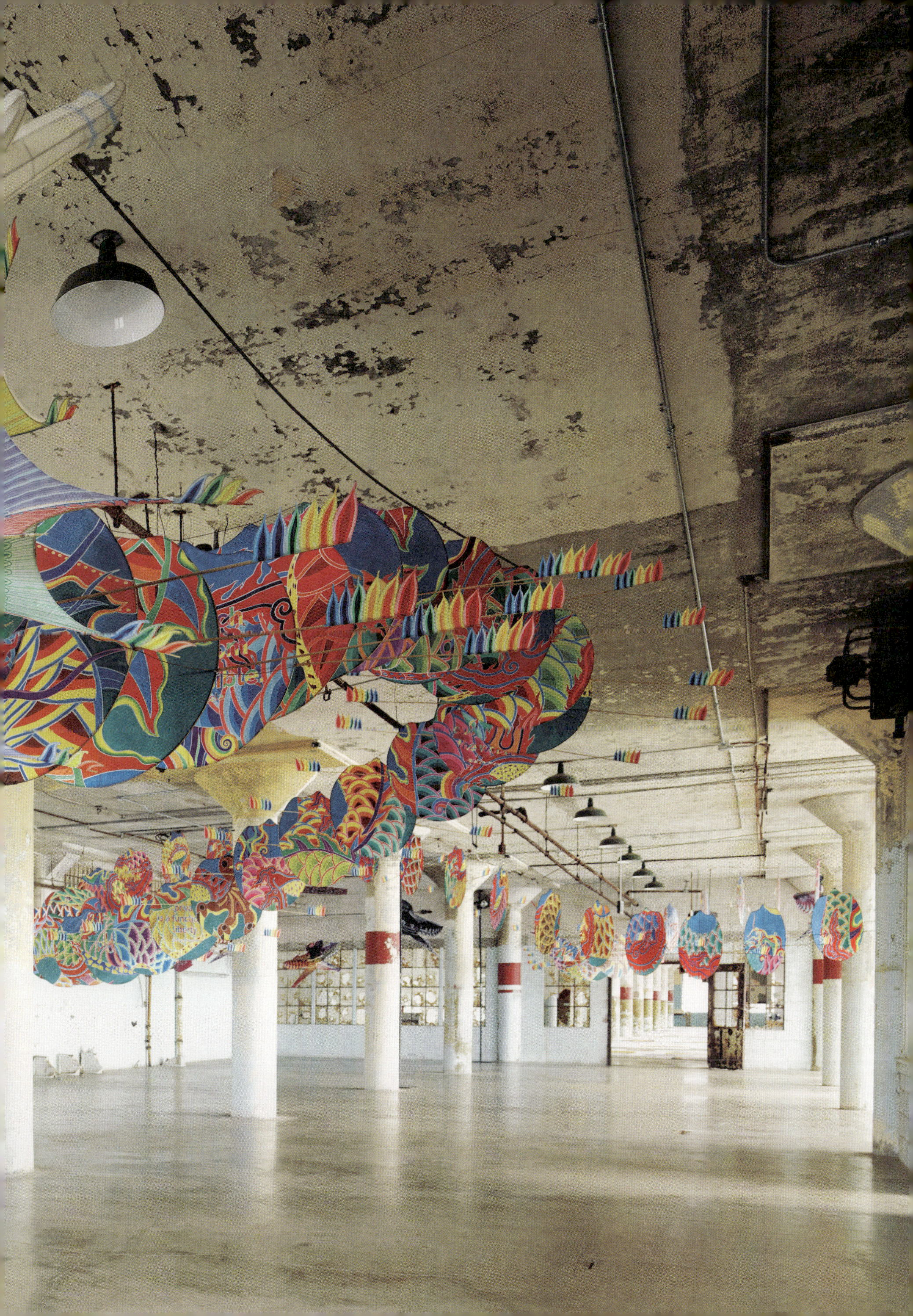

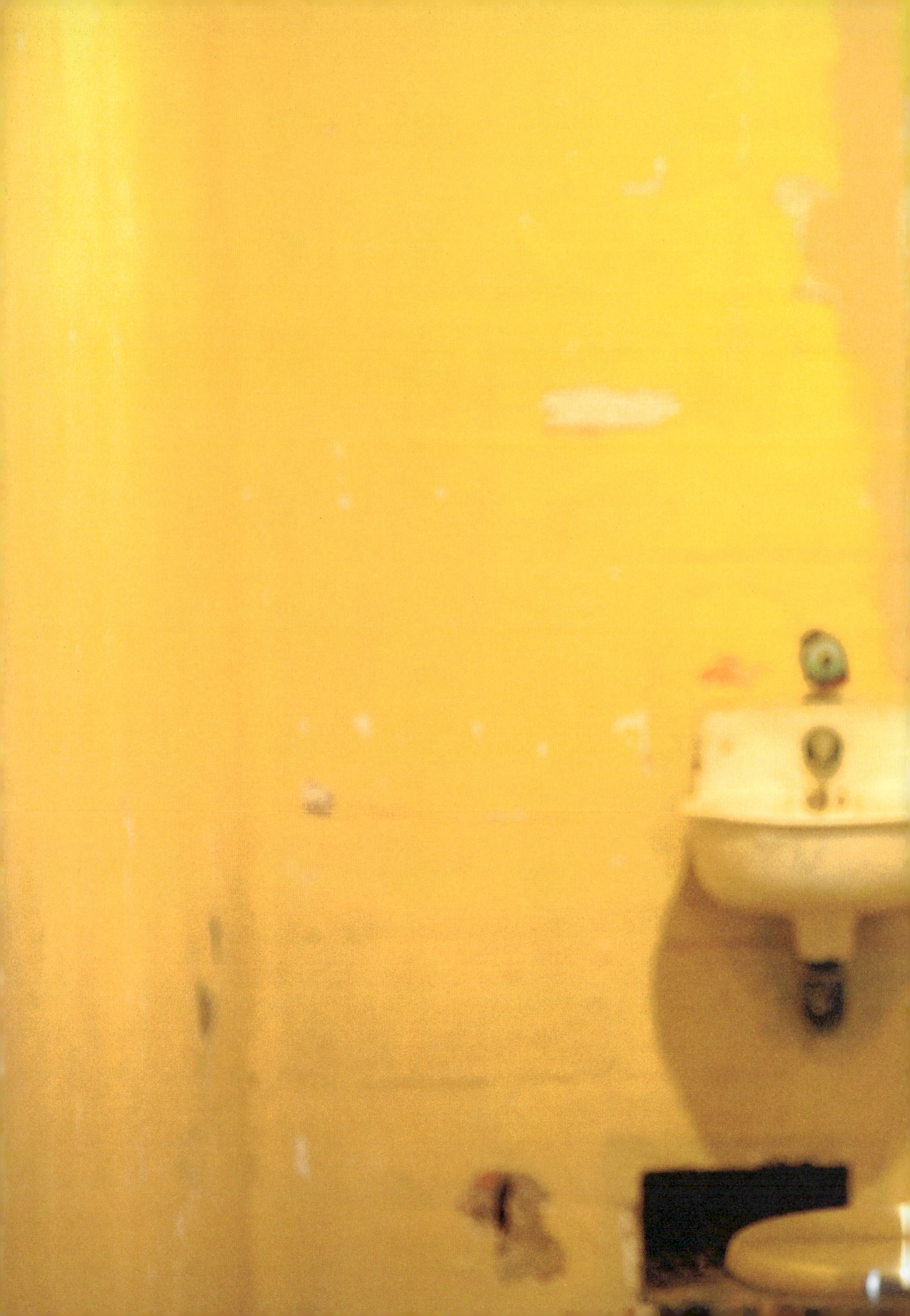

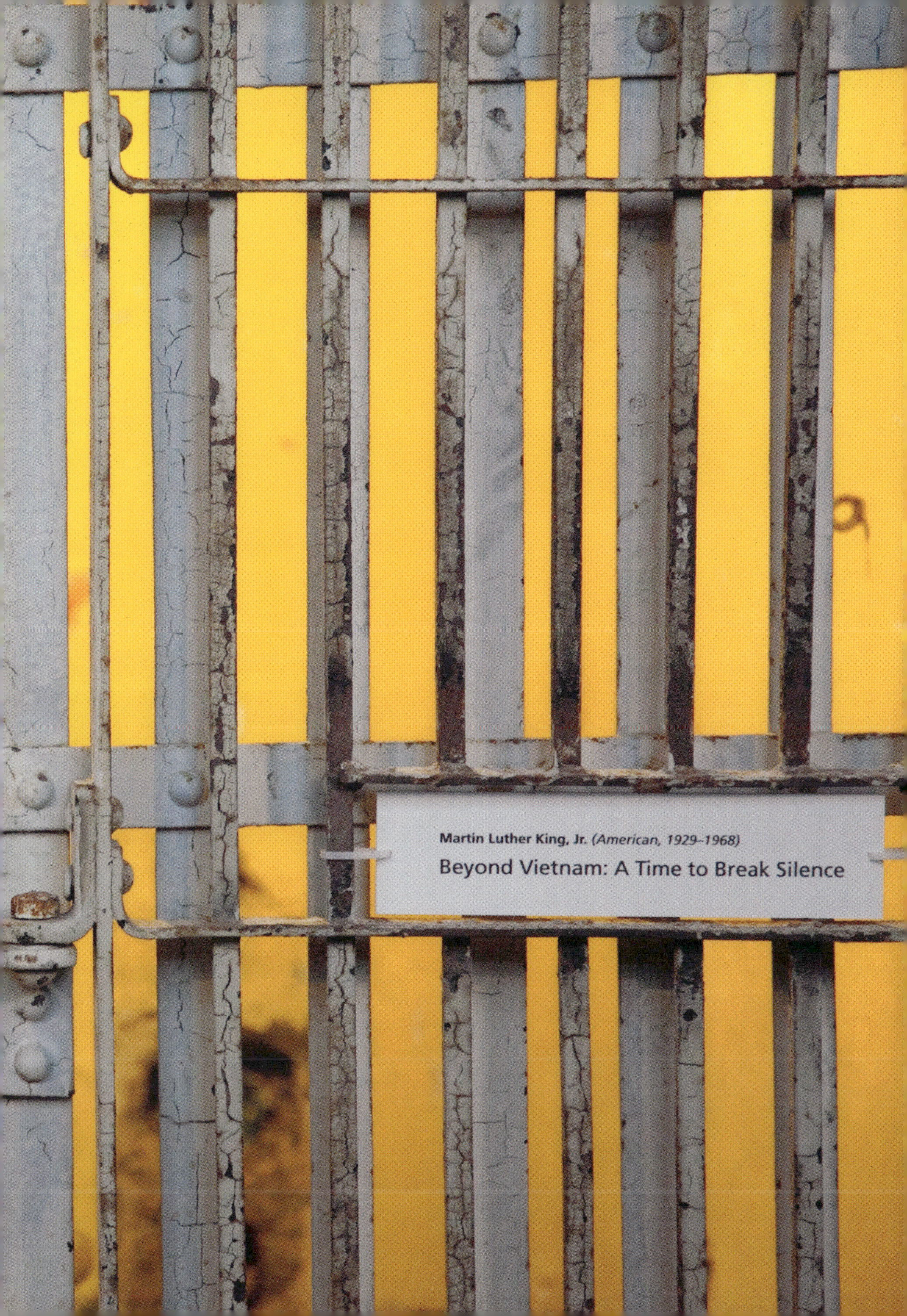
Martin Luther King, Jr. (American, 1929–1968)
Beyond Vietnam: A Time to Break Silence

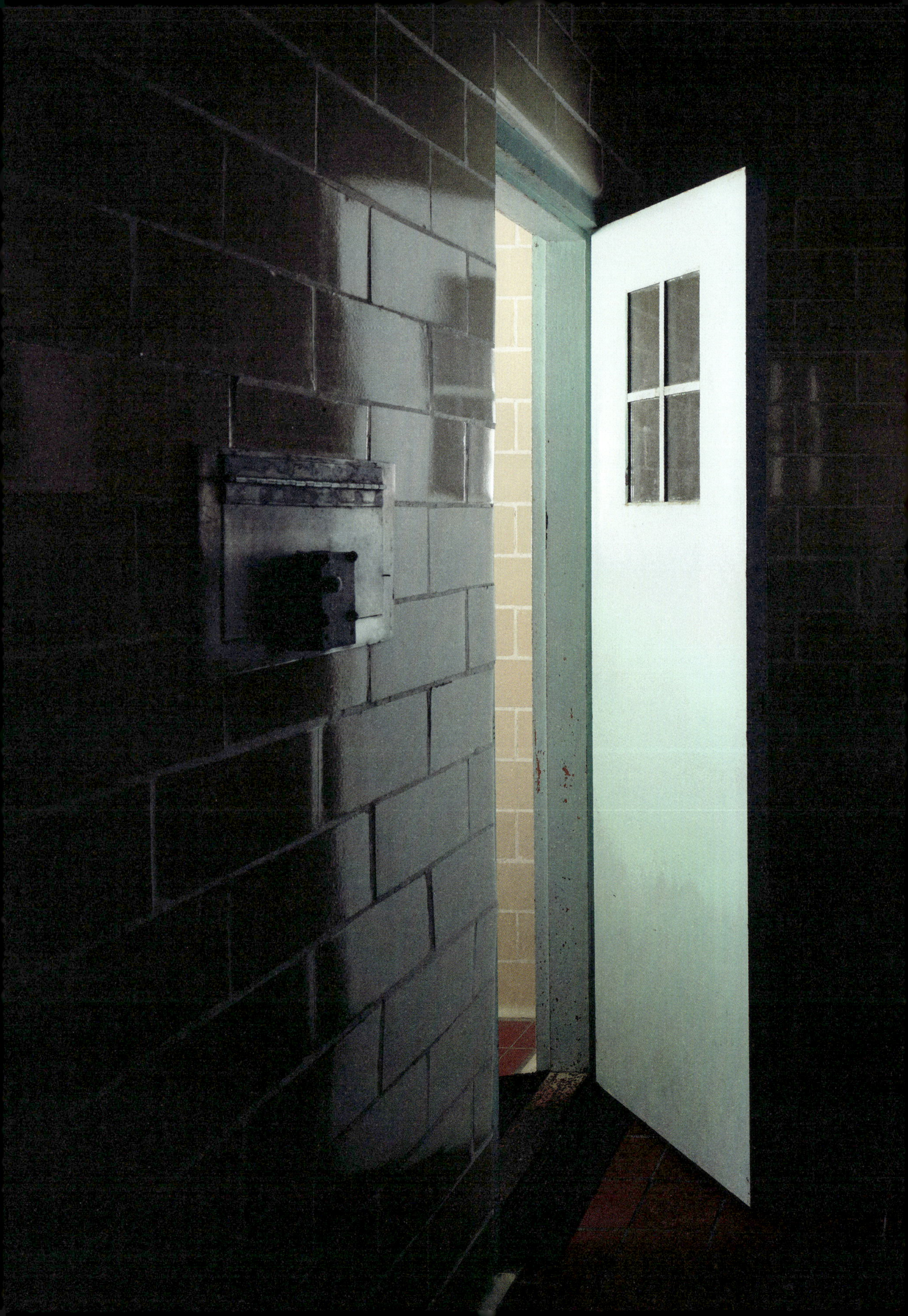

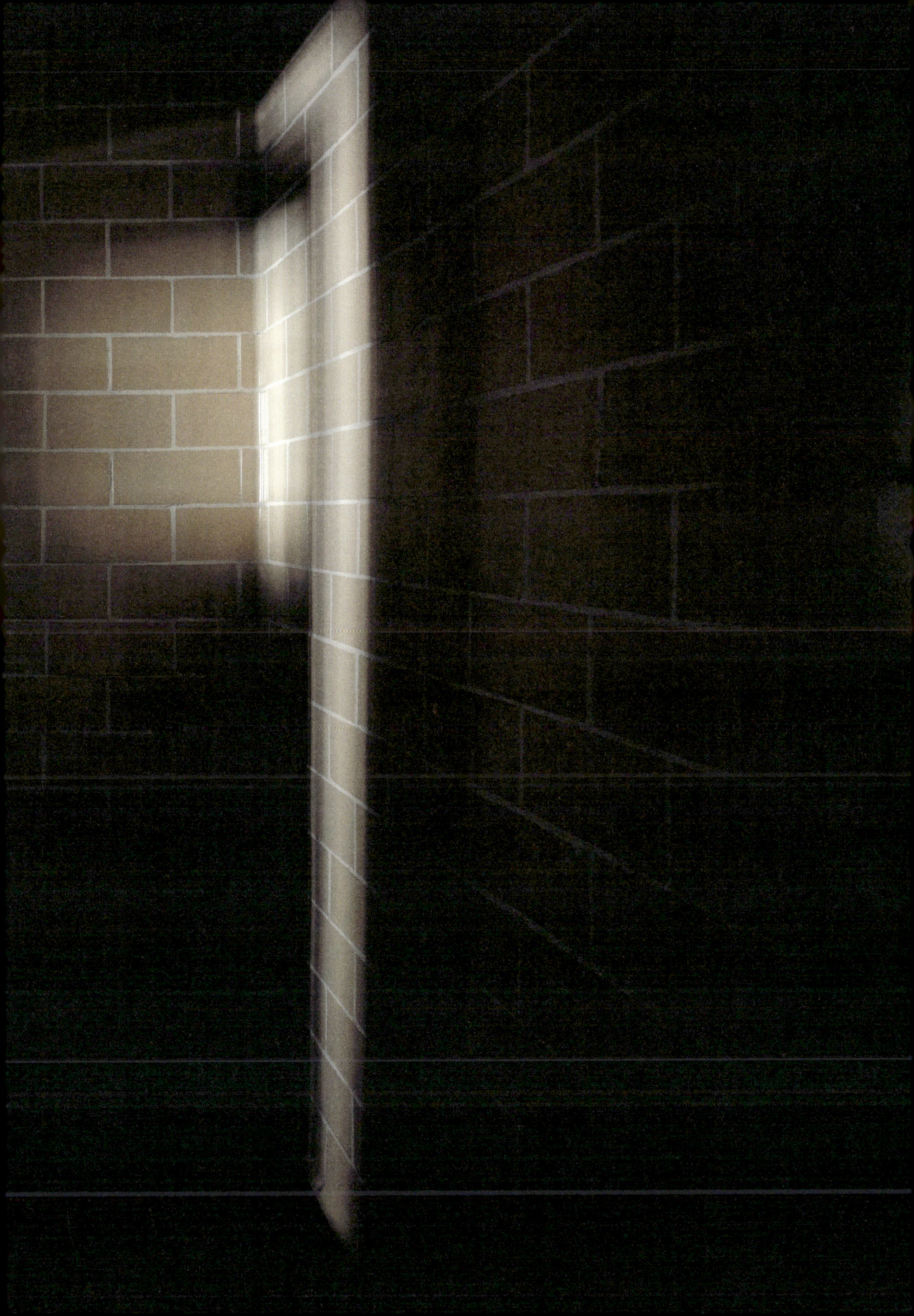

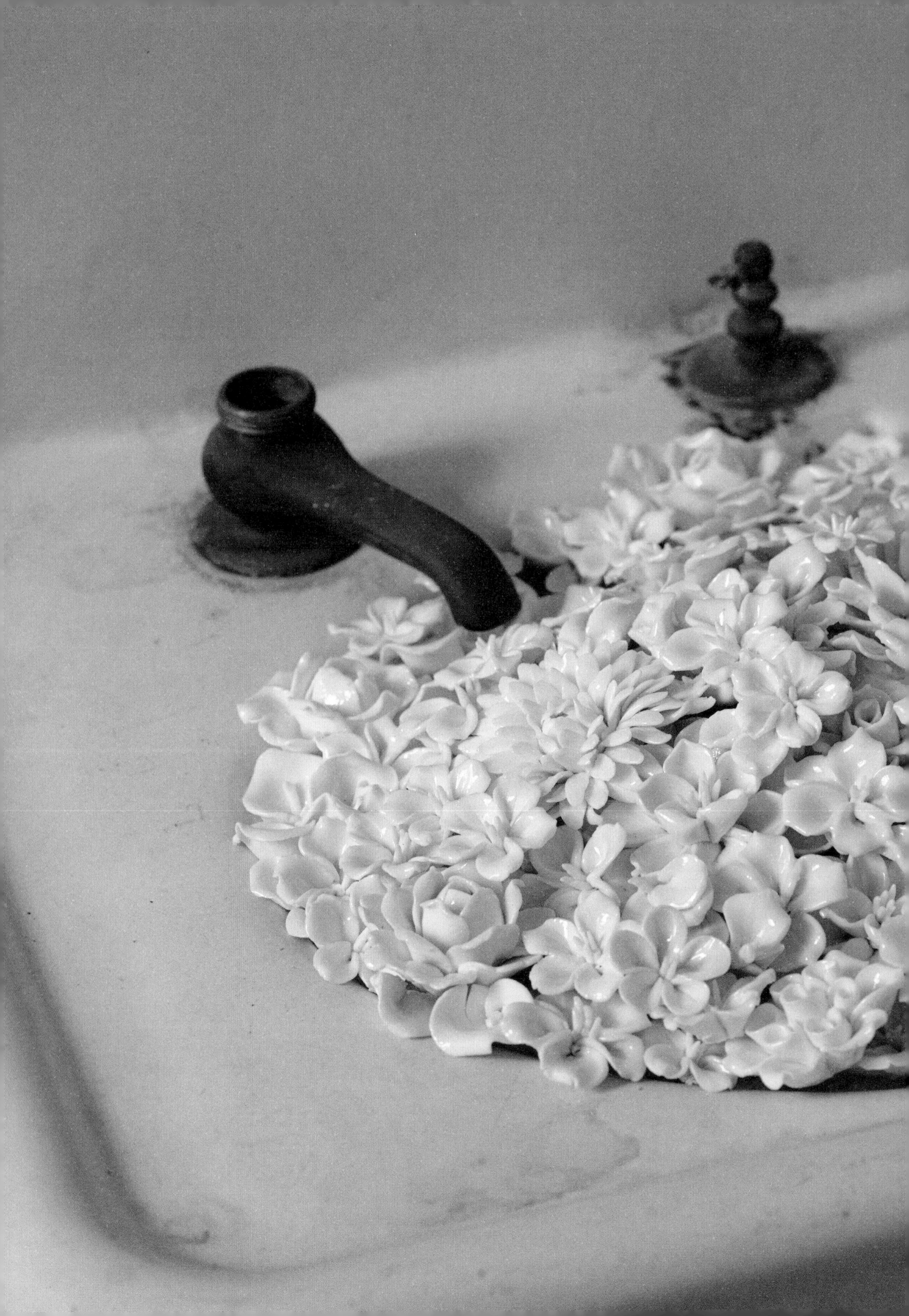

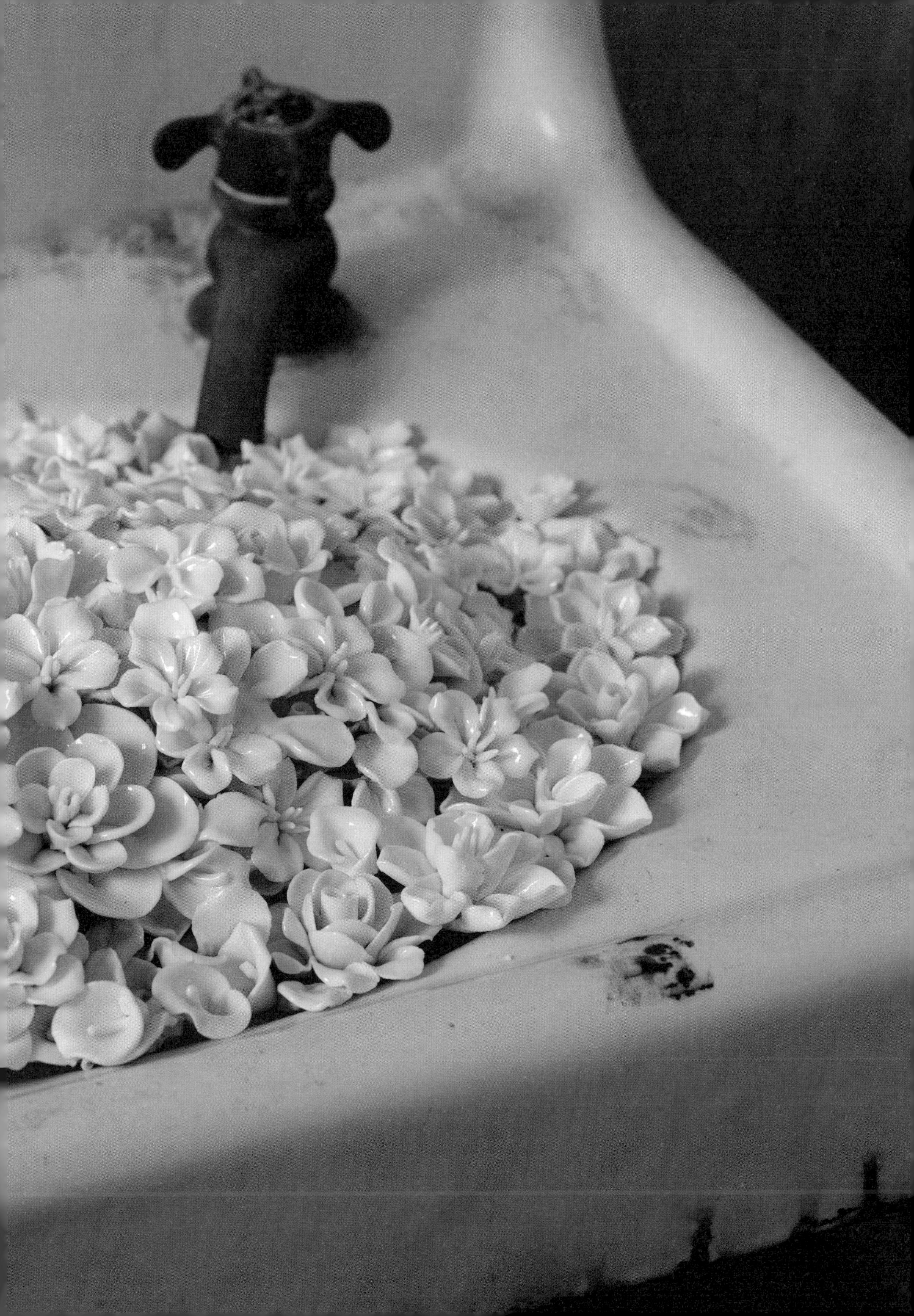

PREFACE

David Spalding Director of Publications, FOR-SITE Foundation

"To be free is not merely to cast off one's chains, but to live in a way that respects and enhances the freedom of others."

—Nelson Mandela

"Never doubt that a small group of thoughtful, committed citizens can change the world.™ Indeed, it's the only thing that ever has."

—Margaret Mead

We can all be agents of change. But sometimes the challenges that surround us make it hard to know where to begin. This book aims to inspire readers to take action in the struggle for human rights, both at home and abroad. It starts with a simple and direct expression of empathy: the sending of a postcard.

The story of *Yours Truly* began with the remarkable exhibition *@Large: Ai Weiwei on Alcatraz*, organized in 2014 by San Francisco's FOR-SITE Foundation in collaboration with the National Parks Service and the Golden Gate National Parks Conservancy. Following his own detention and the loss of his passport at the hands of the Chinese authorities, the outspoken artist and activist Ai Weiwei transformed the former island penitentiary of Alcatraz into an artistic platform. The resulting exhibition engaged the public in a very personal conversation about the plight of prisoners of conscience around the world.

Trace was one of the eight new artworks that comprised the *@Large* exhibition. Made from over 1.2 million LEGO bricks exactingly assembled to spread across the floor of an old prison building, the work depicts the faces and names of 176 brave individuals who have been incarcerated or exiled due to their beliefs, affiliations, and nonviolent expressions of dissent. As the father of a young son, Ai Weiwei understood the gravitational pull that LEGOs could have on children and their families. He hoped to attract the broadest possible audience using his chosen medium, including those who might not otherwise take note of these prisoners and their stories. Nearby binders, containing brief synopses of each prisoner's case, were readily available to visitors who wanted to learn more—and many did, poring over the pages, wondering what they might do to help.

The work's companion piece, *Yours Truly*, answered this question. Located at the exhibition's terminus, *Yours Truly* repurposed the prison's former dining hall into a space of contemplation and communication. There, visitors were invited to compose messages to many of the prisoners seen in *Trace*, using pre-addressed postcards emblazoned with the national birds and flowers of the countries where they were being detained.

Before the exhibition opened, no one was sure how the public, already weary from the ferry ride to Alcatraz and the lengthy tour of the prison, might respond. But from the outset, the room with the postcards was a hive of activity. The seating areas, designed by the artist to resemble picnic tables, quickly filled with people absorbing and discussing the gravity of the prisoners' situations, carefully choosing cards, and quietly crafting messages of hope, compassion, and concern. Art guides, trained to help visitors navigate and respond to this complex material, reported having striking conversations with people for whom the exhibition had proved enlightening. Soon, the completed postcards began piling up faster than anyone had anticipated, until there were well over ninety thousand. Each one is an affecting

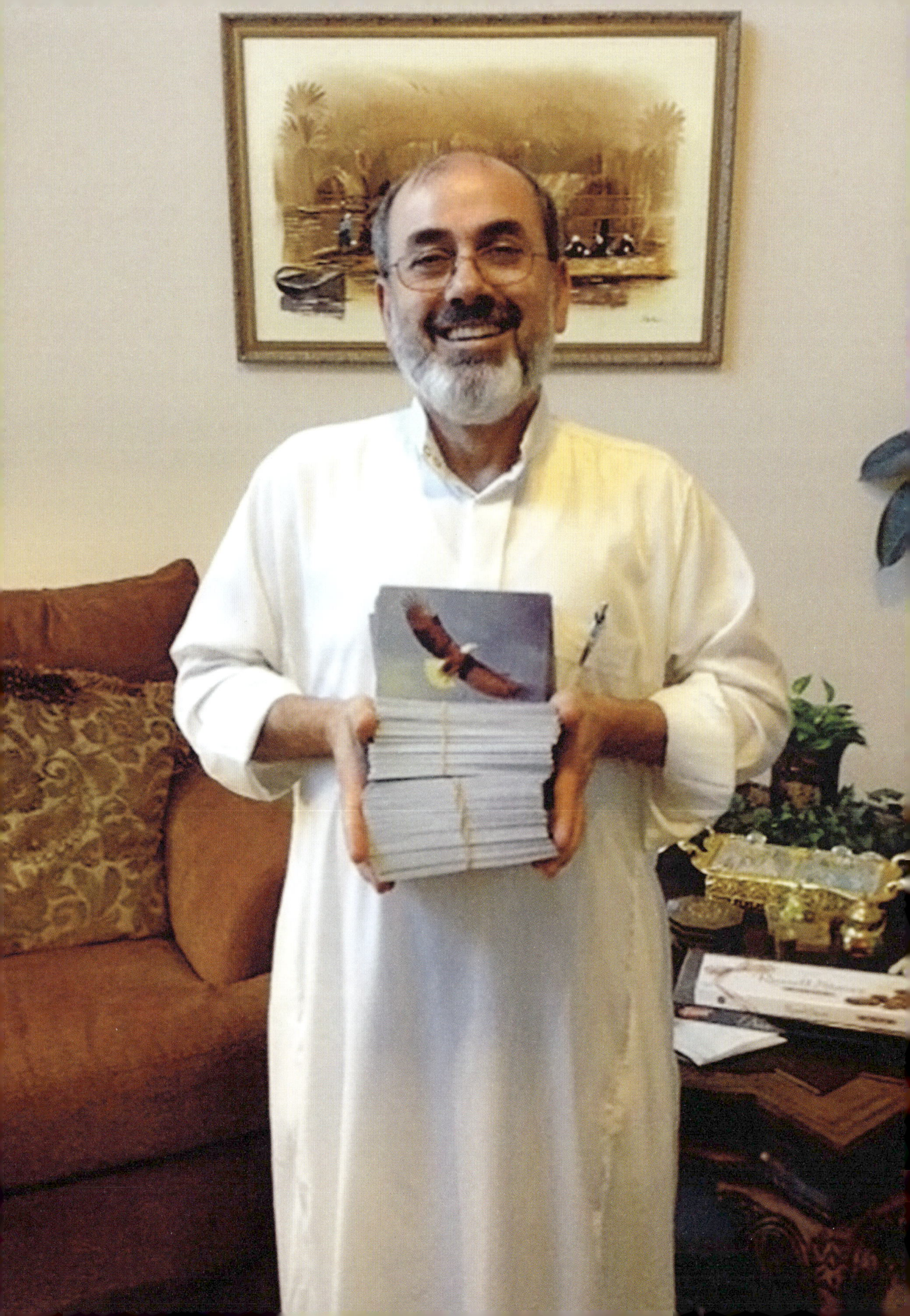

testament to our greatest shared capacity—an awakened sense of empathy.

Over and over again, isolation is said to be the most difficult aspect of incarceration, making solitary confinement one of the cruelest punishments imaginable. Every postcard was a message in a bottle, its arrival at the intended destination more of a wish than an inevitability. One could only hope that those prisoners who were receiving the cards—if any actually were—would be fortified by the knowledge that strangers, often far away, knew their stories and wanted to offer support.

Then something astonishing began to happen. The FOR-SITE Foundation started hearing back from the prisoners and their families. The messages from Alcatraz were getting through, and people had been moved—even sustained—by the public's outpouring of concern for their welfare and causes.

This book documents the experience of *Yours Truly* through photographs of visitors to the exhibition and scans of some of the postcards they wrote, each one an attempt to make someone else's suffering bearable. It also traces the ripples made by the cards when they finally reached their recipients. In the pages that follow, former prisoners of conscience John Kiriakou, Ahmed Maher, Chelsea Manning, Ebrahim Sharif Al Sayed, and Irom Sharmila Chanu, as well as their loved ones, share stories of activism and incarceration and reflect on the impact of the *Yours Truly* postcards. Remarkably, all five of these individuals were released from prison before the book's completion, a testament to their endurance and to the possibility that these postcards aided them on their journeys homeward.

Amnesty International worked tirelessly with the FOR-SITE Foundation and Ai Weiwei to vet the original list of nonviolent prisoners featured in the *@Large* exhibition's postcards and LEGO portraits. In 2015, following the show's closing, the organization honored the artist with its Ambassador of Conscience Award, "a celebration of those unique individuals who have used their talents to inspire many, many others to take injustice personally." This book seeks to extend the incredible reach of Ai Weiwei's original *Yours Truly* project, and to inspire you to take the issue of global human rights personally, by telling the stories of a handful of resilient and relatable individuals and inviting you to send postcards of your own. The four cards attached to the flaps of this book, modeled on the original *Yours Truly* postcards and addressed to prisoners of conscience who remain incarcerated, offer a place to start.

As the rhetoric of racism and xenophobia threatens to cloud the vision of so many, our fundamental human rights feel more fragile than at any time in recent history. If there has ever been a moment to stand up for our beliefs, it is now. The former prisoners of conscience featured in this book did just that, sometimes with grave consequences, but they also changed the course of history. It is more pressing than ever to choose empathy over fear and to ask yourself how you might help those whose rights have already been violated. It is a question to which this book offers one small answer, but the possibilities are limited only by your imagination.

Opposite: Former Iraqi-American prisoner of conscience Shakir Hamoodi with a stack of *Yours Truly* postcards he received during his incarceration, 2014.

Following page: Bags of completed postcards were routinely collected from Alcatraz Island for processing.

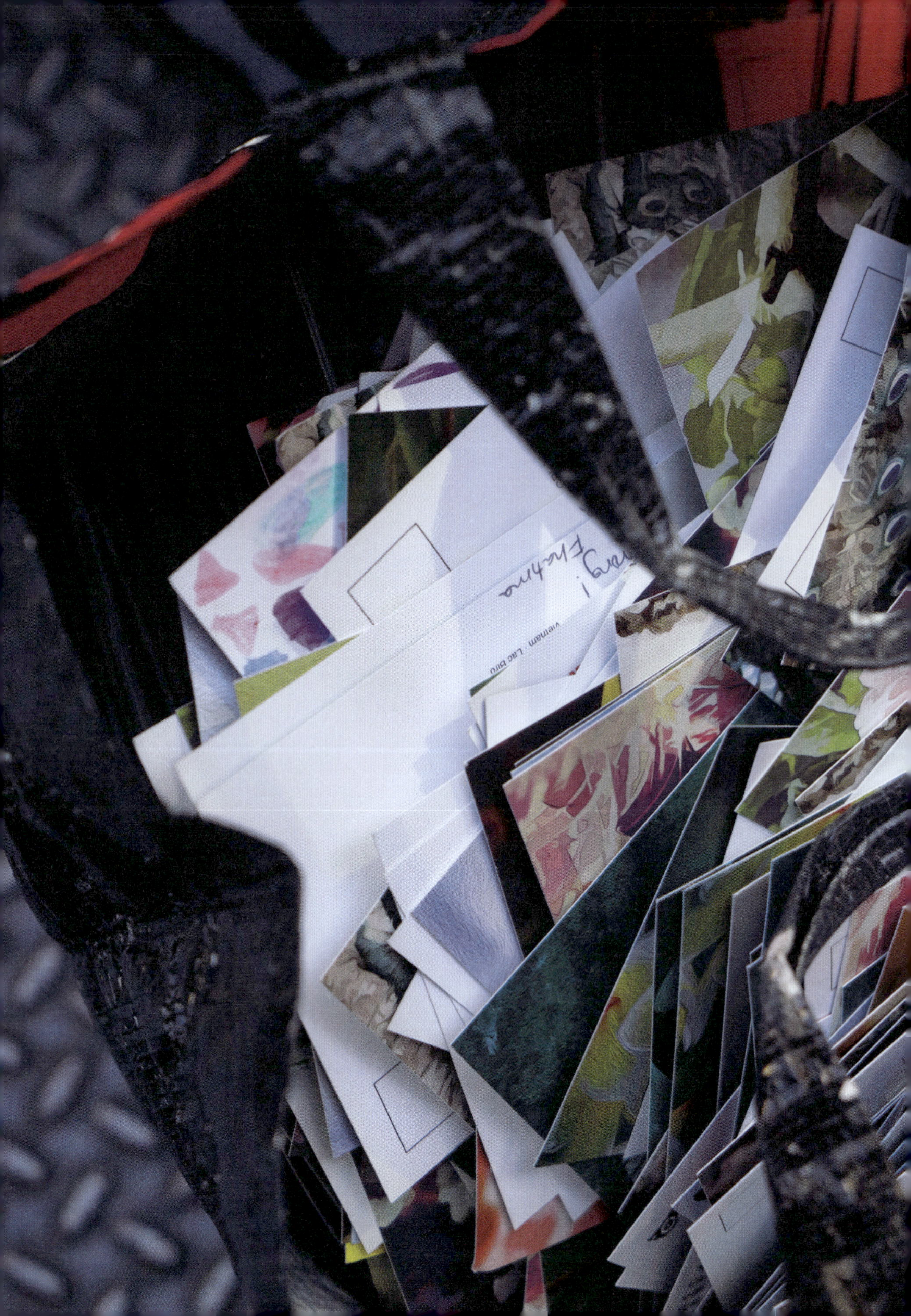

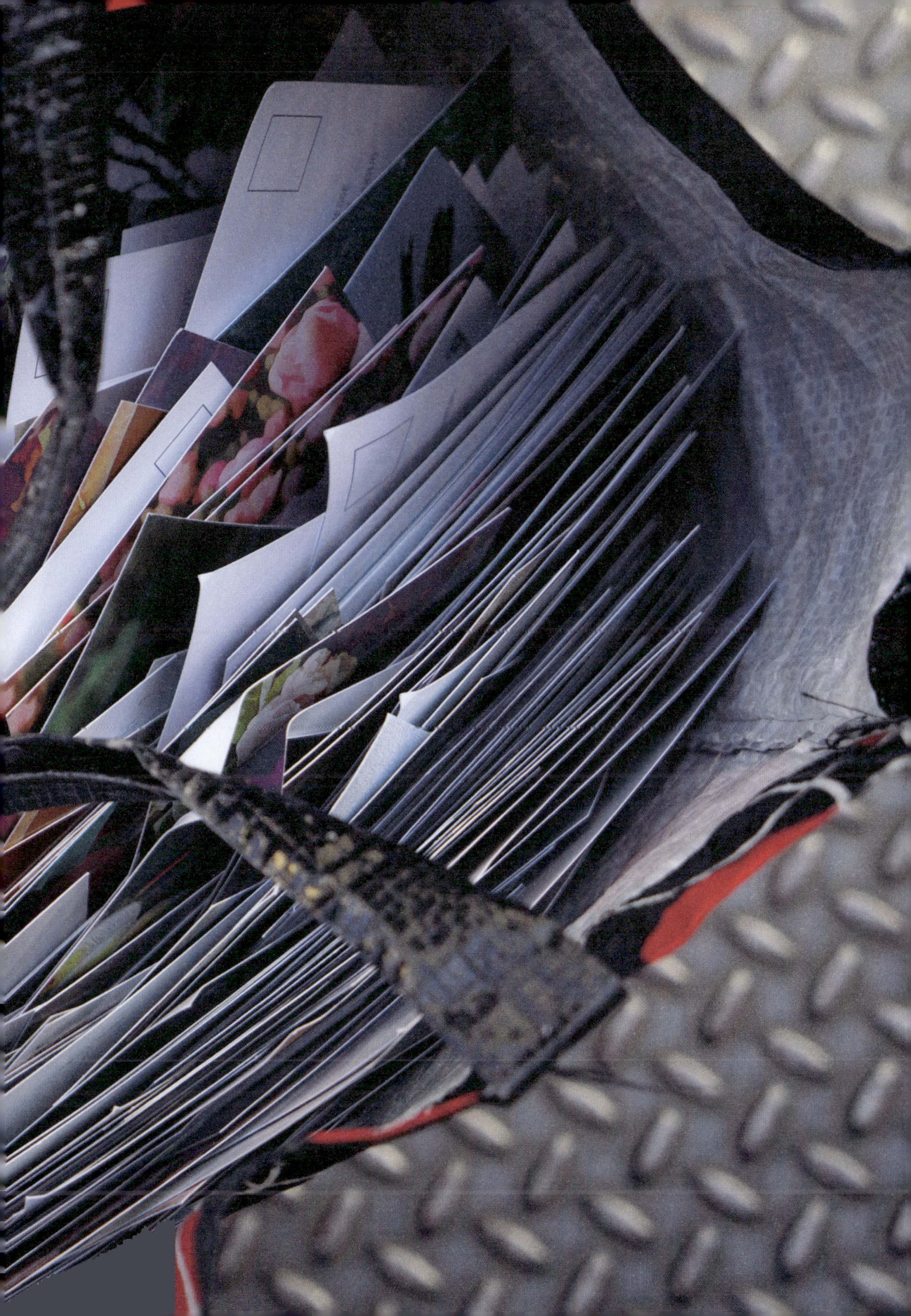

YOU ARE NOT FORGOTTEN: THE STORY OF *YOURS TRULY*

Cheryl Haines Founding Executive Director, FOR-SITE Foundation

The fundamental need for communication is something that Ai Weiwei understands deeply. In 2011, the Chinese authorities detained the artist for eighty-one days, holding him in a secret location and subjecting him to ongoing interrogations—punishment for his public outcries against the Chinese government's disregard for human rights. When I went to Beijing shortly after his release, the artist described the profound sense of solitude he felt while in detention. His captors had repeatedly told him that no one cared that he was missing: Unless he cooperated with them fully, it would be many years before he would see his young son again. For Ai Weiwei, this psychological position was among the most difficult aspects of his incarceration. As he explained to me, "The most terrible thing about jail is not the treatment that you receive, but the isolation."

Yours Truly began as a question Ai Weiwei raised when we were developing *@Large: Ai Weiwei on Alcatraz*, an exhibition of new works addressing the struggle for fundamental human rights, held at the former penitentiary. Wouldn't it be incredible, the artist wondered aloud, if the show could include a call to action? Although during this time, Ai Weiwei was unable to travel beyond China due to restrictions imposed by his government, he was still envisioning new ways to connect and mobilize others on a global scale.

From the start of our work on *@Large*, Ai Weiwei was interested in the fact that from 1934 to 1937, Alcatraz was a silent prison, a cruel penal experiment that reportedly drove some prisoners insane. During this time, inmates were punished if they were found speaking with one another. In response, they invented ingenious ways to make contact, whispering to one another through the empty pipes and leaving notes in library books. Reflecting on his personal experience of detention and the history of Alcatraz, the artist created *Yours Truly*, an interactive project that would invite visitors to send postcards to prisoners of conscience around the world. Through *Yours Truly*, Ai Weiwei wanted to call attention to these courageous activists and let them know that they are not forgotten.

The 116 prisoners ultimately featured in *Yours Truly*, as well as the individuals highlighted in this book, were imprisoned for a variety of nonviolent activities carried out in the name of human rights and social justice. In many instances, they were merely criticizing the unjust policies of their governments. While reviewing these cases, I was appalled to discover how unthreatening many of these "illegal" acts seem, but people have nonetheless been arrested, because their governments felt that their expressions of dissent had the potential to create social unrest. In choosing cases to include in this project, we also had to consider whether simply receiving the postcards might further endanger the prisoners and their families. I am grateful to our partner in this endeavor, Amnesty International, for shepherding us through the selection process. Their Write for Rights campaign was another source of inspiration. Every day, this incredible organization makes great efforts to ensure that the dream of global human rights can someday become a reality for all of us.

During the run of the exhibition, it was fascinating to observe how visitors chose the individuals they wrote to. Sometimes they picked postcards based on the beauty of their illustrations. The front of each card depicts the national bird or flower of the nation where the prisoner is being detained. These are meant not only to be visually pleasing for the cards' intended recipients, but also to operate as a sign to the guards and prison administration, potentially casting a shadow of shame over these national symbols. Other visitors selected specific cards because they had been to the country in question or were familiar with a particular prisoner of conscience's story. I was surprised to discover that some visitors had once been prisoners of conscience themselves and wanted to show their solidarity for those still imprisoned. Children made some of the most fascinating choices, often adding beautiful illustrations to complement their frank, thoughtful voices.

We scanned approximately ten thousand of the nearly ninety-three thousand postcards before sending them out into the world. In reviewing them, I was moved by the range of emotions and depth of feeling that people expressed as they offered words of comfort and encouragement to these strangers whose stories had inspired them.

During the run of the exhibition, I had many powerful interactions with visitors to *Yours Truly*. One day, a Nepalese woman approached me with her son, who must have been only eight or nine years old. She was pleased to meet me and communicated her thanks for the project. It turned out that they had traveled from San Jose by bus and ferry to see *@Large*, and though there were no Nepalese prisoners of conscience represented (she reminded me that there are many), she and her son were delighted by the opportunity to reach out to some of these amazing people. They ended up staying all day, filling out as many postcards as they had the energy and the time to complete. I was touched by the fact that this woman had made it a priority to share ideas of freedom of speech and human rights with her son through this shared activity. Together, they celebrated the brave individuals who were included in the project, even if the prisoners didn't come from their own cultural background. Moments like these made me feel the project had been a success, even if we could not be sure whether the cards would reach the prisoners.

In fact, it turned out that many cards did reach their destinations, and the communication was not entirely one-sided. It was quite surprising when the FOR-SITE Foundation started to hear back from some of the prisoners and their relatives, who informed us that the postcards were getting through. The family of the Egyptian activist Ahmed Maher was among the first to reach out, relaying their deep appreciation for the sentiments of support. One of the most astonishing things occurred when the family of Bahraini dissident Ebrahim Sharif al Sayed traveled from various parts of the world to San Francisco to experience the exhibition and to thank the FOR-SITE Foundation for our efforts on his behalf. Maher and Sharif's stories are outlined in greater detail in the pages that follow. Sharif was released on June 19, 2015, not long after *@Large* closed, but he was rearrested less than a month later, following another speech in which he expressed the need for change in his country. "In our case, there is no going back to building a wall of fear," Sharif said. "The government is only strong when we are cowards and is weak when we are courageous." One can only hope that the postcards we mailed to Sharif and many others will encourage their inspiring fortitude in the face of such adversity.

There are many challenges in today's world. Every day, people are forced to flee their homes and countries because they are being persecuted for their ideological beliefs. There are countries that are building walls and barriers. There is a palpable sense of a global shift toward fear. Xenophobia is on the rise, and many people are expressing the desire to withdraw and withhold resources from "outsiders." These and myriad other issues sometimes seem so overwhelmingly enormous that one wonders—what can one person do other than to keep an open heart?

One of the truly successful aspects of *Yours Truly* is that it gave visitors the sense that they could do something. It encouraged them to act—to make a difference in someone's life by simply sending a postcard. I saw people walking out of the *Yours Truly* installation elated, moved, and excited that they had participated, somehow, in the larger quest for human rights.

@Large, and particularly *Yours Truly*, has been a springboard for my own curatorial practice through the FOR-SITE Foundation. It has made me realize that we all have a responsibility to put something back into the world. Since *@Large*, I try to ensure that my curatorial work considers and responds to some kind of social issue. I'm deeply grateful for the experience I have had working with Ai Weiwei, collaborating with our partners, and interacting with the public in a way that I have rarely had the chance to do in the contemporary art world.

To receive a message from someone you've never met, someone who is perhaps eight thousand miles away, who is learning of your story and your courage for the first time—I can only hope that this might offer prisoners of conscience the encouragement to endure their situations, and perhaps to remain resolute in their dissent and hold the course. This is the takeaway from *Yours Truly*: despite what sometimes appear to be insurmountable odds, through our collective efforts, we can and will change the world for the better.

Below: Ai Weiwei with FOR-SITE Executive Director Cheryl Haines at the artist's Beijing studio, Spring 2014.

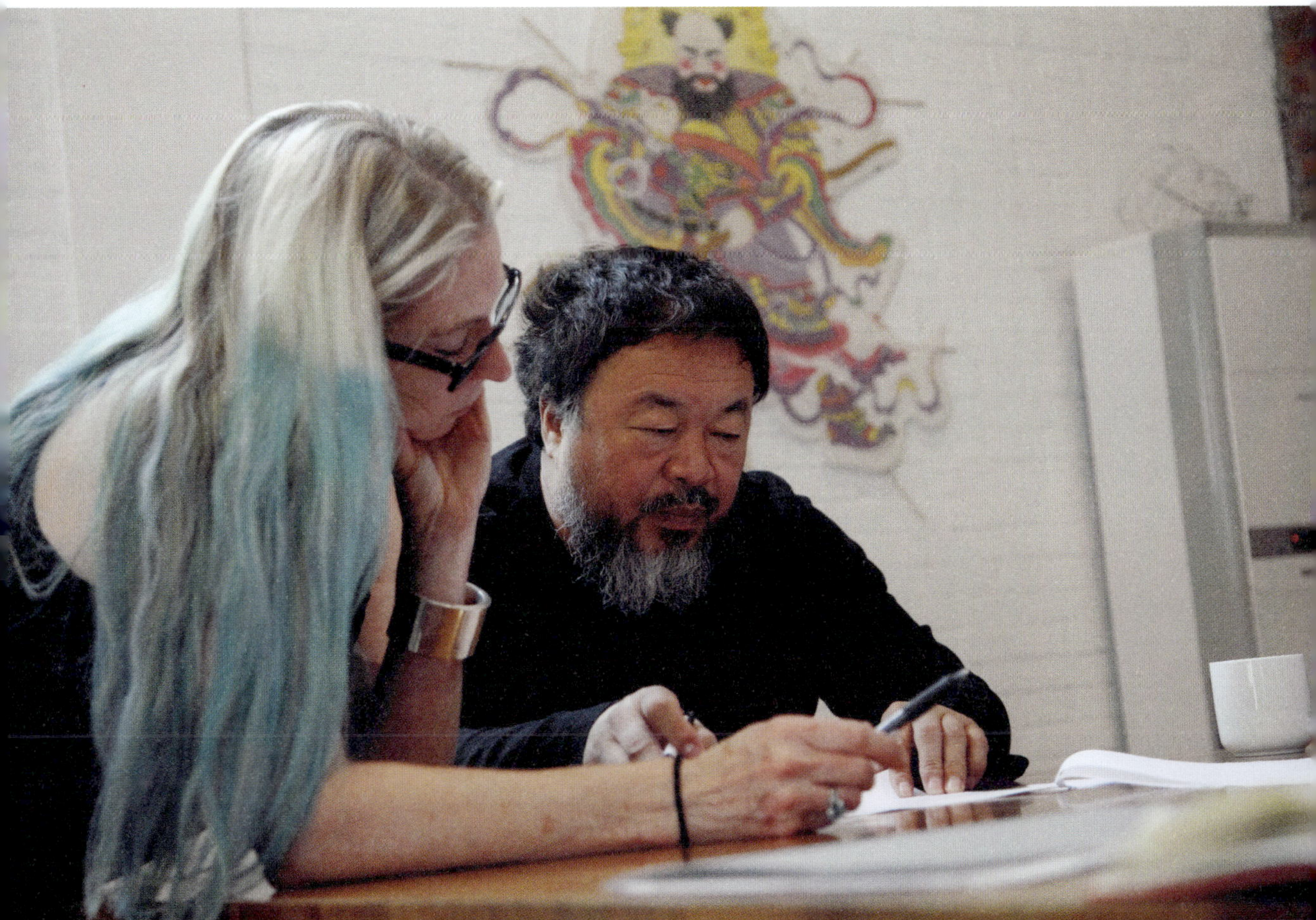

ARTIST'S NOTE

Ai Weiwei

Today, there are many prisoners of conscience in jails around the world. To me, these people are the heroes of our time. They have lost their freedom simply for trying to improve their conditions through peaceful writing and non-violent protest. Now, as a result, they remain imprisoned by their governments. Without intervention, many of them might stay in jail for the rest of their lives, forgotten by the public. Hidden in dark corners, in unknown places, these prisoners' names may never be celebrated like the names of those considered to be the founders of our civilizations. But while their work is less visible, it will never be less important. We must understand that if we are able to live peacefully within a civilized society, it is through their efforts.

Yours Truly was intended to create the possibility for people to develop their feelings about these issues and then to get involved through the act of writing a postcard. To someone jailed or living in exile, a postcard can be an essential form of communication. My father, the poet Ai Qing, was part of a generation of writers, poets, and artists who could not liberally express their ideas without losing their freedom. They were punished for having different ideals, different attitudes, and different characters, and the punishment could include losing their lives. My father was jailed and then exiled. From the late 1950s onward, I grew up in a remote and impoverished area in Xinjiang Province, in westernmost China, where my family was forcibly relocated. I still remember this time, when we were living in the Gobi Desert. The conditions there were very difficult and did not support life. It was as if nobody knew where we were. One day, my father received a postcard. It simply read, "Today is the anniversary of the publication of your poem *Dayanhe—My Nurse*," one of his most famous works. The card was unsigned, because at that time, people were scared to reach out to us, but this fear didn't cause them to forget my father or his writing.

My father was deeply touched by the card. He had been living in the middle of the desert, thinking that no one could possibly remember him. He often mentioned this card to me, and it helped me to understand the weight of art and literature, which remains in people's hearts.

In 2011, I was detained by the Chinese government in an almost hostage-like situation for eighty-one days. I felt like a miner trapped in a collapsed mine, not knowing if anyone up top was looking for me or if there were any other miners trapped down there with me. The soldiers stood by my bed all night long, in two-hour shifts. They stood silent and ramrod straight, next to the bed, their eyes not leaving me for a second, even when I closed my own. Every time I made a request, they had to look at their watches before giving permission. I would say, "Squad leader, sir, I want to scratch my head." And I couldn't scratch my head until he said I could. Then he would look at his watch again. I would say, "I need the toilet" or "I want to stretch my legs." Everything required their explicit permission. Yet, during my detention, it was the feeling of isolation that was the hardest to bear. My detainer told me that he had not seen anyone who had not been broken down, or in his words "finished," after two years. Knowing that someone else appreciates and shares your values can be the most rewarding thing for those who endure such hardship, which oftentimes can be extreme.

As an artist, I live in a society where freedom is a most precious quality. Through *Yours Truly*, I hope to encourage others to send postcards to prisoners of conscience, so that they will know that people still care about their condition. I want us to show these prisoners that they are not forgotten, and to remind the authorities that these people in jails represent a larger ideology that is shared by the society.

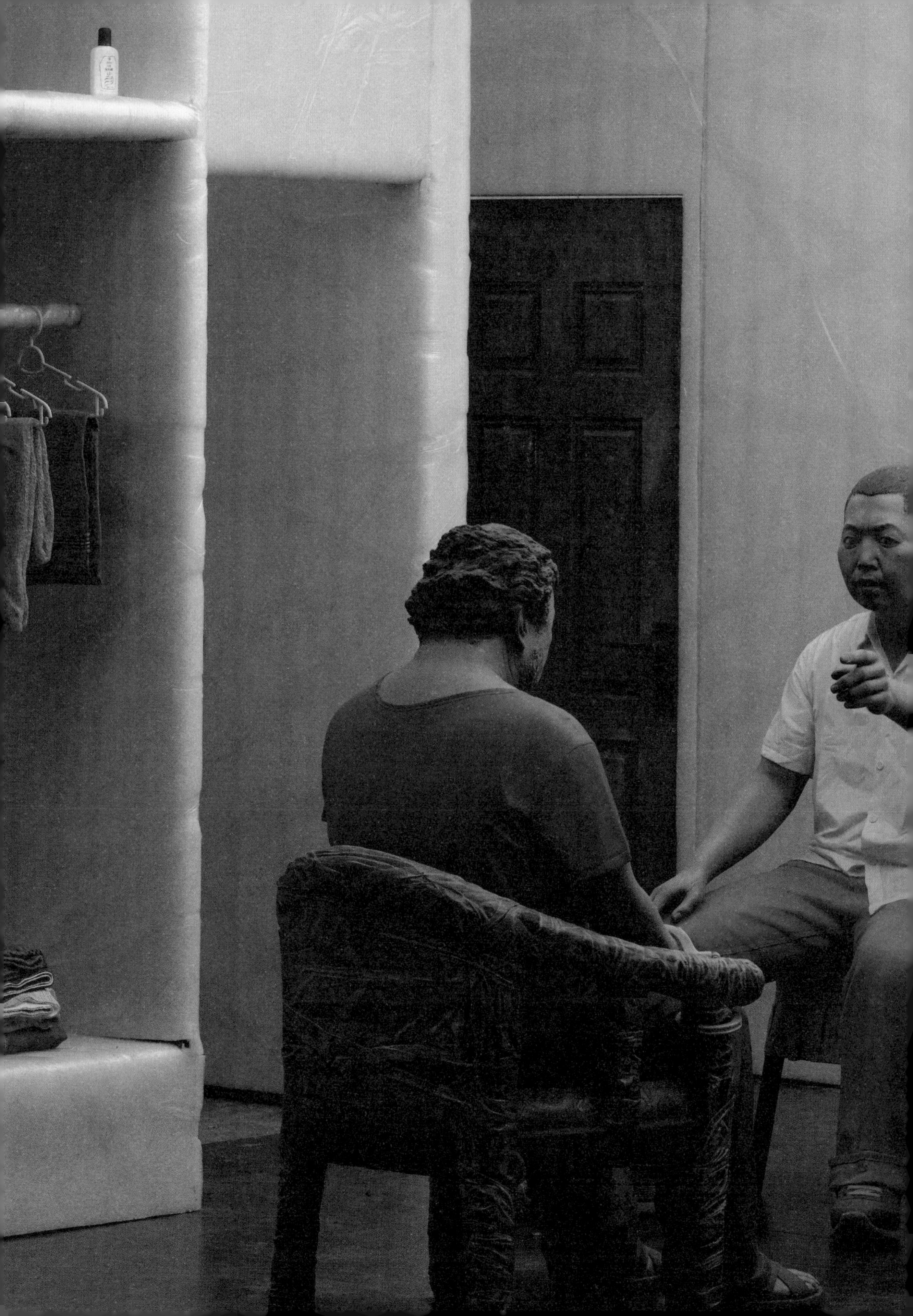

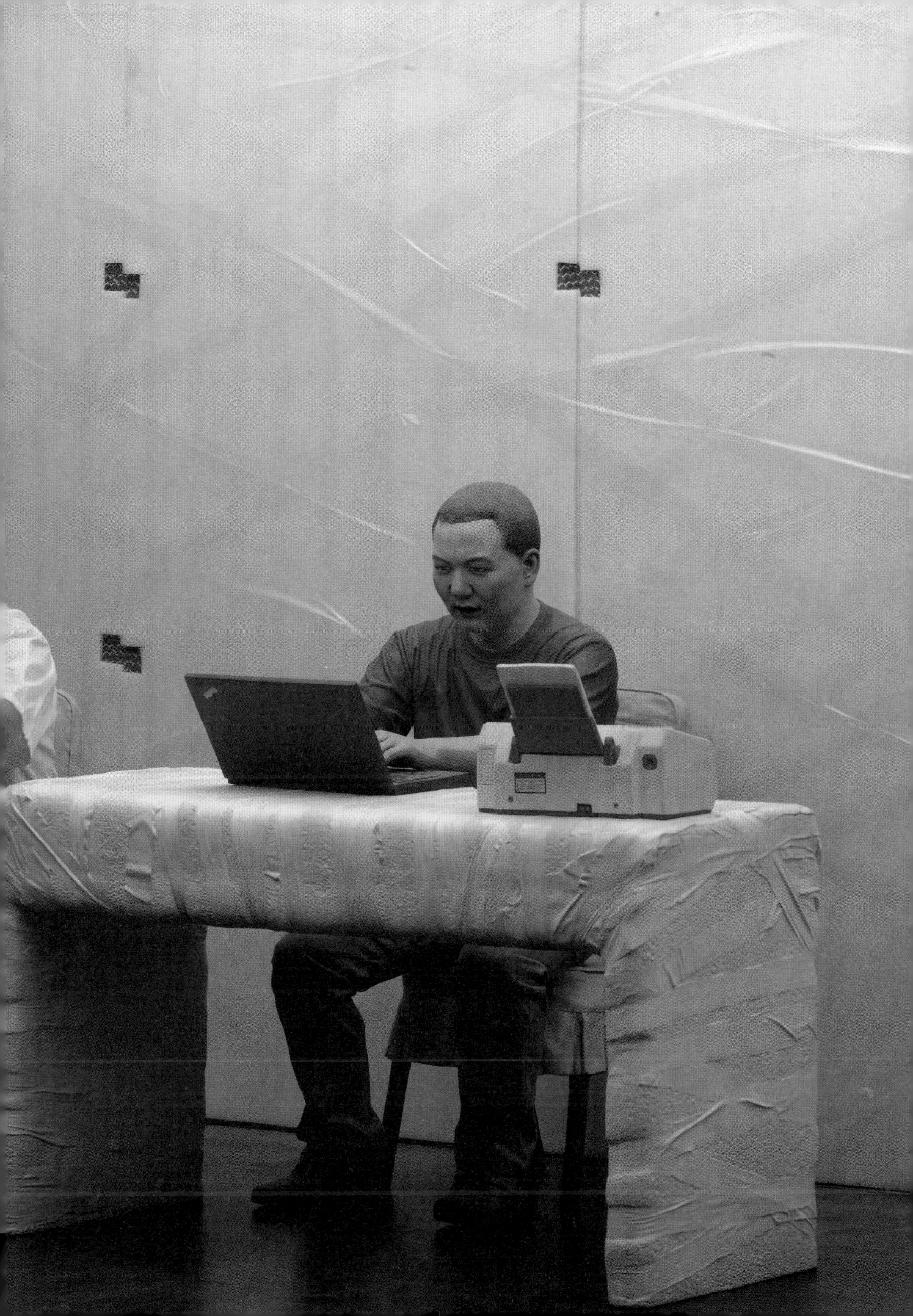

Unfortunately, I don't think the world will ever be a place where we can live without fear. There always seems to be a need to fight for our basic human rights. Each day, we must struggle—and sometimes even make sacrifices—in our efforts to protect these values. For those freedom fighters and activists who have been imprisoned, one of the most important things is knowing that their efforts have been worthwhile, that there are others who share their beliefs and who can extend their efforts. For me, the overwhelming success of *Yours Truly* comes from the fact that we have started a dialogue between people living in a peaceful democratic society and those who have paid with their lives and their freedom to protect those basic values. When people write these postcards, share such messages, and show care for those in dire conditions, it proves that we believe that if even one person's human rights have been violated, we all suffer. We have to see humanity as one.

Opposite: Ai Weiwei in front of the door to his Beijing studio, 2014.

Previous page: Ai Weiwei, *S.A.C.R.E.D. (Accusers)*, 2011–2013.

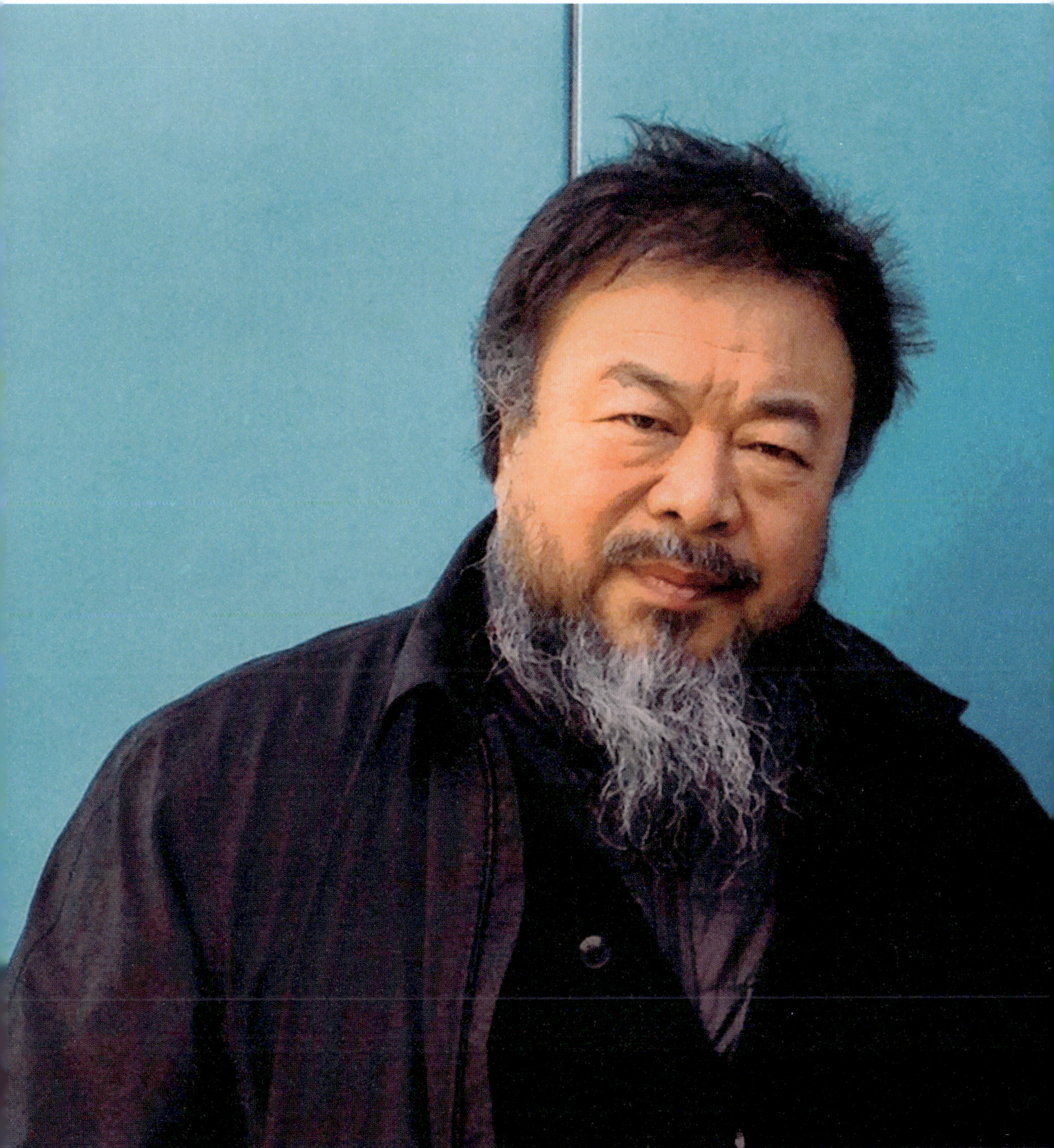

TRANSFORMATIVE ACTS

Jasmine Heiss Former Senior Campaigner, Individuals at Risk Campaign, Amnesty International USA

In the era of the twenty-four-hour media landscape, we are confronted each day by stories that confound the moral imagination. Our constant immersion in news and social media serves up a daily helping of fresh human rights crises: Entire families "disappeared" in Syria; young men shot to death by the police in the streets of Rio de Janeiro or Chicago; journalists thrown behind bars in Ethiopia. The cumulative effect can be one of paralysis. In the face of such sweeping horrors, it's quite easy to feel small, powerless, and unable to make a difference.

In this context, the humble act of writing a letter or a postcard becomes anything but humble. It is, instead, an act of daring. The choice to put pen to paper and reach out to a president, parliamentarian, or prisoner is a leap of faith in the idea that one human voice can help shape the world. It is a courageous choice to take injustice personally.

Amnesty International's fifty-year legacy of campaigning for prisoners around the world is built on this belief, on small acts of daring, and on millions of people who commit to taking injustice personally. And we know that it has an impact. Each year, we see prisoners released after Amnesty's letter-writing campaigns. We see torture survivors winning accountability and reparations, and we hear directly from people all over the world that messages of solidarity have helped to shine a light in the darkness. Individuals who have been released after receiving Amnesty International's letters have told me, "You gave me hope; I finally felt that I was not alone."

For many prisoners, the experience of incarceration is one of isolation. It is often meant to strip a person of community, communication, and autonomy—even dignity. For prisoners across the world, prison bars can be a message: You are alone, forgotten, and incapable of moving the tremendous mechanism of state power. Prisoners like those featured in Ai Weiwei's *@Large* are largely people who engaged in some of the most difficult work imaginable before being jailed for their activism, identity, or beliefs. Many prisoners of conscience are struggling to create systemic, lasting changes in societies where free speech is not tolerated, where dissent is quashed, where the choice to voice their opinions and concerns comes with the risk of being silenced—yet they continue to struggle for dignity, justice, and rights.

Ai Weiwei understands both the crippling sense of isolation and the transformative power of hope more intimately than most. He has experienced firsthand the isolating effects of incarceration and house arrest. Yet his work on Alcatraz loudly proclaims the one thing that the Chinese authorities will never be able to strip from him: his humanity. Creative expression, whether manifest in music, poetry, sculpture, painting, theater, or dance, is a profoundly human act. It affirms the very fundamental dignity of the human spirit that the Universal Declaration of Human Rights is predicated on. What's more, Ai Weiwei's choice to wield art as a force for the justice and freedom of others affirms a shared humanity across borders and through prison bars in a world that seeks to deny it. Using art to galvanize action turns the fundamentally human act of creative expression into an act of creative resistance.

Such acts are transformative. I'll never forget the case of Yorm Bopha, the Cambodian housing rights activist. She was a powerful voice on behalf of her community, a woman who was leading the way and holding the Cambodian government accountable. Arrested on what we believe were spurious charges and imprisoned for three years, she was part of Amnesty International's Write for Rights campaign in 2013. In roughly forty-eight hours, we generated more than 250,000 appeals for her in advance of her appeals hearing, and she was released. She was reunited with her family, including her young son. As soon as she was released, she took up a megaphone again and was outside the government offices, demanding that her community, her family, and her people be given housing, water, and other fundamental human rights.

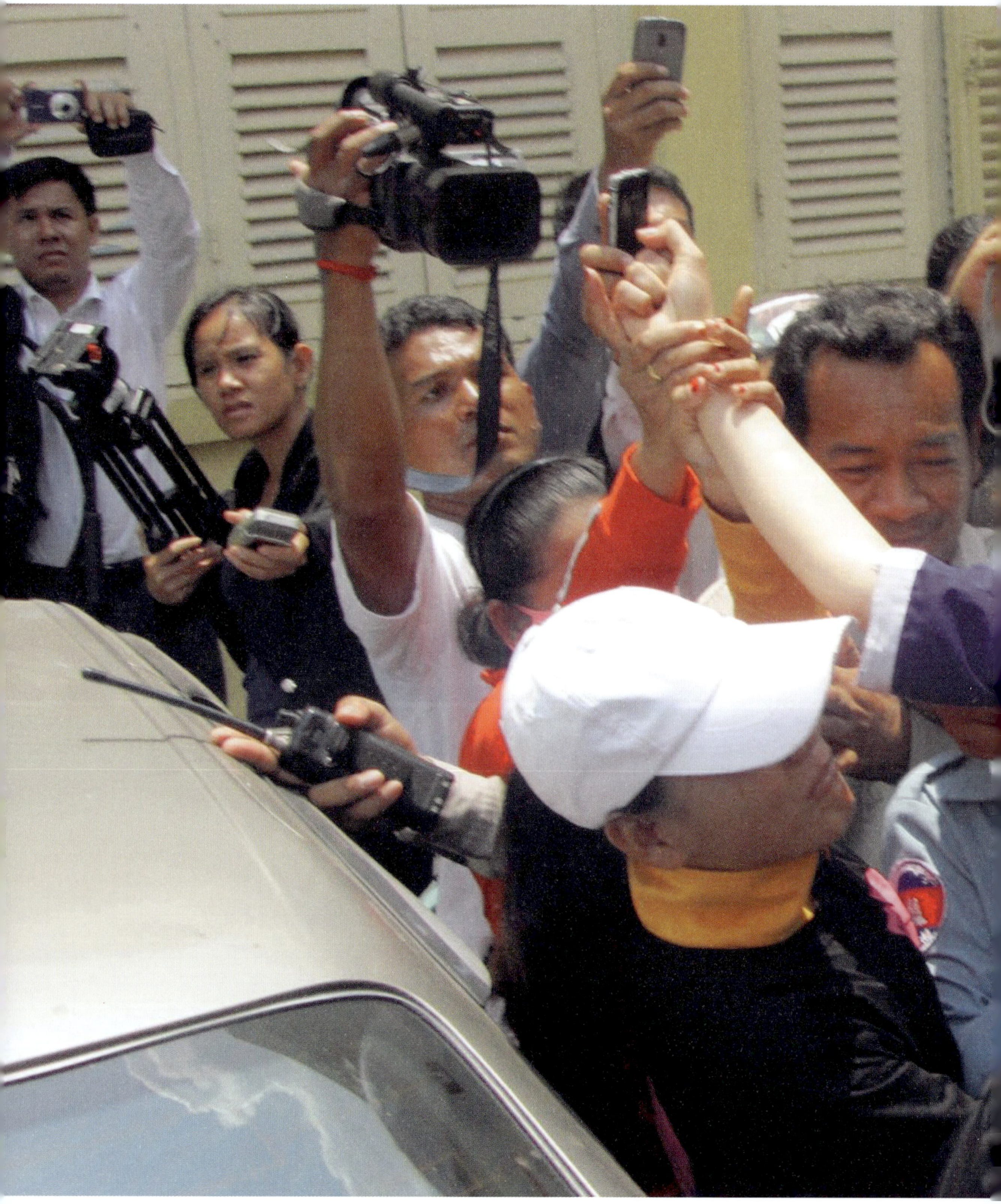

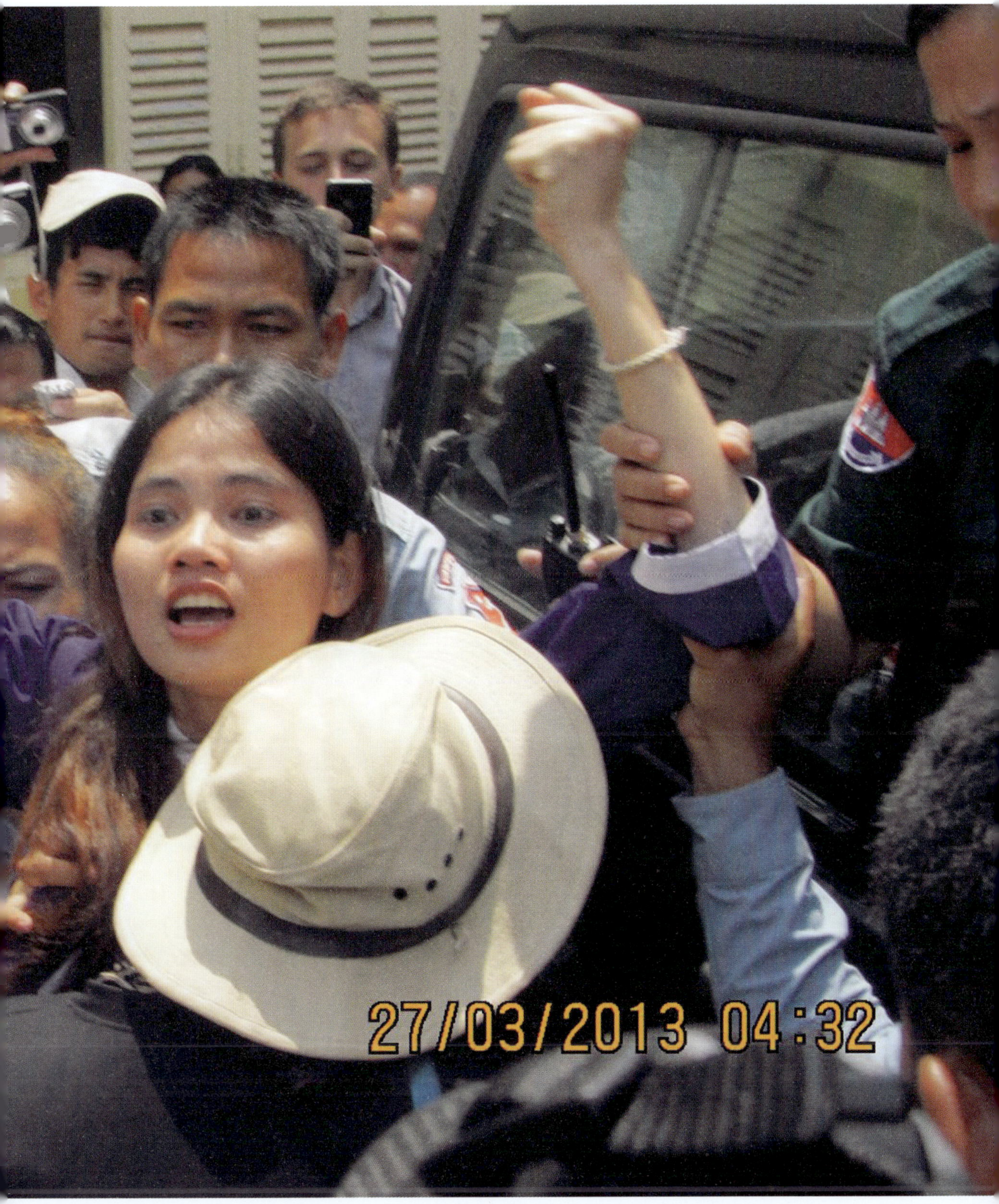
27/03/2013 04:32

She thanked us, but an even more powerful form of gratitude comes from knowing that people like Yorm Bopha, after they are released, continue to be forces of change. When we advocate for the release of prisoners of conscience, we are not just freeing them from behind bars. In many cases, we are freeing forces that are going to bring true change to their communities, to their countries, and to the world.

The importance of Ai Weiwei's decision to breathe life into such an exhibition on Alcatraz cannot be understated. For nearly three decades, Alcatraz was one of the most notorious prisons in the country. While the prison itself has been transformed, the human rights crisis of mass incarceration in the United States has only deepened. The country is the world's leading jailer, with nearly a quarter of the world's prison population, despite being home to only 5 percent of the world's total population. Displaying the portraits of prisoners from across the world in a US penitentiary helps situate the United States within the global context of incarceration. Furthermore, the inclusion of figures such as Martin Luther King, Jr., Edward Snowden, and Chelsea Manning in *@Large* is a reminder that politicized imprisonment is not something that only happens outside of US borders; rather, the United States continues to grapple with a troubling legacy of human rights abuses.

During the run of *@Large: Ai Weiwei on Alcatraz*, at least twenty-three prisoners of conscience featured in the exhibition were released. In the months that followed, even more people finally walked free. While it's impossible to know with certainty the impact of such a project, we do know that in some cases, when the odds have seemed insurmountable, global bursts of pressure such as those generated by the *@Large* exhibit can generate transformative changes in the lives of individuals. Our global solidarity and support can not only free people from prison; when government officials know that the world is watching, it can also help prevent people from being returned to those prison cells.

I would like to tell Ai Weiwei how deeply grateful I am to be reminded that I live in a world that is filled not only with atrocity, but also with people who are courageous, creative, and committed to surmounting incredible odds. Ai Weiwei is someone who, unable to leave his country, still found a way to make his voice heard—not only across borders and oceans, but also across barriers of nationality, language, race, gender, and class. When someone can survive his or her own experience of isolation and use it as a tool to become a more powerful advocate for others around the globe, I am reminded that the world I want to live in could someday become a reality. It is a world that Ai Weiwei helps coax into being every day by choosing dignity, humanity, and resistance.

Opposite: Postcards pre-addressed to prisoners freed during the *@Large: Ai Weiwei* on Alcatraz exhibition.

Previous page: Yorm Bopha raises her fists in defiance as she is placed in a van and returned to Prey Sar Prison, Phnom Penh, Cambodia, March 27, 2013.

Following page: Completed *Yours Truly* postcards, sorted by country and prepared for mailing

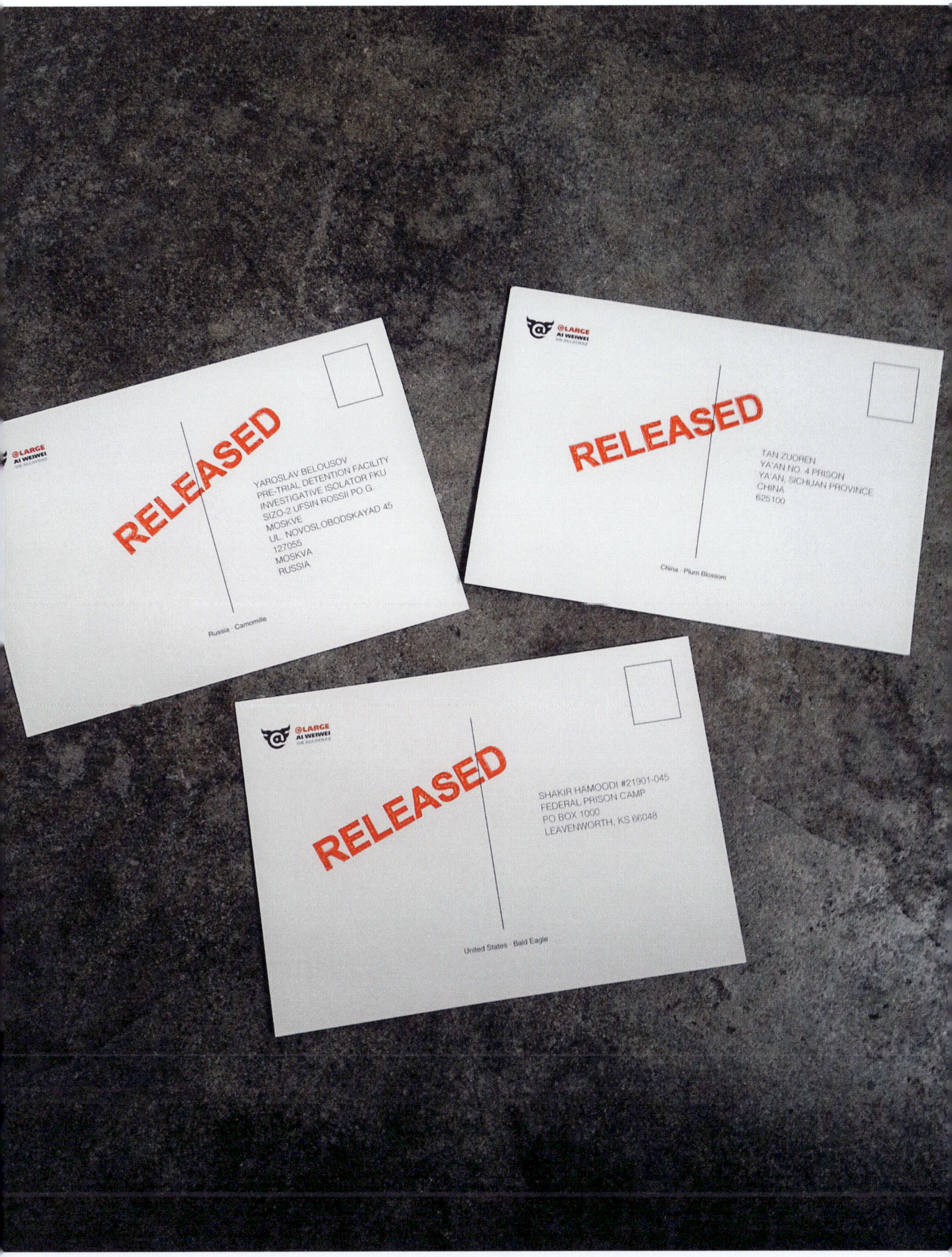

@LARGE
AI WEIWEI
RELEASED
YAROSLAV BELOUSOV
PRE-TRIAL DETENTION FACILITY
INVESTIGATIVE ISOLATOR FKU
SIZO-2 UFSIN ROSSII PO G.
MOSKVE
UL. NOVOSLOBODSKAYAD 45
127055
MOSKVA
RUSSIA
Russia · Camomille
@LARGE
AI WEIWEI
RELEASED
TAN ZUOREN
YA'AN NO. 4 PRISON
YA'AN, SICHUAN PROVINCE
CHINA
625100
China · Plum Blossom
@LARGE
AI WEIWEI
RELEASED
SHAKIR HAMOODI #21901-045
FEDERAL PRISON CAMP
PO BOX 1000
LEAVENWORTH, KS 66048
United States · Bald Eagle

GUO XIAOJUN
TILANQIAO PRISON WARDEN
LIU JINBAO
147 CHANGYANG ROAD
SHANGHAI, CHINA
200082
@LARGE
AI WEIWEI
ON ALCATRAZ
Mr. Karma,
I disagree

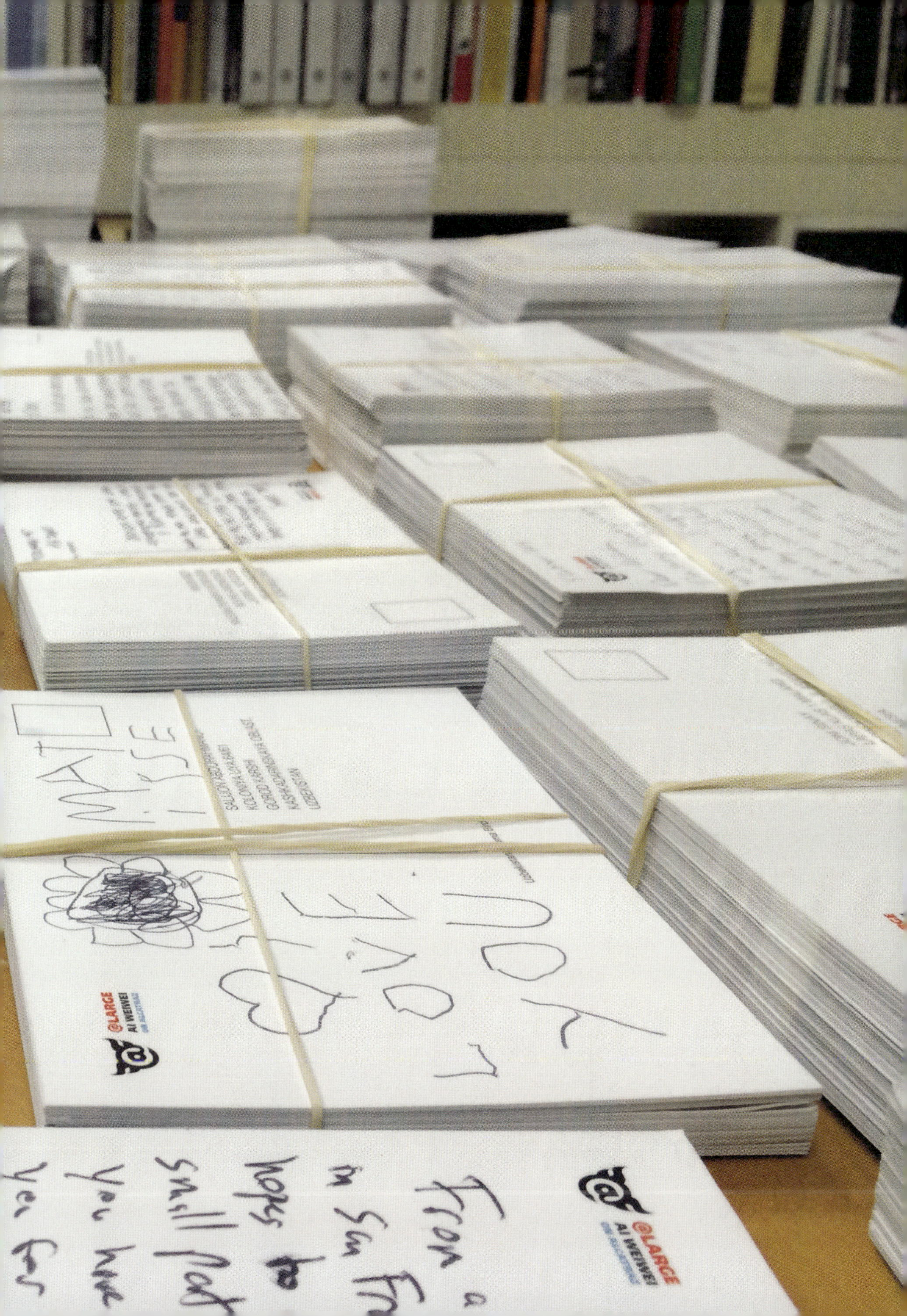

This and following pages: Visitors to *@Large* completing postcards destined for prisoners of conscience

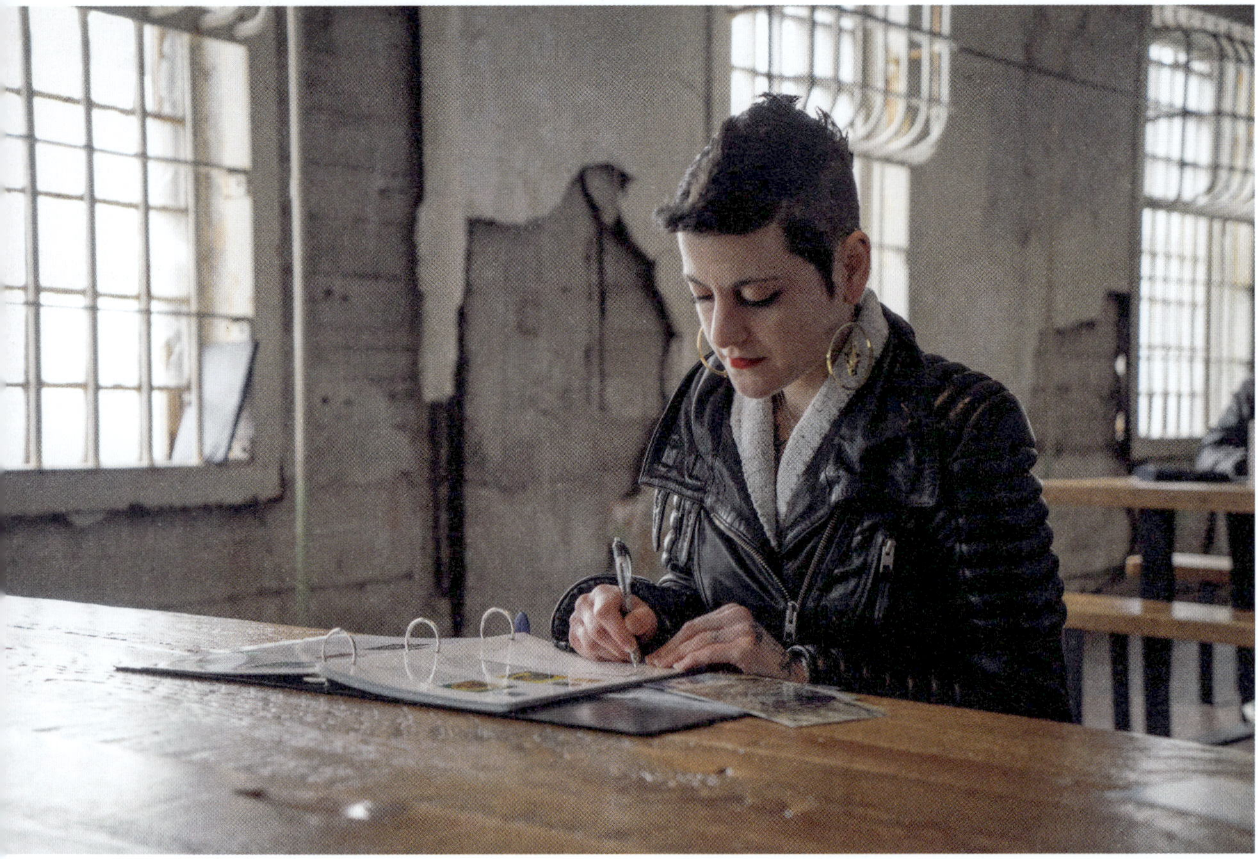

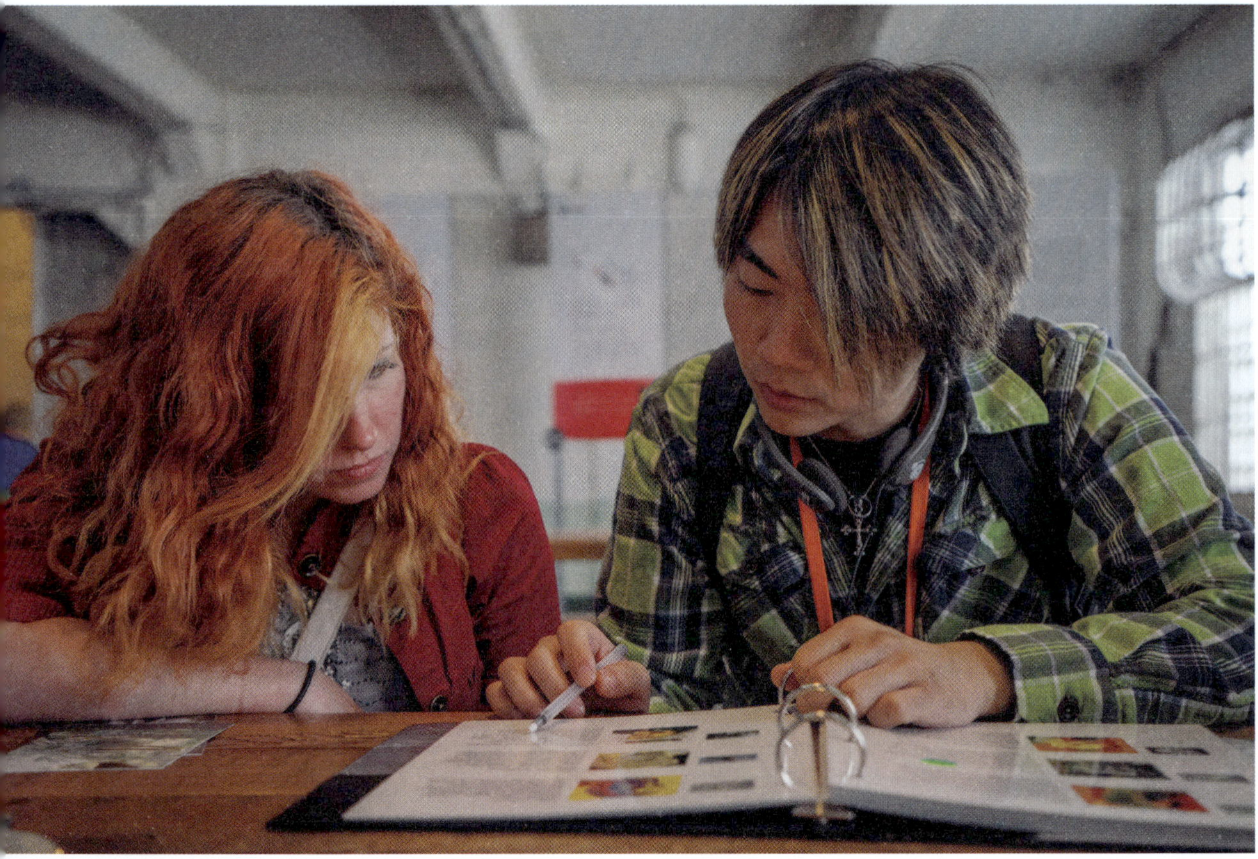

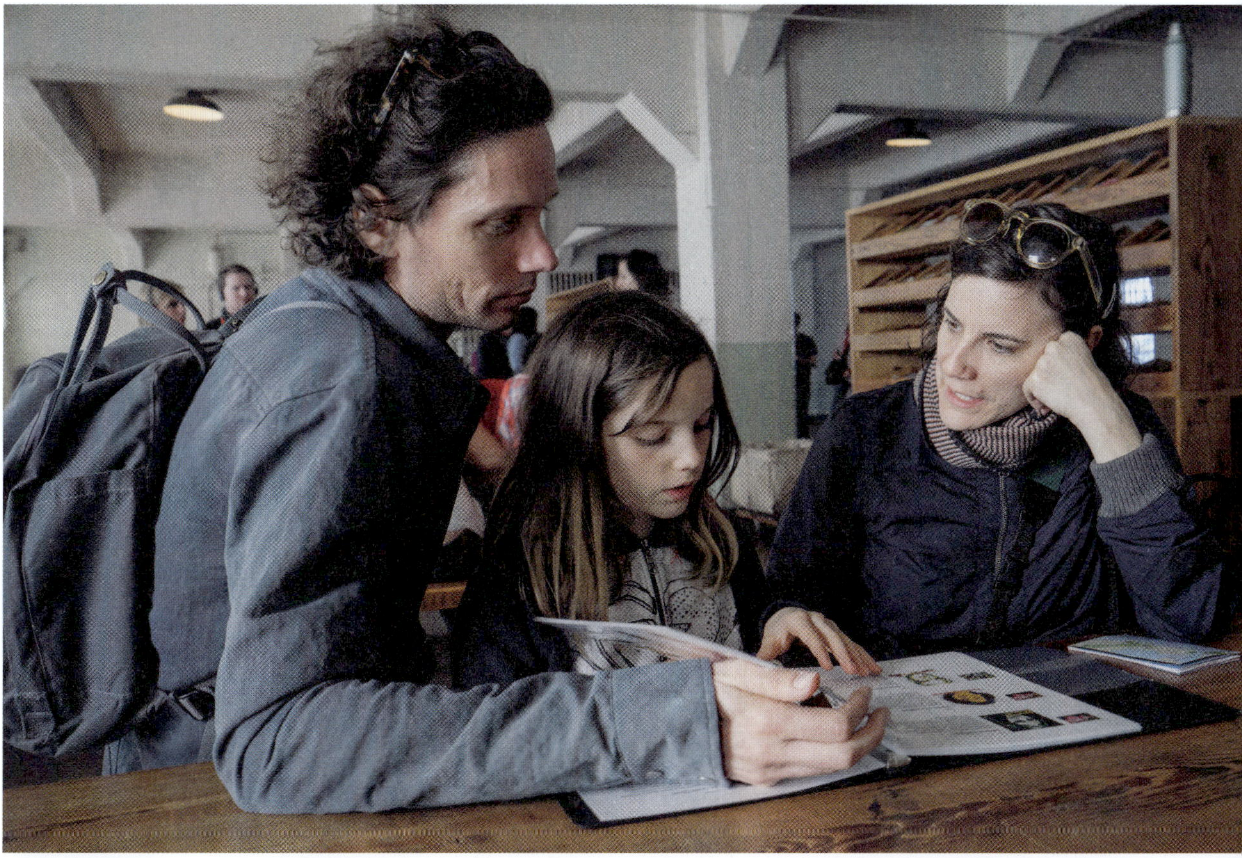

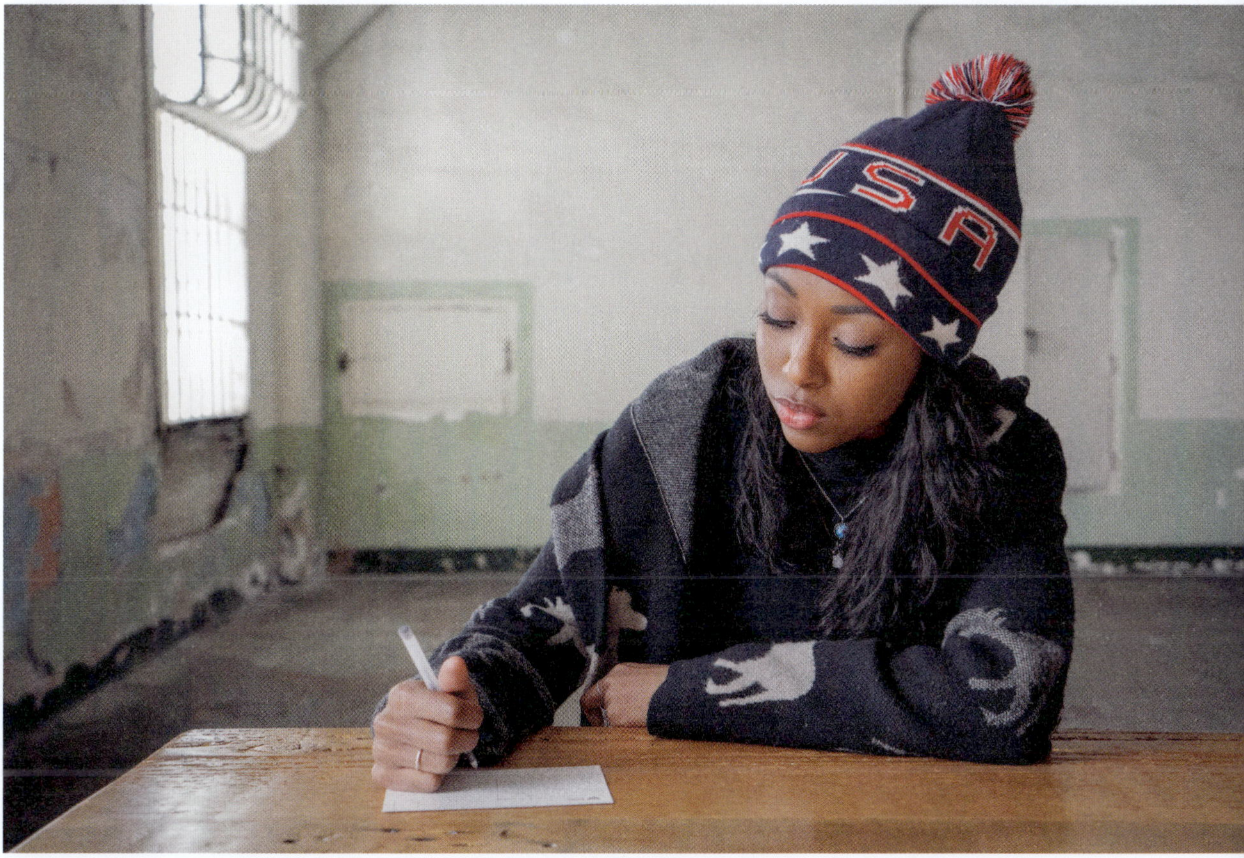
USA

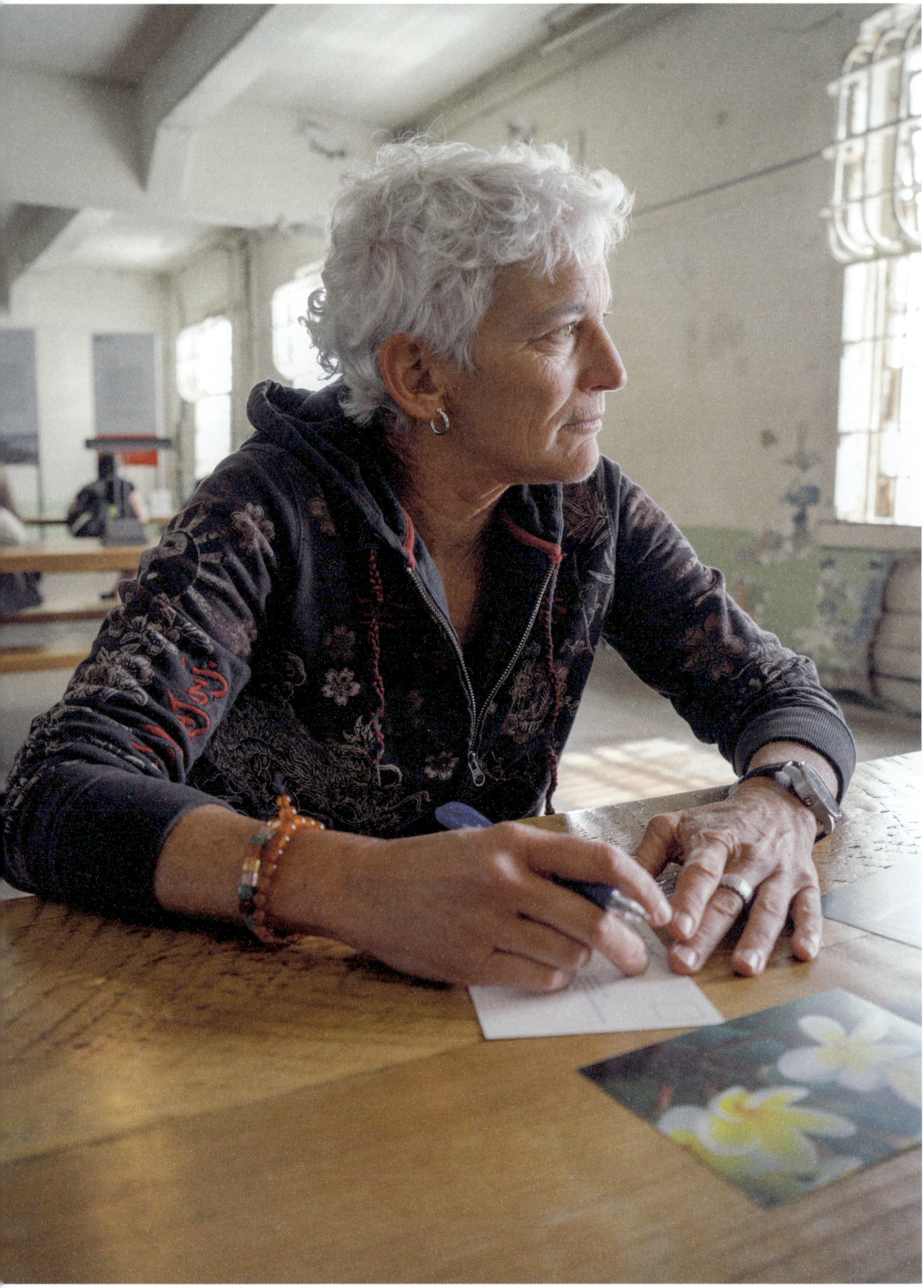

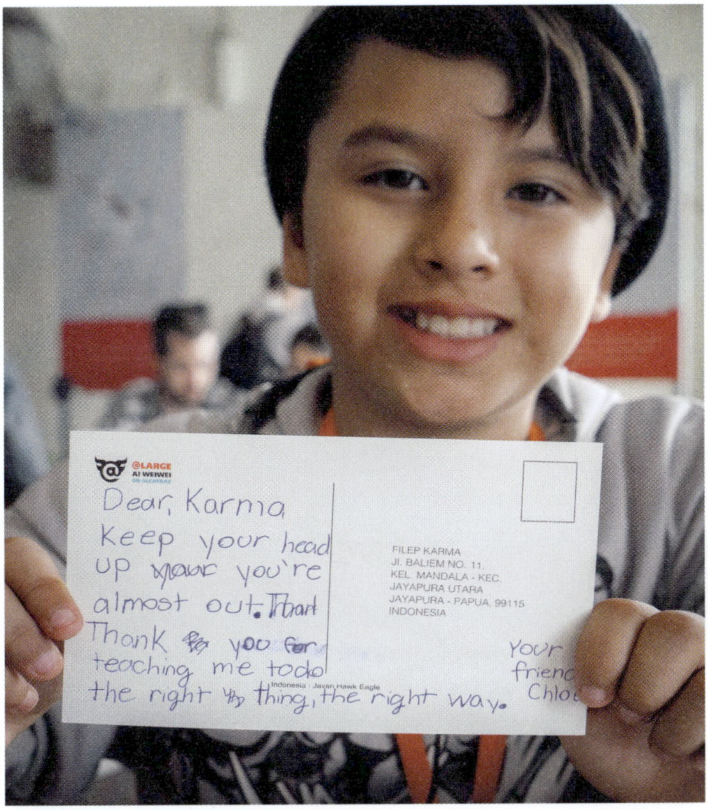
@LARGE
AI WEIWEI
Dear, Karma
Keep your head up you're almost out.
Thank you for teaching me todo the right thing, the right way.
Your friend Chlo
FILEP KARMA
Jl. BALIEM NO. 11
KEL. MANDALA - KEC.
JAYAPURA UTARA
JAYAPURA - PAPUA, 99115
INDONESIA
Indonesia : Javan Hawk Eagle

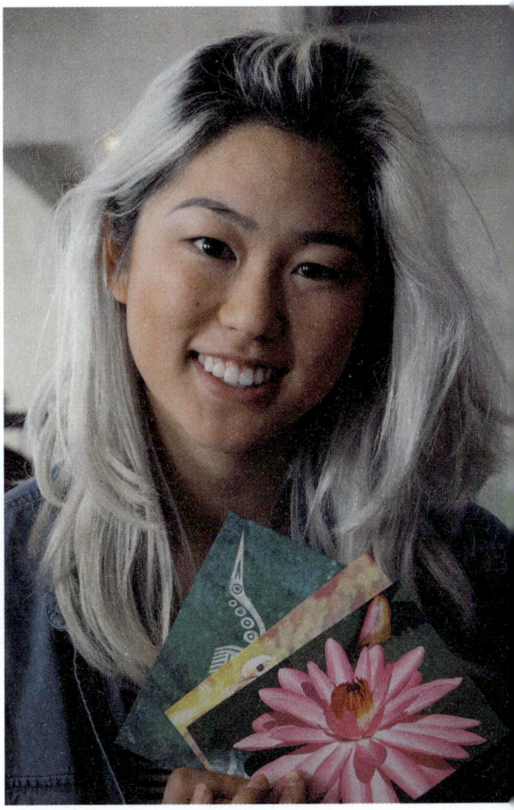

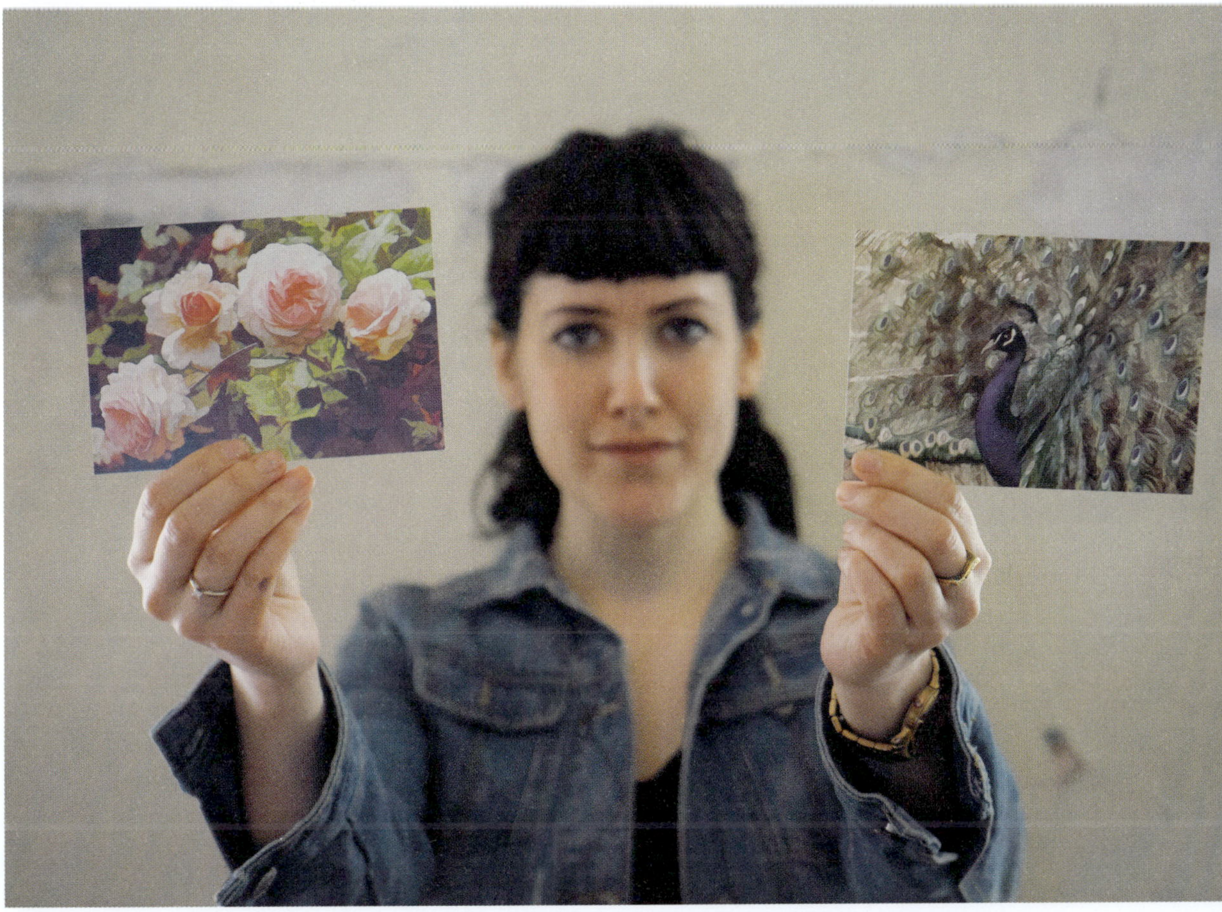

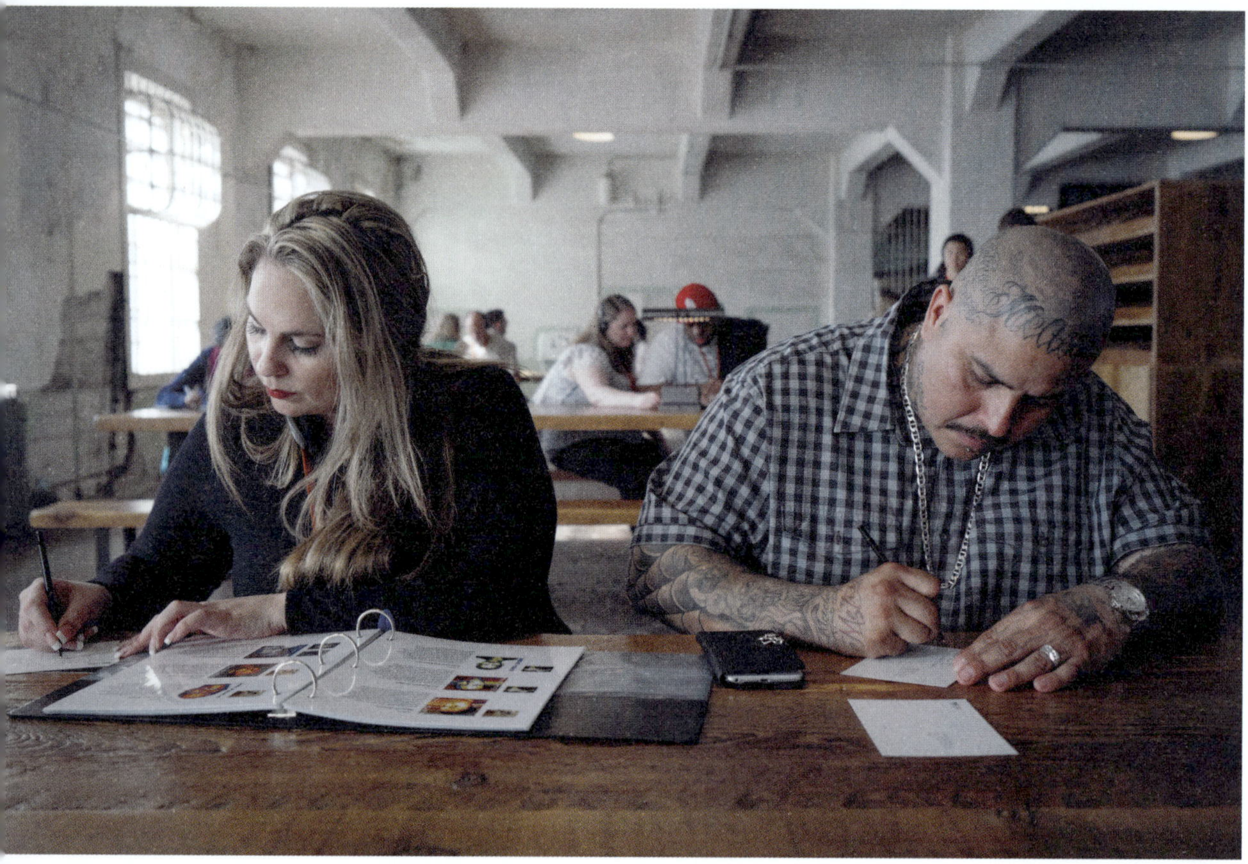

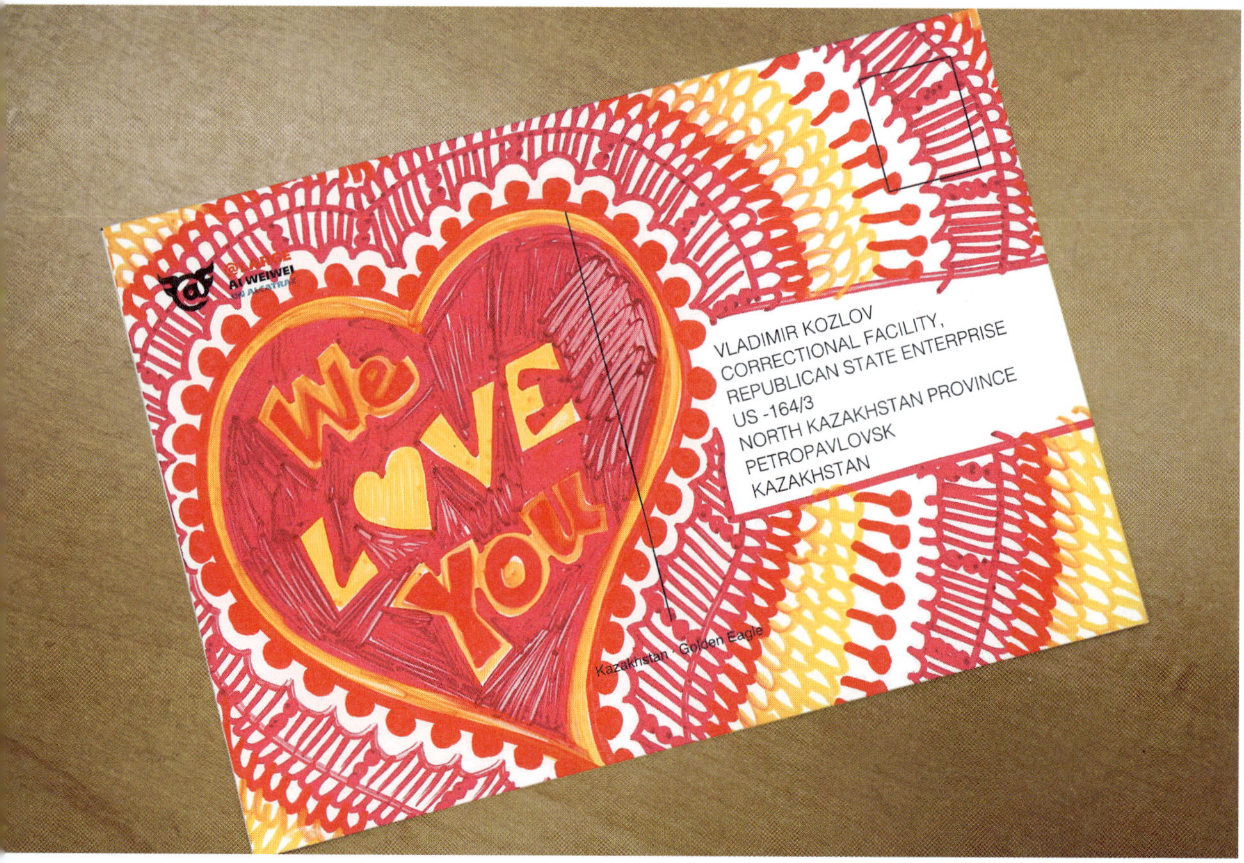
AI WEIWEI
We LOVE YOU
VLADIMIR KOZLOV
CORRECTIONAL FACILITY,
REPUBLICAN STATE ENTERPRISE
US -164/3
NORTH KAZAKHSTAN PROVINCE
PETROPAVLOVSK
KAZAKHSTAN
Kazakhstan · Golden Eagle

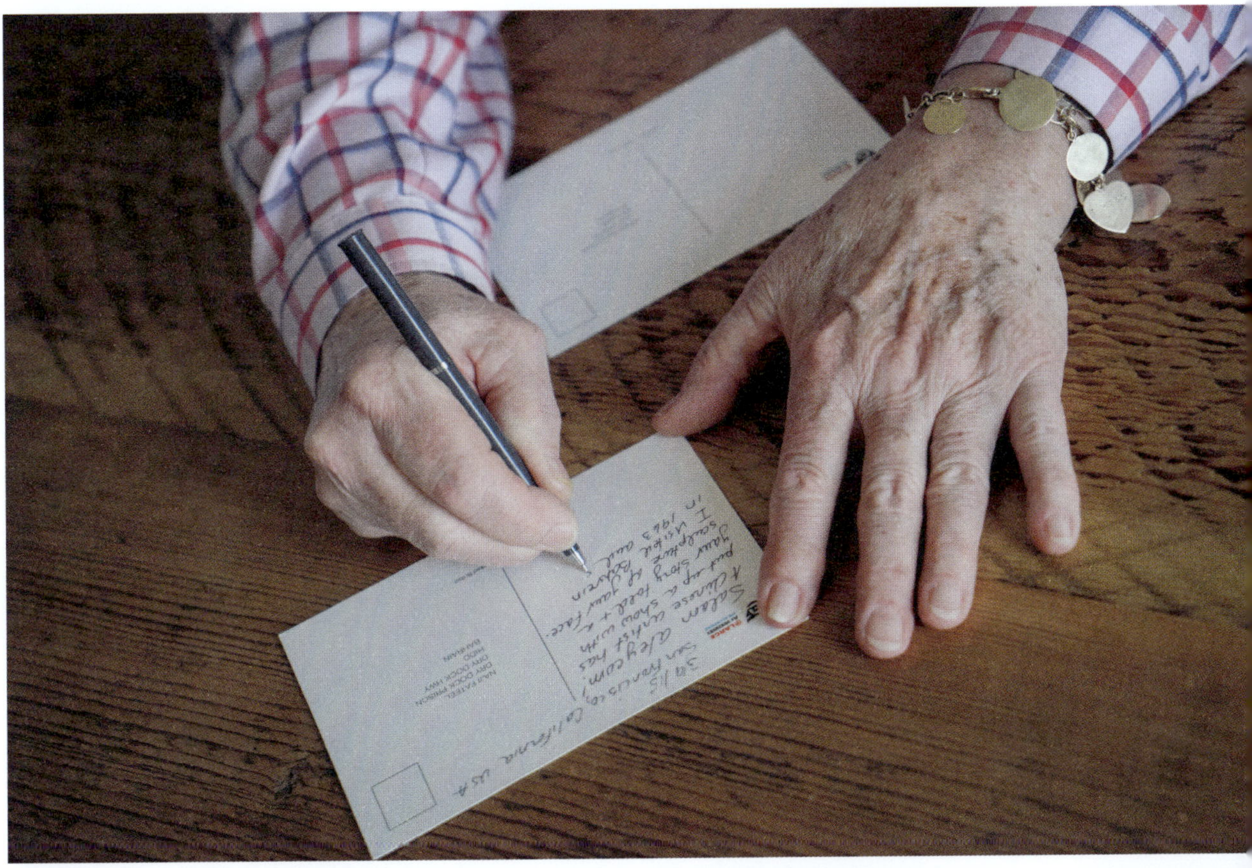

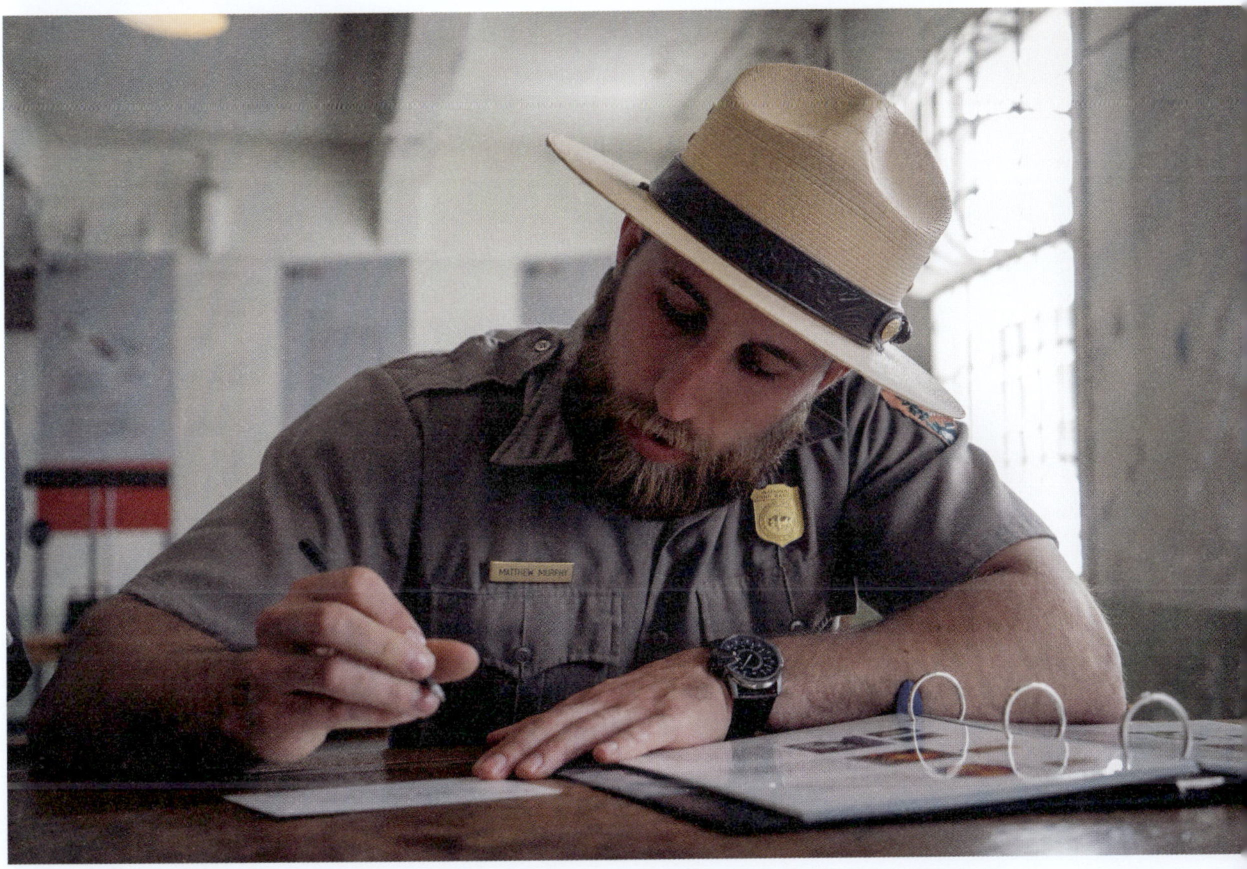
MATTHEW MURPHY

Below and opposite: A sampling of the thousands of *Yours Truly* postcards completed during *@Large: Ai Weiwei on Alcatraz*

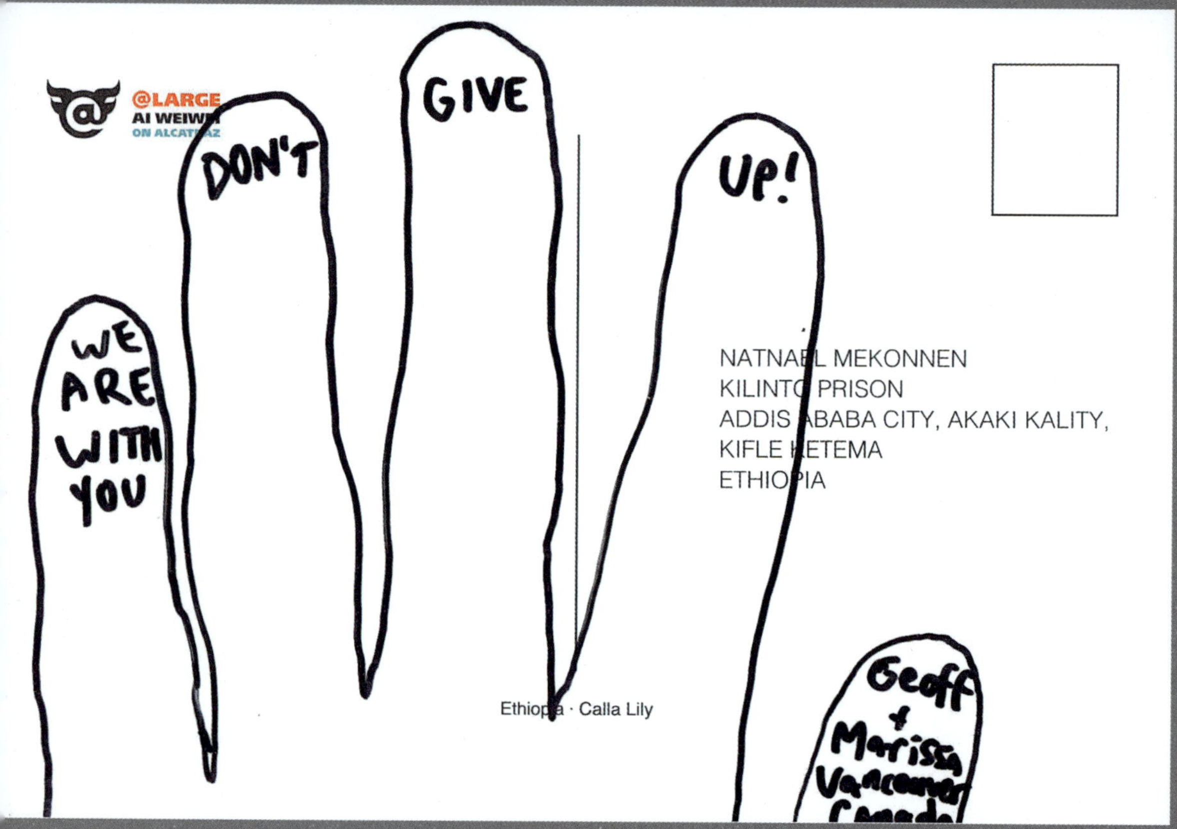

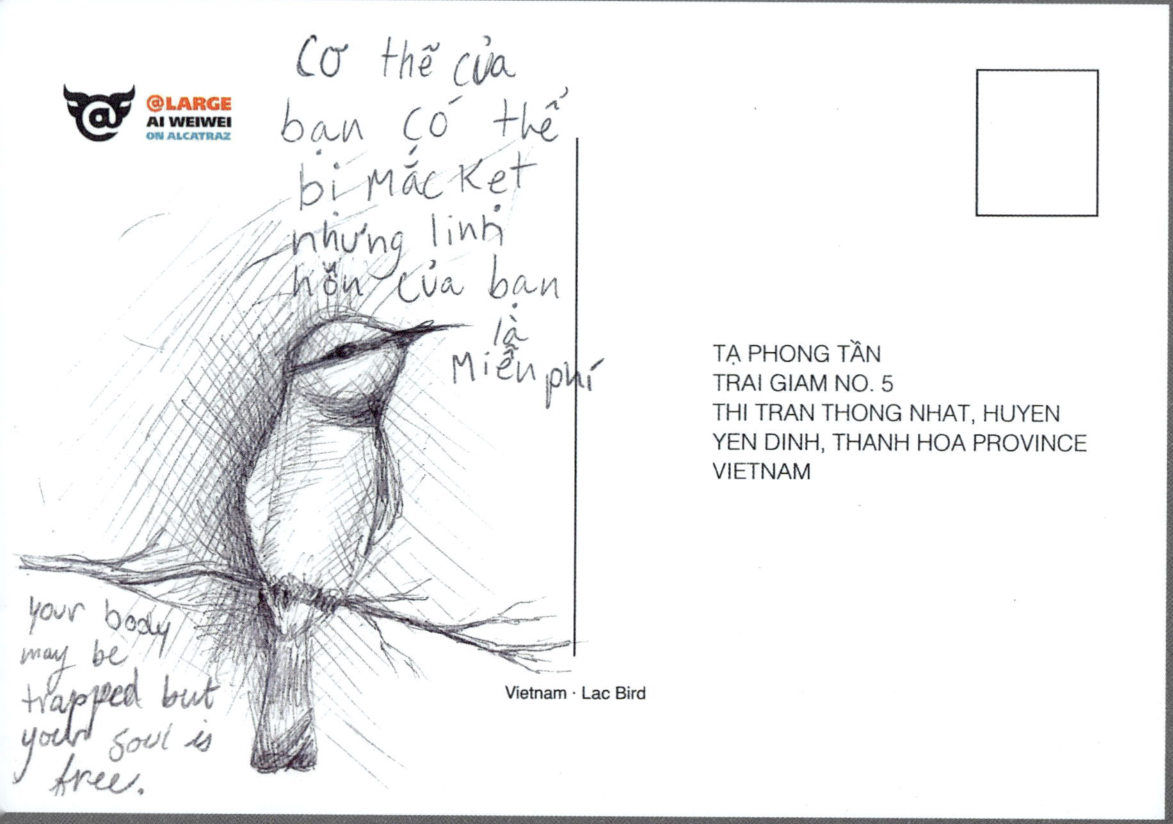

@LARGE
AI WEIWEI
ON ALCATRAZ

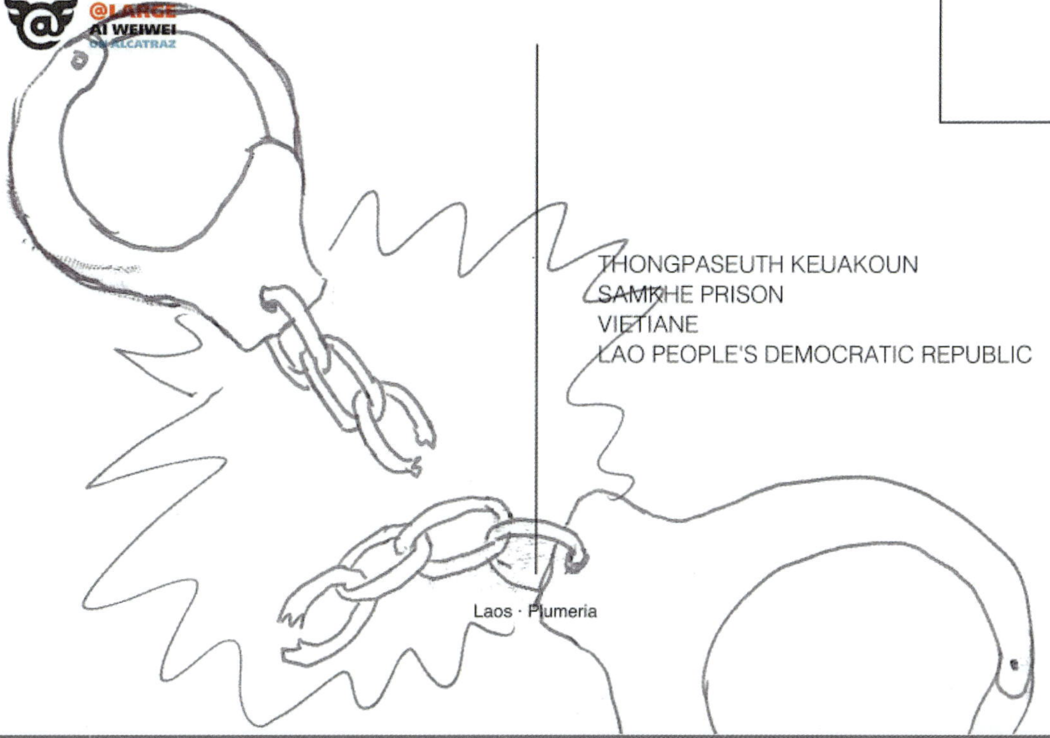

THONGPASEUTH KEUAKOUN
SAMKHE PRISON
VIETIANE
LAO PEOPLE'S DEMOCRATIC REPUBLIC

Laos · Plumeria

@LARGE
AI WEIWEI
ON ALCATRAZ

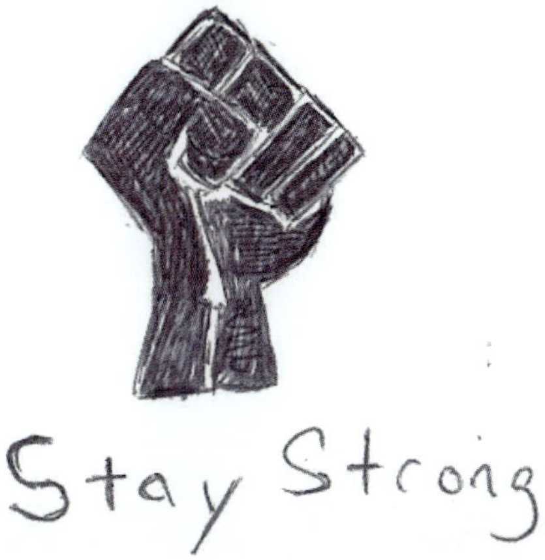

ANDREI BARABANOV
INVESTIGATIVE ISOLATOR
SIZO-2 BUTYRKA
UL. NOVOSLOBODSKAYA, 45
127055
MOSCOW
RUSSIA

Russia · Camomille

Postcard art featured in *Yours Truly*

Bahrain

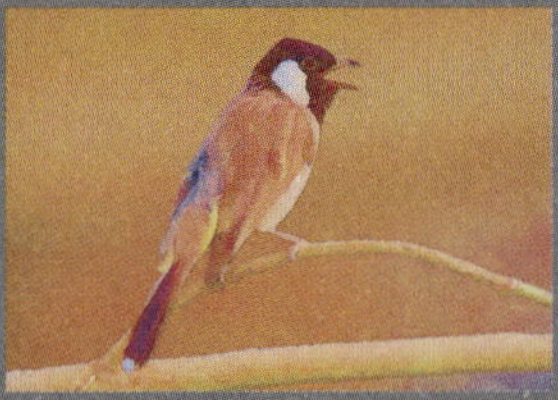

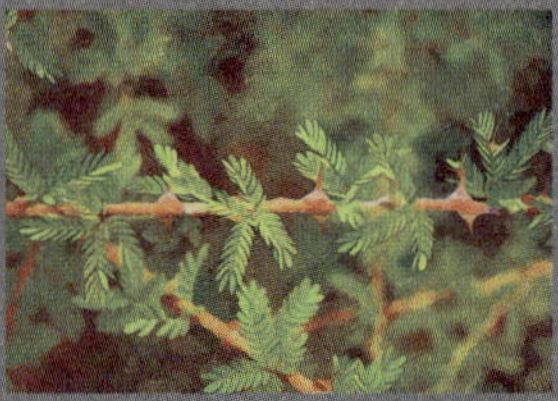

Belarus

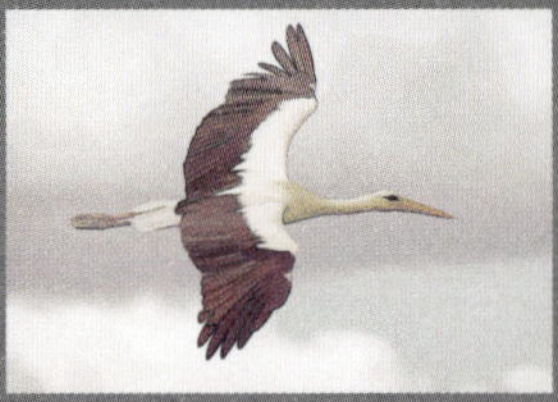

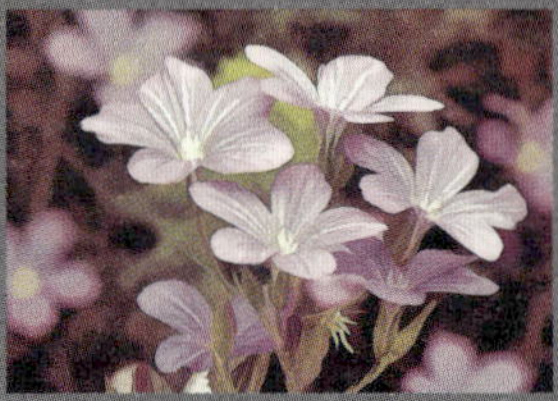

Cameroon

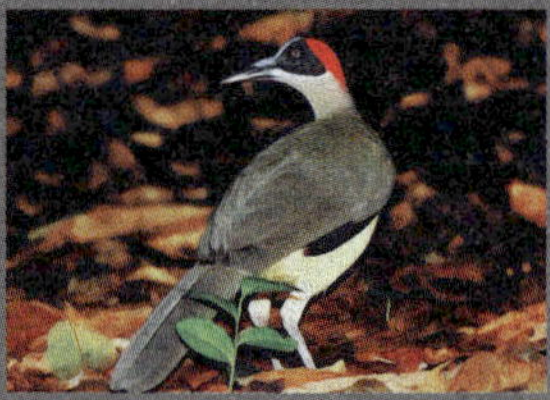

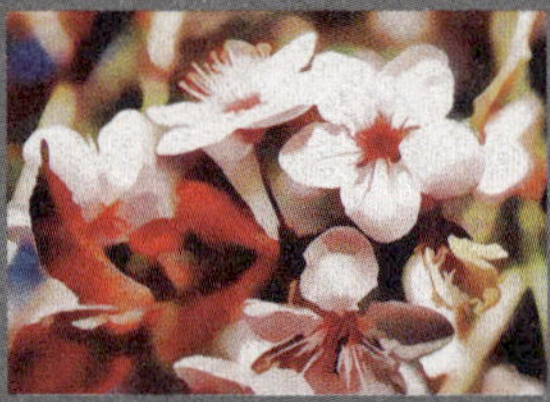

China

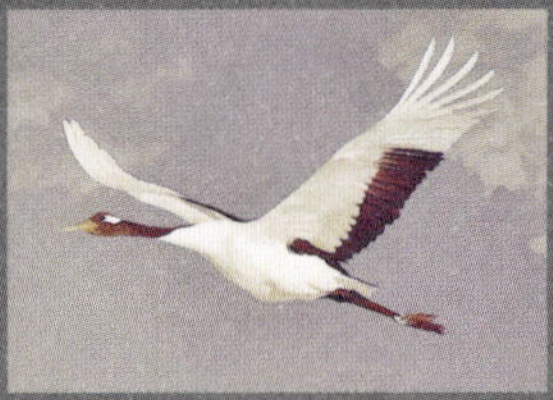

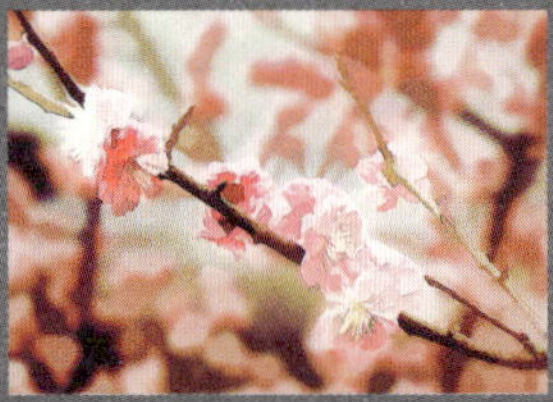

Cuba

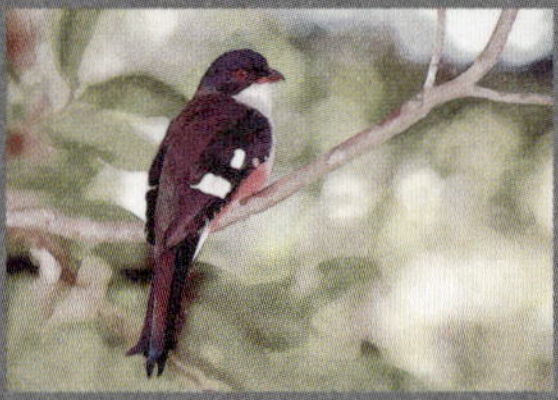

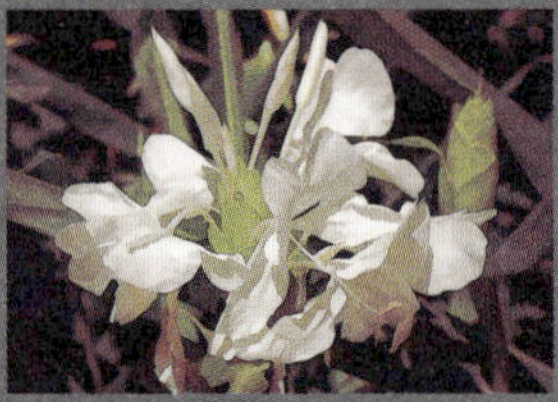

Egypt

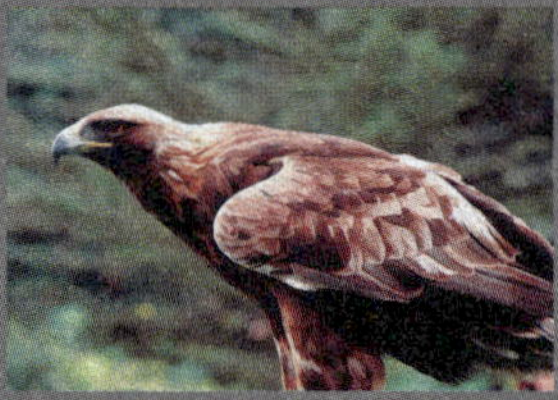

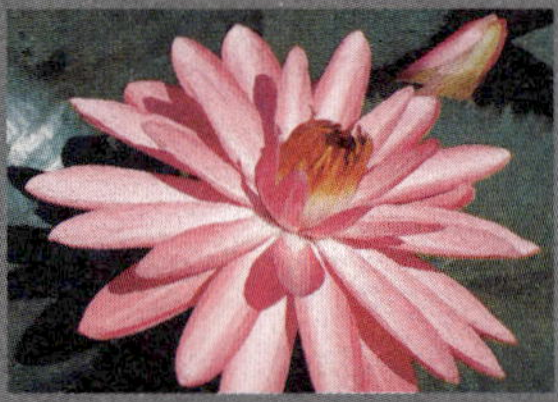

Cameroon

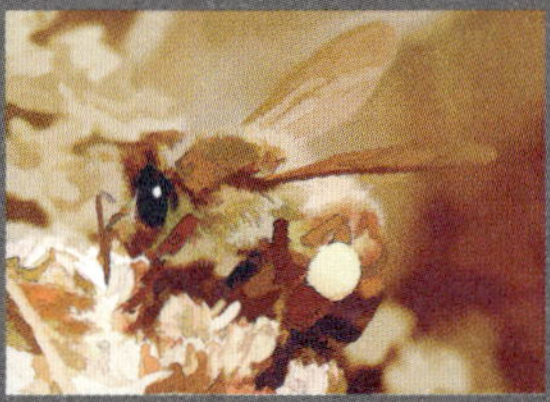

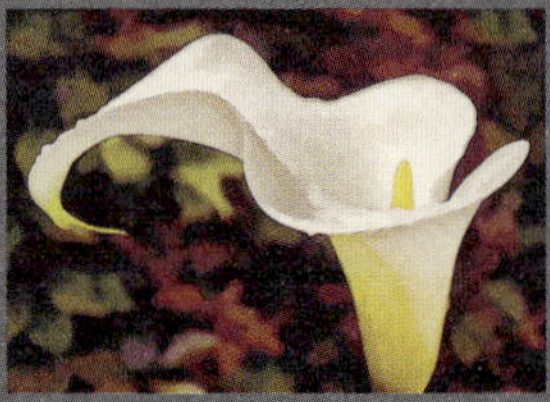

China

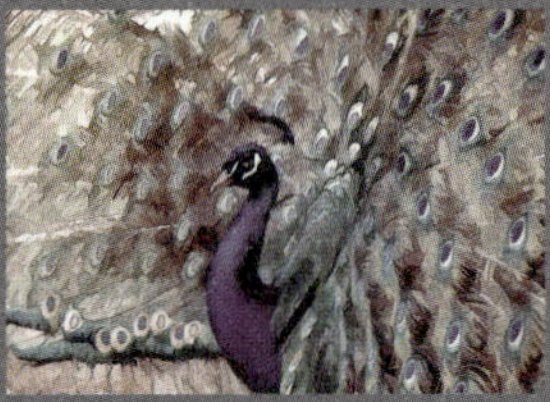

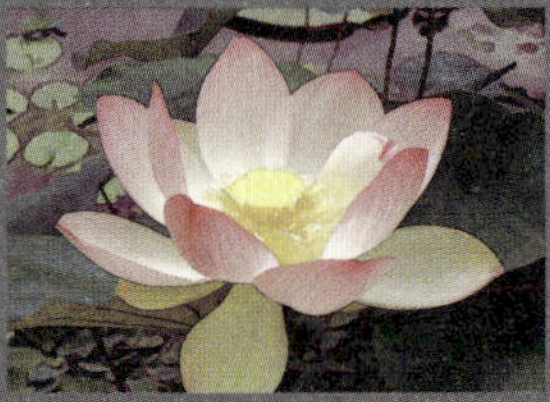

Indonesia

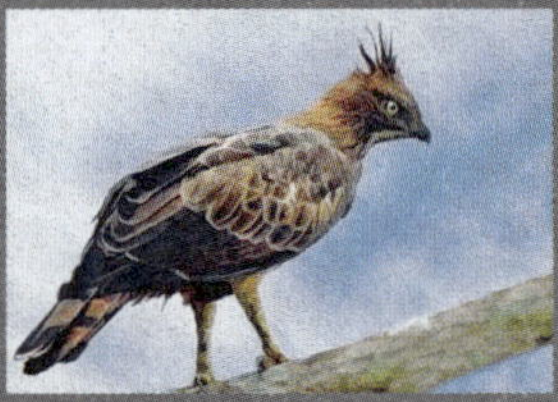

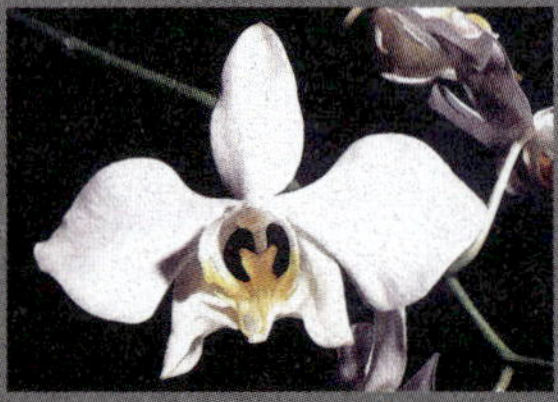

Iran

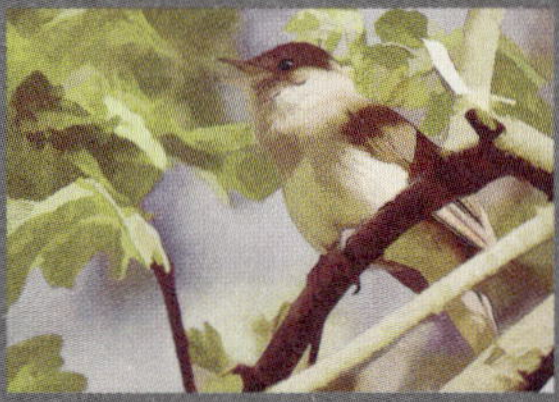

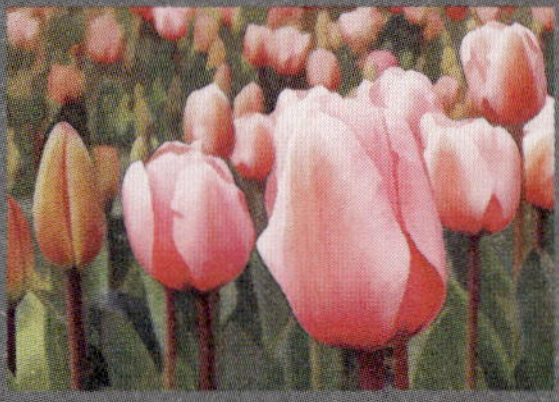

Iraq

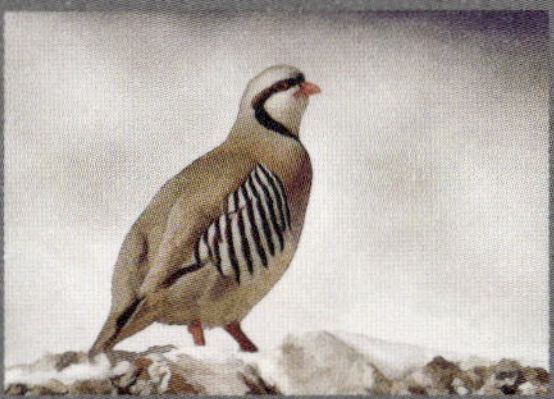

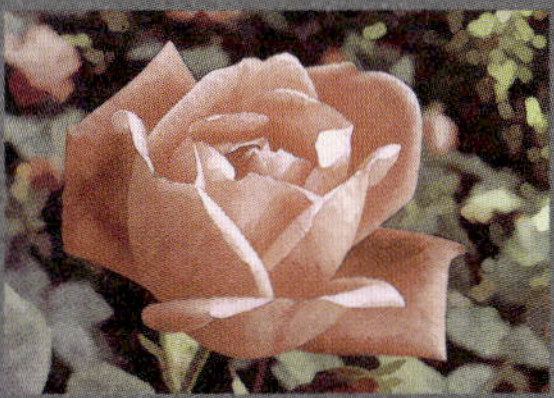

Kazakhstan

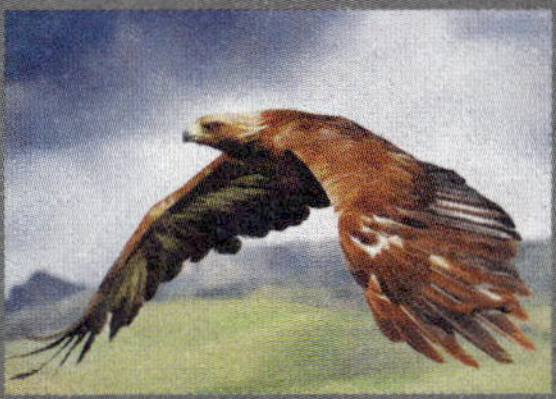

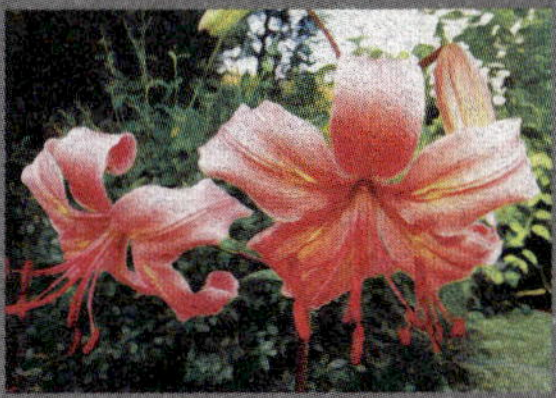

Kuwait

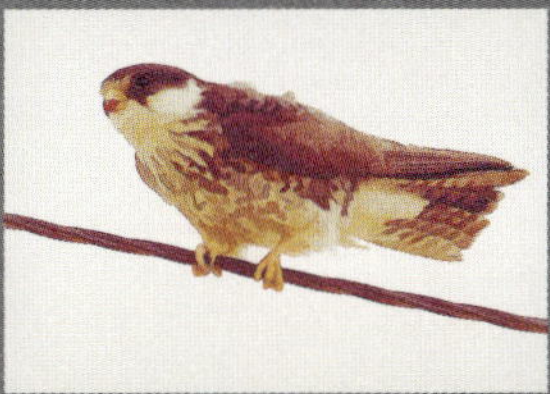

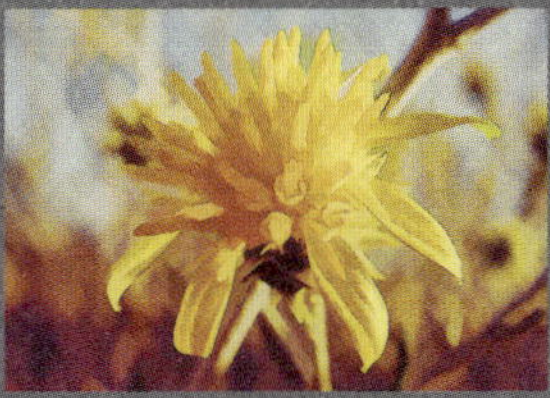

Kyrgyzstan

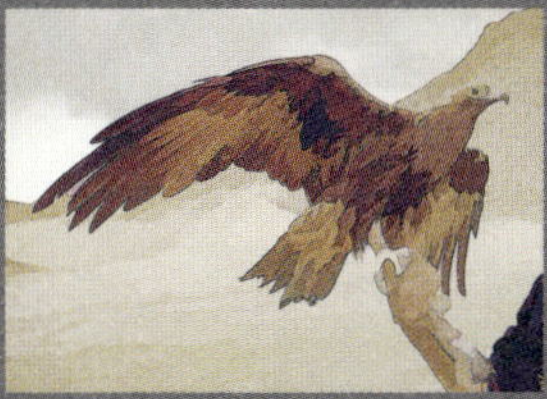

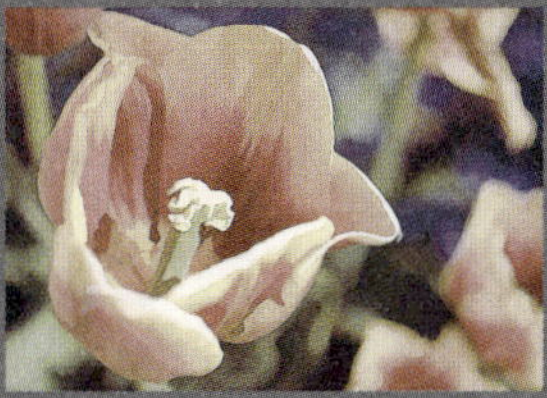

Laos

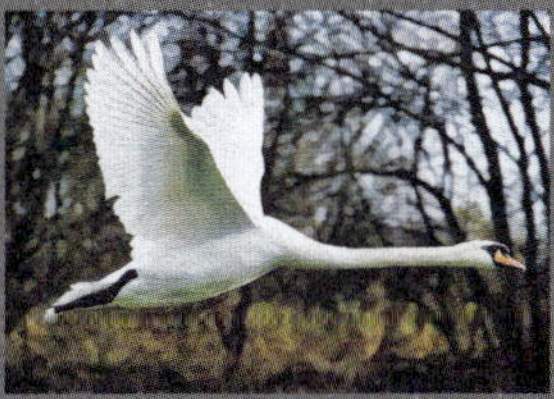

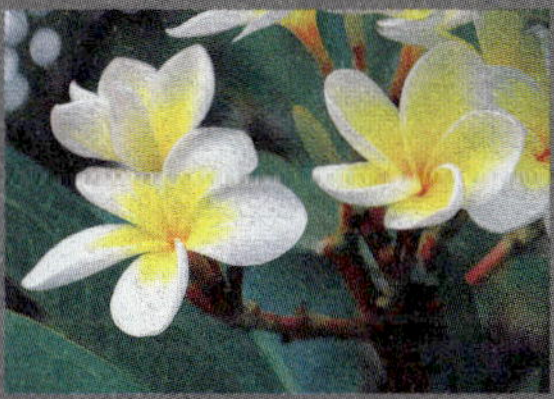

Qatar

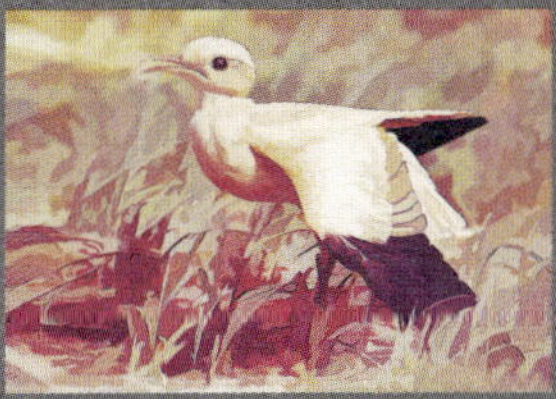

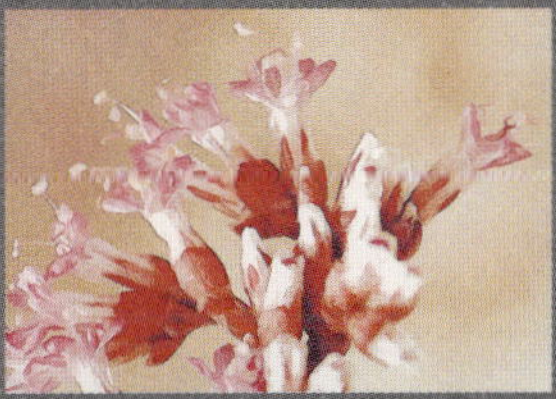

Russia

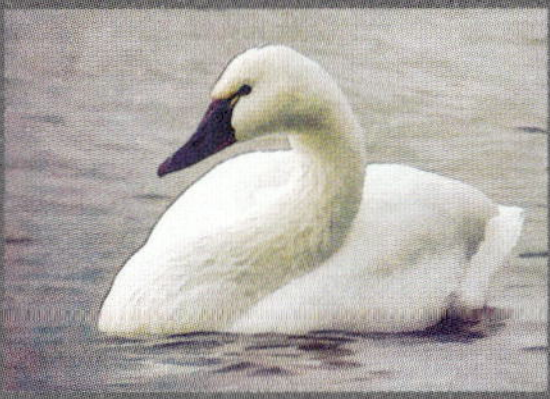

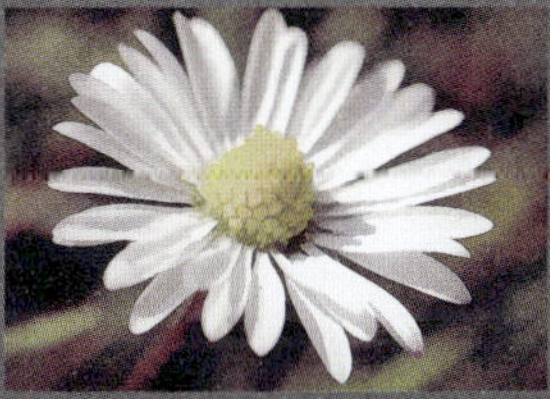

Saudi Arabia

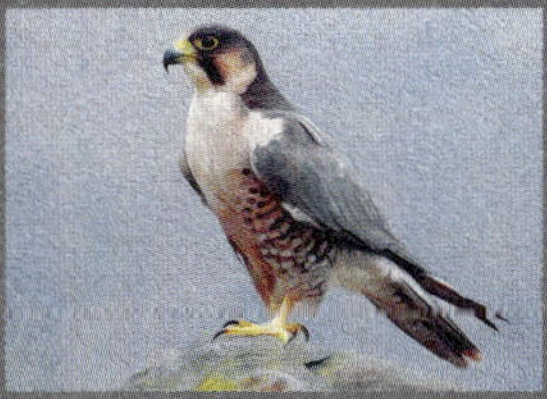

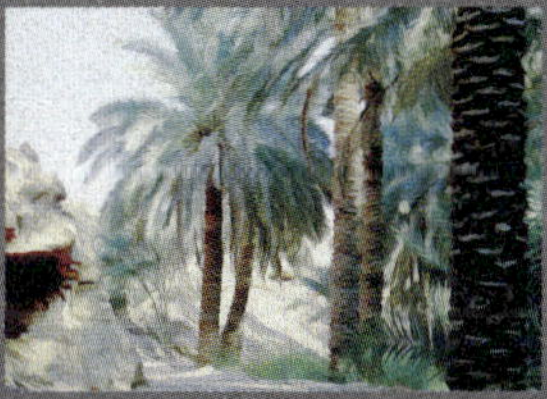

Thailand

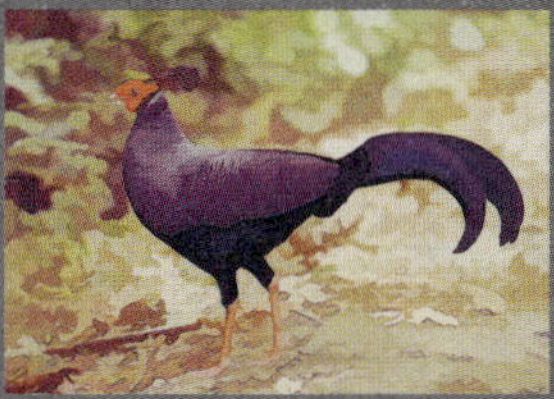

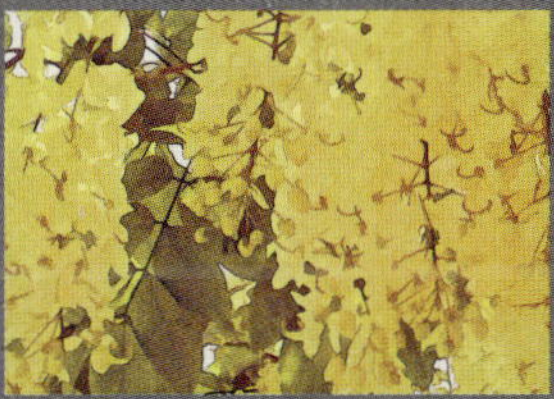

United States

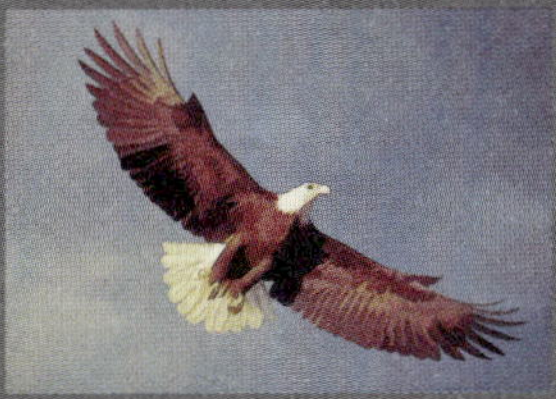

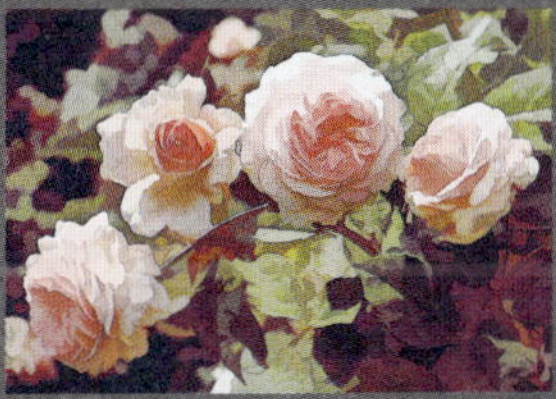

Uzbekistan

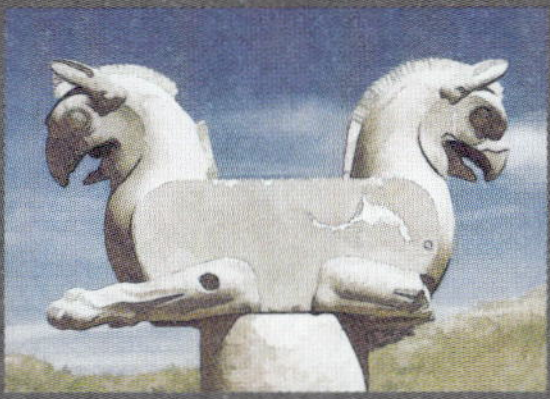

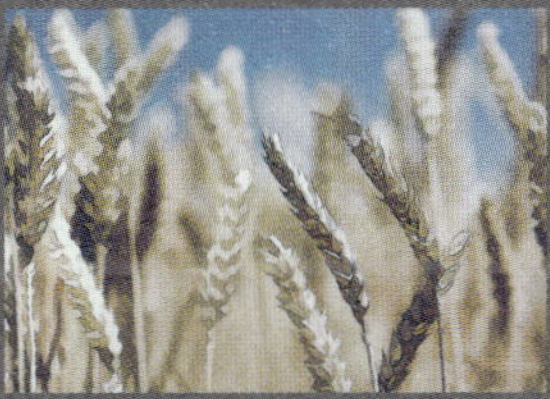

Vietnam

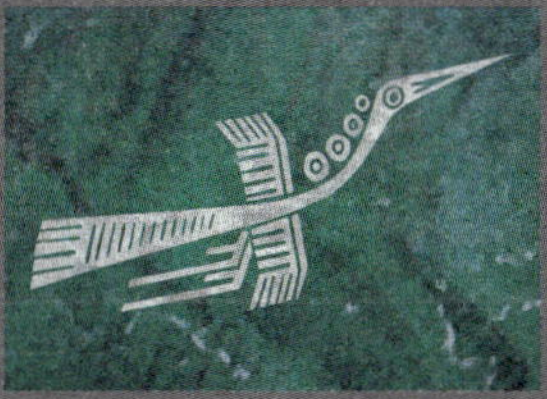

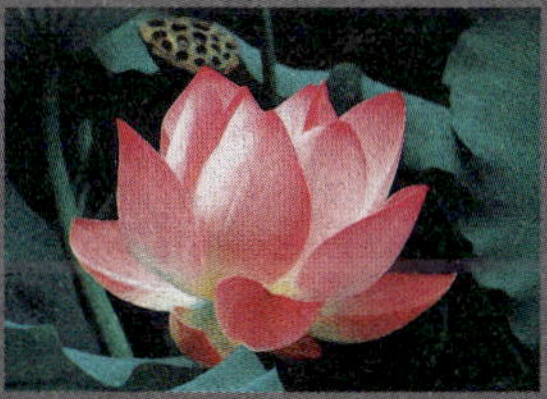

Prisoners of conscience featured in *Yours Truly*

Bahrain

Mahdi Abu Deeb
Ali 'Esa Mansoor al-'Ekri
Abdulhadi al-Khawaja
Salah al-Khawaja
Abdulla al-Mahroos
Abdel-Jalil al-Miqdad
Mohamed Habib al-Miqdad
Abdulhadi 'Abdullah Hassan al-Mukhodher
Sa'eed Mirza al-Nuri
Abduljalil al-Singace
Naji Fateel
Abdulwahab Hussain
Mohamed Hasan Jawad
Hasan Mshaima'
Ebrahim Sharif

Belarus

Mikola Statkevich

Cameroon

Dieudonné Enoh Meyomesse

China

Chen Wei
Chen Xi
Gao Zhisheng
Gong Shengliang
Guo Quan
Kunchok Tsephel Gopey Tsang
Li Bifeng
Li Tie
Liu Xianbin
Liu Xiaobo
Gheyret Niyaz
Runggye Adak
Tan Zuoren
Tenzin Delek Rinpoche
Ilham Tohti
Wang Bingzhang
Xu Zhiyong
Nurmuhemmet Yasin
Alimjan Yimit
Zhang Lin
Zhao Changqing
Zhu Yufu

Cuba

Iván Fernández Depestre

Egypt

Ahmed Douma
Ahmed Maher

Ethiopia

Reeyot Alemu
Andualem Arage
Natnael Mekonnen
Eskinder Nega
Woubshet Taye

India

Irom Sharmila Chanu

Indonesia

Filep Karma
Joni Sinay
Johan Teterisa

Iran

Abolfazl Abedini
Sayed Hossein Kazemeyni Boroujerdi
Arzhang Davoodi
Bahareh Hedayat
Fariba Kamalabadi
Jamaloddin Khanjani
Navid Khanjani
Omid Kokabee
Sa'id Metinpour
Sayed Ziaoddin Nabavi

Afif Naeimi
Kamran Rahimian
Saeid Rezaie
Hossein Ronaghi Maleki
Mahvash Sabet
Keyvan Samimi
Mohammad Seifzadeh
Reza Shahabi
Abdolfattah Soltani
Behrouz Tavakkoli
Vahid Tizfahm

Iraq
Walid Yunis Ahmad

Kazakhstan
Vladimir Kozlov
Roza Tuletaeva

Kuwait
Hamad al-Naqi

Kyrgyzstan
Azimjan Askarov

Laos
Seng-Aloun Phengphanh
Thongpaseuth Keuakoun

Qatar
Mohammed al-Ajami

Russia
Andrei Barabanov
Yaroslav Belousov
Sergei Krivov
Denis Lutskevich
Aleksey Polikhovitch
Artiom Saviolov
Yevgeny Vitishko
Stepan Zimin

Saudi Arabia
Abdullah al-Hamid
Mohammad Fahad al-Qahtani
Suleiman al-Rashudi

Thailand
Somyot Prueksakasemsuk

United States
Shaker Aamer
Shakir Hamoodi
John Kiriakou
Chelsea Manning

Uzbekistan
Salijon Abdurahmanov
Azam Farmanov
Gaybullo Jalilov
Isroil Kholdorov
Dilmurod Saidov
Akzam Turgunov

Vietnam
Lu Van Bay
Tran Vu Anh Binh
Doan Huy Chuong
Thich Quang Do
Nguyen Van Hai
Ngo Hao
Nguyen Doan Quoc Hung
Ho Thi Bich Khuong
Nguyen Xuan Nghia
Le Quoc Quan
Ta Phong Tan
Tran Huynh Duy Thuc
Vo Minh Tri
Le Thanh Tung

Note: Research for Yours Truly *was completed in June 2014. The status of these individuals may have changed since that time.*

FIVE PORTRAITS OF FORTITUDE

First and foremost, *Yours Truly* is a project about people—starting with the 116 brave individuals who inspired an outpouring of hope and encouragement from visitors to Alcatraz Island. Of those prisoners of conscience, five are highlighted in the pages that follow, offering readers insights into the beliefs that have sustained them and the inordinate challenges they have faced for upholding the value of human rights. John Kiriakou (US), Ahmed Maher (Egypt), Chelsea Manning (US), Ebrahim Sharif Al Sayed (Bahrain), Irom Sharmila Chanu (India), and their loved ones share their stories and reflect on *Yours Truly* as a source of strength. A brief biography introduces each subject and outlines the complex political realities that led to his or her arrest. Each profile is complemented by a poignant selection of postcards that were completed and sent during Ai Weiwei's exhibition. Remarkably, all five of these former prisoners are now free—suggesting that even our smallest gestures of kindness can be forces of change.

Opposite: Cellhouse bars on Alcatraz Island

Following page: Ai Weiwei, *Yours Truly*, 2014; interactive installation: custom-designed postcards, racks, and furniture; part of *@Large: Ai Weiwei on Alcatraz*, Alcatraz Island, 2014–2015

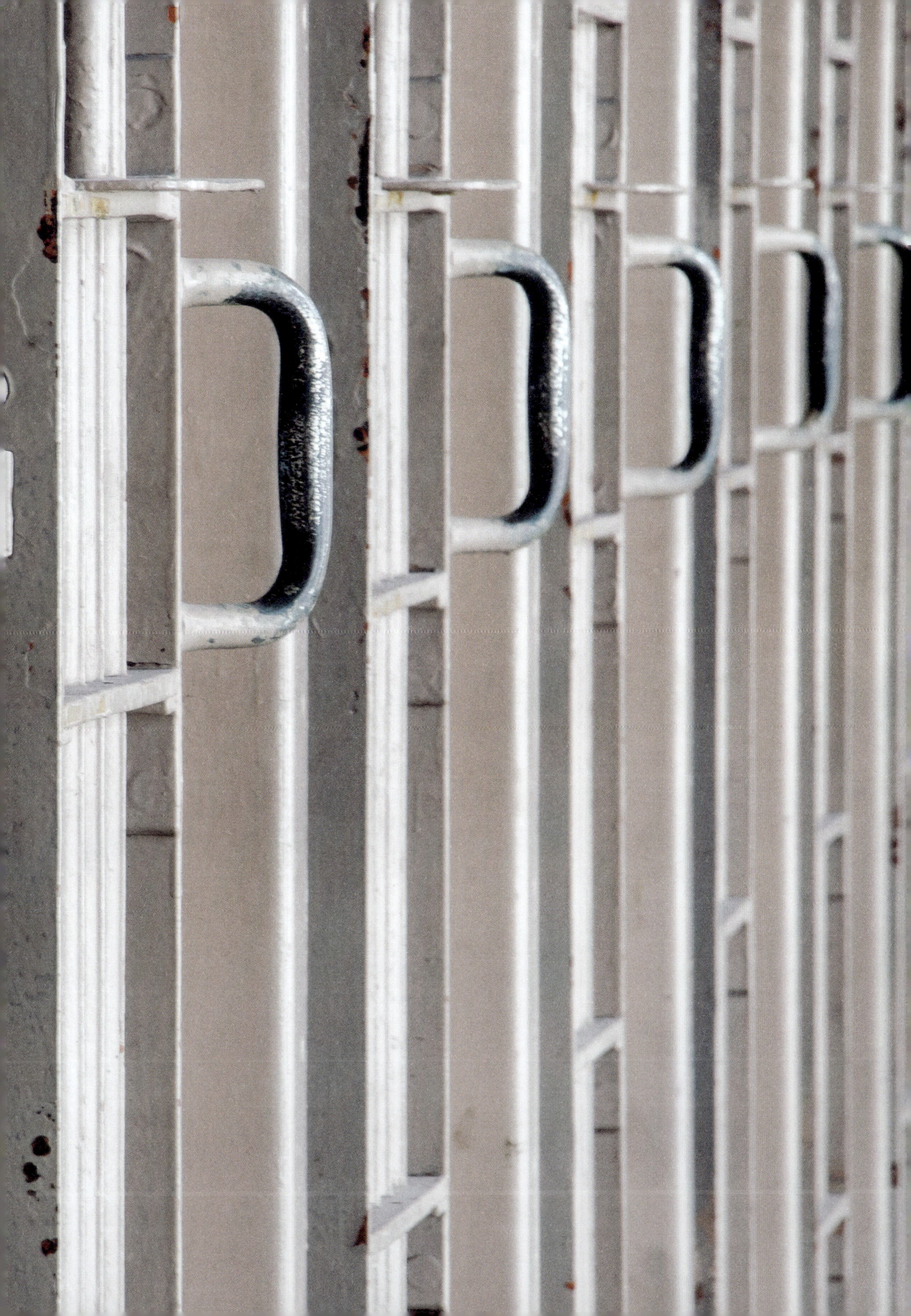

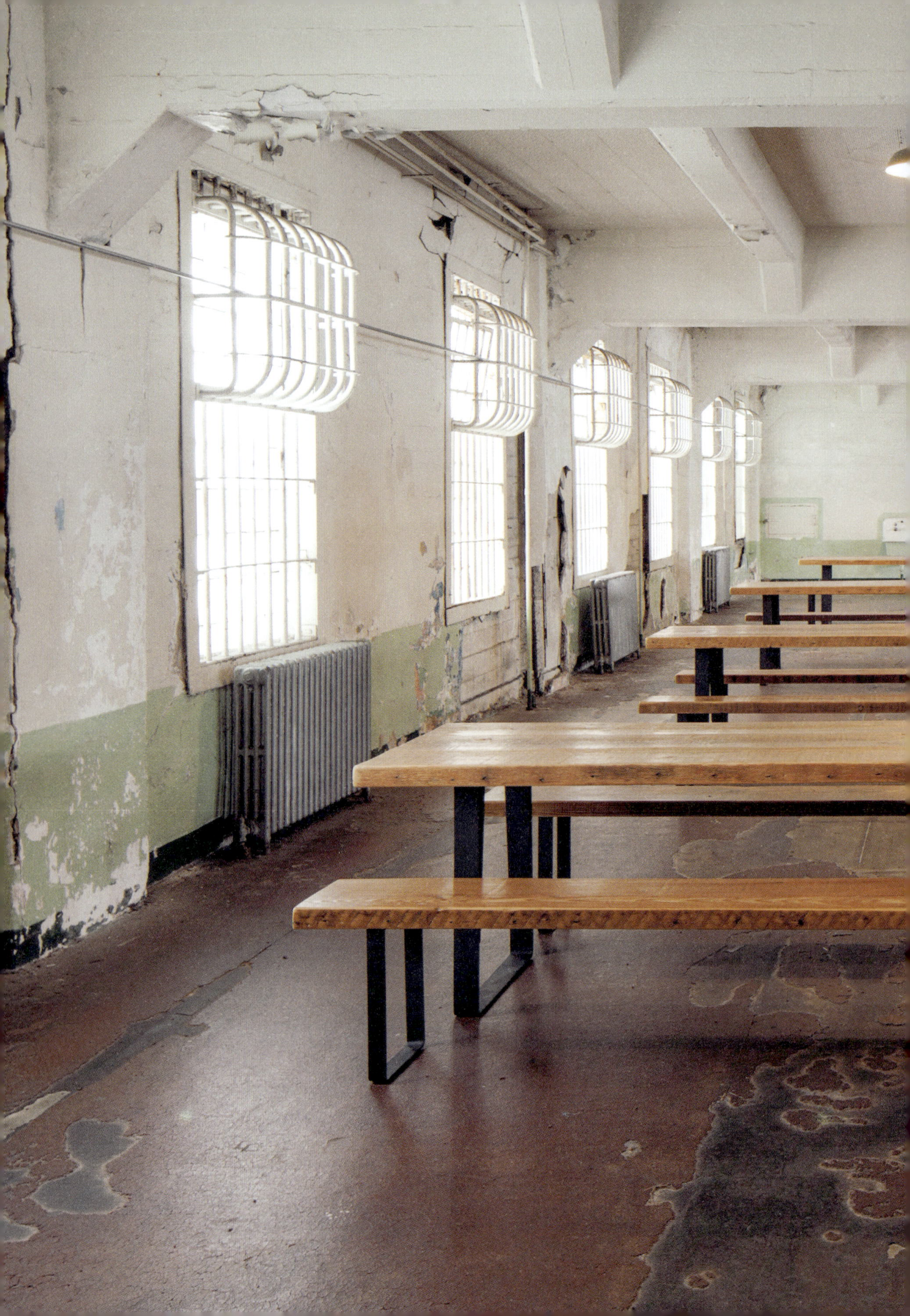

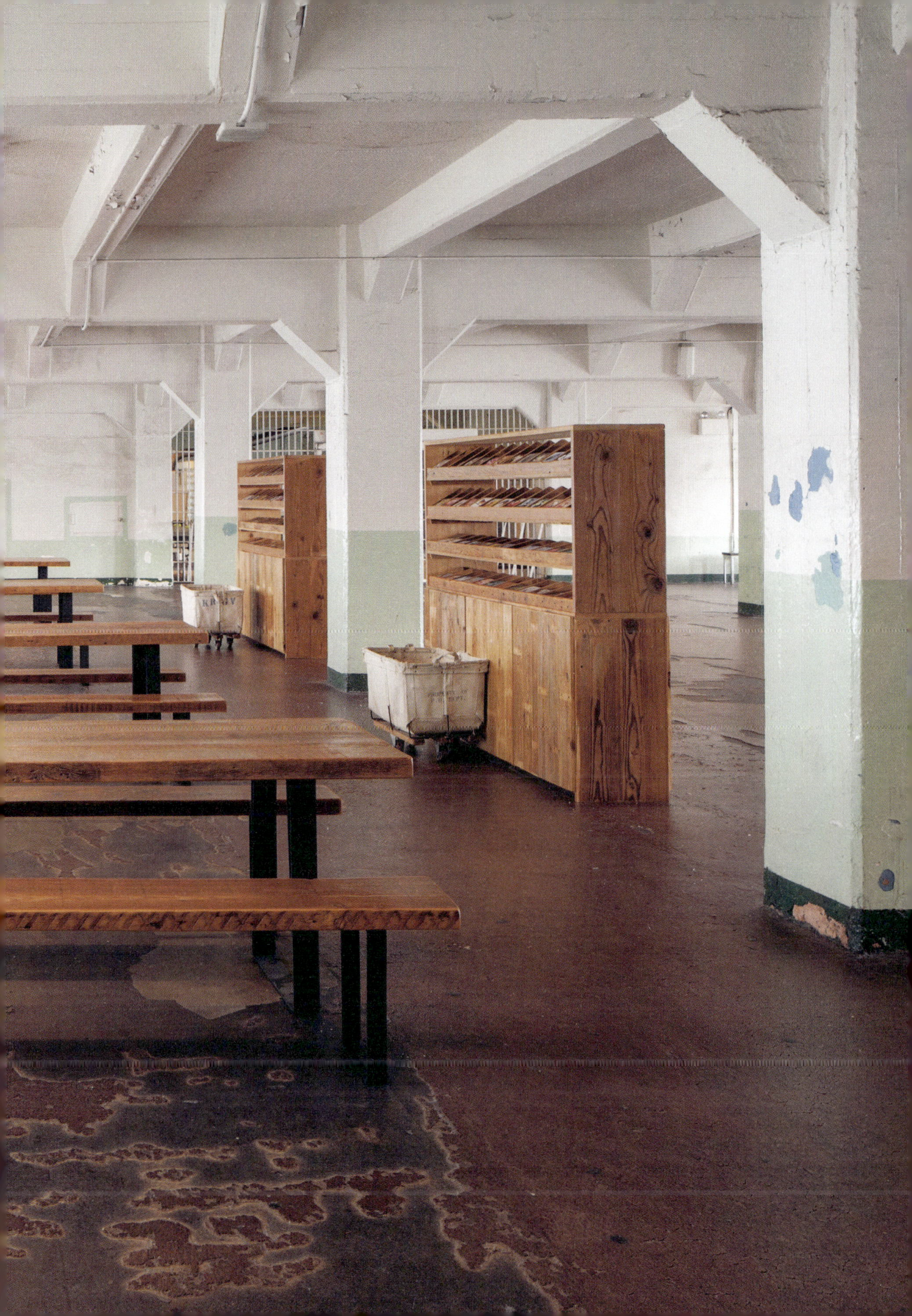

JOHN KIRIAKOU

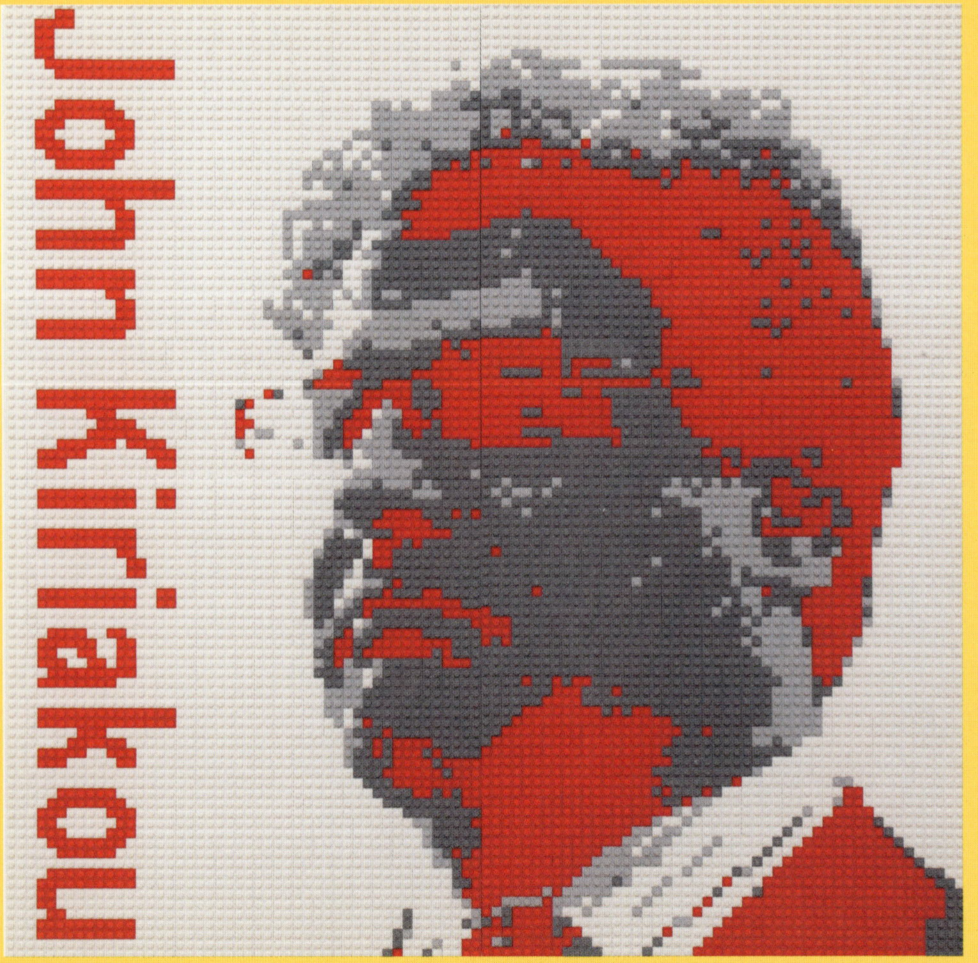

John Kiriakou is an associate fellow with the Washington, D.C., think tank Institute for Policy Studies and an acclaimed author and public speaker, addressing topics that include the war on terror, surveillance, and the prison system. A former CIA officer, Kiriakou was imprisoned for revealing information about the US intelligence community's use of torture.

In 2002, Kiriakou became the chief of counterterrorism operations in Pakistan. He led a CIA team in the March 2002 raid and capture of Abu Zubaydah, then thought to be al-Qaeda's third-ranking official. Following Abu Zubaydah's capture, Kiriakou was appointed executive assistant to the CIA's deputy director for operations, where he served as the agency director's principal Iraq briefer.

Kiriakou left the CIA in March 2004. He later served as a senior investigator on the Senate Foreign Relations Committee and as senior intelligence advisor to Committee Chairman Senator John Kerry. Kiriakou also authored a best-selling book, *The Reluctant Spy: My Secret Life in the CIA's War on Terror*, and worked as an intelligence consultant for ABC News. Over the course of his career, Kiriakou received twelve CIA Exceptional Performance Awards, the CIA's Sustained Superior Performance Award, the Counterterrorism Service Medal, and the State Department's Meritorious Honor Award.

In 2007, Kiriakou appeared on ABC News, becoming the first CIA officer to confirm that the CIA had used waterboarding on detainees and describing waterboarding as "torture." Kiriakou's interview revealed that this practice was official US policy, approved at the highest levels of the government.

The US government began investigating Kiriakou immediately after his media appearance. Five years later, he was charged with multiple felonies related to his whistle-blowing. He became the sixth whistle-blower indicted by the Obama administration under the Espionage Act—a law designed to punish spies.

Opposite: LEGO portrait of John Kiriakou by Ai Weiwei.

Eventually, in order to avoid a trial that could have resulted in separation from his wife and five children for up to forty-five years, he opted to plead guilty to one count of a reduced charge in exchange for a thirty-month sentence.

In 2012, the same year he was charged, Kiriakou was honored with the Joe A. Callaway Award for Civic Courage, an award given to individuals who "advance truth and justice despite the personal risk it creates." Two days prior to sentencing, his portrait was included in artist Robert Shetterly's series *Americans Who Tell the Truth*, which depicts citizens who courageously address issues of social, environmental, and economic fairness.

On February 28, 2013, Kiriakou reported to federal prison in Loretto, Pennsylvania, where he continued to speak out in a written series called "Letters from Loretto." His first installment, which provided a portrait of prison life, was covered and reprinted by major media outlets worldwide. In November 2013, the Peace and Justice Center of Sonoma County, California, honored Kiriakou as its Peacemaker of the Year.

Since his release on February 3, 2015, Kiriakou has continued to be a vocal advocate for whistle-blower protections, prison reform, and increased government transparency. He was awarded the prestigious PEN First Amendment Award from the PEN Center USA in August 2015. In 2016, Kiriakou was awarded the Blueprint International Whistleblower Prize.

In the text that follows, adapted from an interview given to FOR-SITE's Cheryl Haines, Kiriakou tells the story of his whistle-blowing and incarceration and reflects on the impact of the postcards he received via *Yours Truly*.

When I returned to headquarters from Pakistan in 2002, where I had worked as a CIA analyst, the United States had already captured Abu Zubaydah, who at the time was the first senior al-Qaeda capture that the country had undertaken. When I got back to headquarters, a senior officer in the CIA's counterterrorism center asked me if I wanted to be what he called "certified in the use of enhanced interrogation techniques." I asked what that meant. "We're going to start to get rough with some of these guys that we capture," he said. He described what these techniques were and I told him no, that didn't sound like something I would be interested in. I told him it sounded like torture to me and that I had a moral problem with torture and was not interested.

I was one of two people out of fourteen who were approached and said no. And so I moved on to another position. In the intervening months, I learned that we had begun torturing Abu Zubaydah, and later, when we captured other al-Qaeda figures, such as Khalid Sheikh Mohammed and Ramzi bin al-Shibh, that we were torturing them as well. I kept that to myself for a long time and resigned from the CIA in 2004. Then, in late 2007, Brian Ross of ABC News called me and said that he had a source who told him that I had tortured Abu Zubaydah. I said that was absolutely untrue; I was the only person who was kind to Abu Zubaydah. I have never tortured anybody. I've never raised a hand to anybody, and his source was a liar. He said that I was welcome to come onto the show and defend myself.

In the meantime, that same day, and the previous day, President George W. Bush appeared on television and reacted to a report from Human Rights Watch that stated that the United States had been torturing prisoners. The president said that this was not true. He looked right in the camera and he said, "This government does not torture people." I knew that this was a lie. He went on to say that if there was torture taking place, that it was the result of a rogue CIA officer, or a rogue CIA operation. I also knew that this was a lie. I knew that we were indeed torturing prisoners, that torture was official US government policy, and that the president himself had personally signed off on the order to begin torturing prisoners.

I decided to go on ABC News and confirm that we were torturing prisoners and that torture was our policy. I gave quite an extensive interview. My wife went with me. I asked her to go just to make sure that I wasn't saying anything that was classified. Keep in mind that Human Rights Watch had already broken the story that the US government was using torture; Amnesty International announced that we were using torture; the American Red Cross and the International Red Cross, too, both said we were torturing prisoners—so I didn't think I was saying anything new, but it turned out that I was the first current or former CIA officer to confirm the use of torture as policy.

Honestly, I didn't see any other choice. I'm a firm believer in the fact that the truth always comes out. You can't keep the truth bottled up, so the truth is always the best policy. I had been silent for five years, and I decided to tell the truth.

At that point, I didn't have any idea about the potential consequences of speaking out. I assumed that there were going to be former CIA colleagues who would cut me off, but I could live with that. I don't want to be associated with torturers. But I really believed this was going to be a story with a two-day life span. I didn't think that this act was going to become world-wide news, and I didn't believe it was going to change the course of my life, but that's what happened. People often ask me if, given the choice, would I do anything differently. And the answer really is that I would change nothing. My punishment and jail time is all water under the bridge. The important thing is that torture is now illegal in the United States, as it should be, and if I even had a minor role in that, it was all worth it.

Still, when you decide to take on your government, there's an incredible price to pay. First of all, the government has unlimited resources, so you can't fight them until the bitter end. You're going to have to give up at some point, because they'll ruin you financially. They'll ruin you socially. They'll separate you from your friends and from people who would be your natural allies. They'll ruin you professionally. So, in considering your actions, you have to think about the consequences and determine whether or not it's still worth it. And for me, it was still worth it.

I was actually very fortunate. My very first day in prison, there was an announcement for mail call, so I went to mail call not expecting anything. But I had received a postcard from a woman from somewhere in Ohio whom I had never met. I thought that was sweet: My very first day of prison and this woman thought to send a postcard in advance so that it got there the same day that I did.

It turned out that her postcard was the first of seven thousand pieces of correspondence that I received in the twenty-three months that I was in prison. I made a decision very early on that I was going to answer every letter I received. If people were kind enough to take the time to think of me and to write a letter, which is hard to do these days, I would answer. People are busy and everybody relies on email, so if people were going to be that kind, I was going to respond to every letter. I ended up receiving approximately 7,000 letters from about 650 different people. And then one day in a letter, someone wrote, in an aside, "Oh by the way, you're included in this exhibition on Alcatraz."

And I thought, "What's that supposed to mean?" I just dismissed it. And then I got a copy of the magazine *The Week*. And there was a little piece about *@Large*, and I wondered if that was what the person had been referring to in the letter. And then the postcards started coming. The first

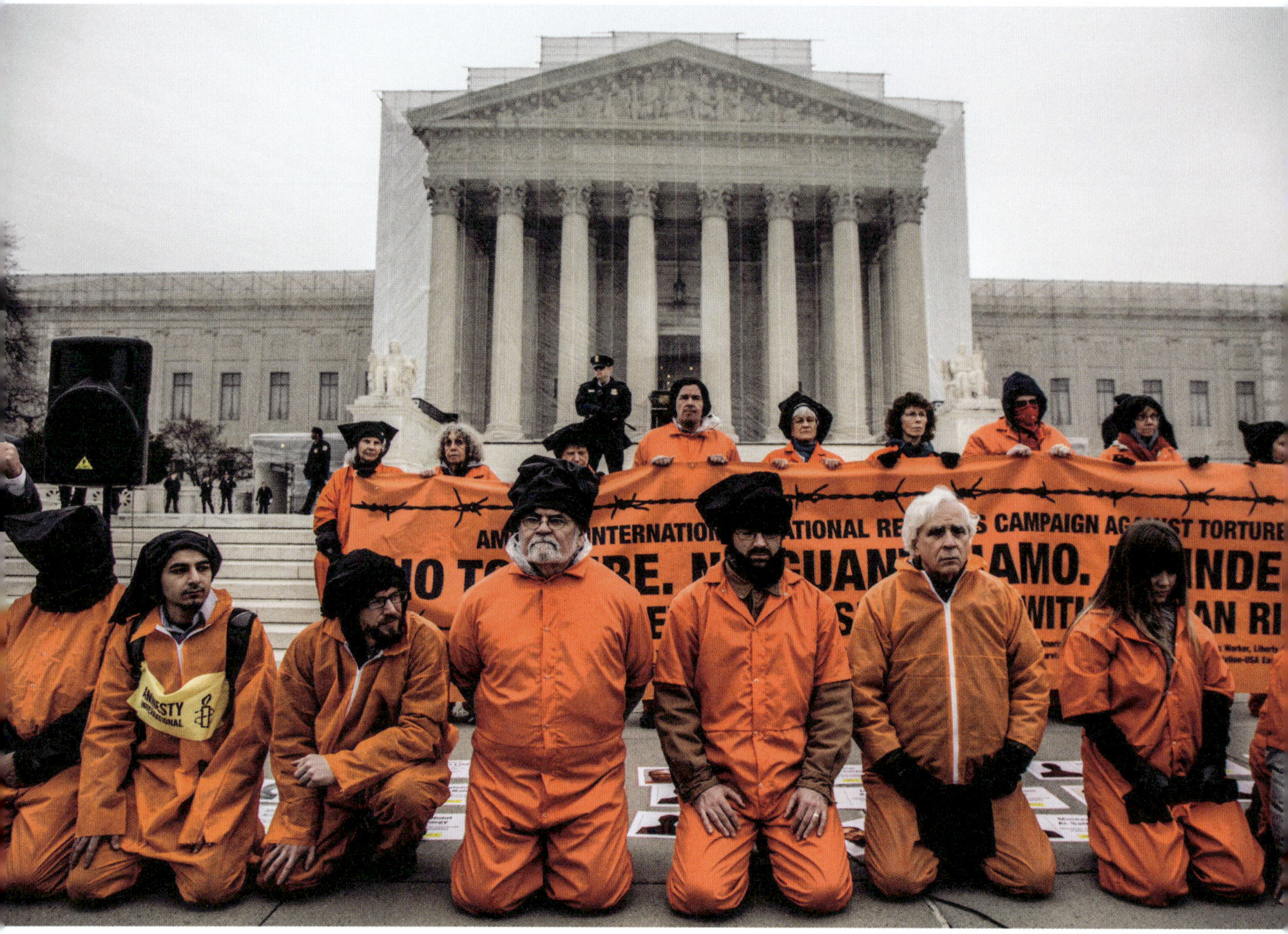

day that I got postcards, I got about two hundred of them, wrapped in rubber bands. And I said to myself, "What in the world is this?" It was a huge stack! The corrections officer handling the mail that day handed it to me as a stack, so I fingered through them very quickly and they were all the same, with eagles and roses on their fronts, and they all had messages written on them by the senders.

I looked at one of the guys that I lived with, and he asked, "What are those?" I didn't know, so we went back to the room. I spread them out over the bed, message side up, and people started wandering into my room and asking what all these postcards were. I told them I wasn't sure, though I thought they might have something to do with an art exhibition on Alcatraz Island. The next day, I got another two hundred and fifty, and I said to myself, "Oh my gosh, this must be a big deal." Then a man in Texas, who was a regular correspondent, printed some information from the Internet and said, "Hey, you're in this Ai Weiwei show." I said, "Ai Weiwei!" I ran straight to the telephones and I called my wife, and I asked, "Have you ever heard of Ai Weiwei?" And she said, "Yes, he's a Chinese artist and dissident, right?" And I said, "Yeah. He did a show at Alcatraz. I'm only getting bits and pieces of information, but can you go online and see what it's all about?" In prison, we could only talk for fifteen minutes and then I'd have to wait for forty-five minutes before I could call again. So I waited a little while and then I called my wife back. She told me that it was a really big deal that I was in this exhibition called *@Large*. Well, as the days and weeks passed, I got more and more postcards, and I was so proud of each

Opposite: Members of Witness Against Torture and Amnesty International dressed as Guantanamo detainees protesting in front of the US Supreme Court to mark the detention center's eleventh anniversary.

one. My only regret was that most people didn't include an address or an email address, because I really wanted to write back and say, "Thank you so much for thinking of me, this really made my day." It really did.

Finally, I heard my name announced on the speaker system: "Kiriakou, report to the mail room." I went down to the mail room and there was another stack of around five hundred postcards. The corrections officer said, "Kiriakou, you better cut this out! You're starting to make me angry!"

I said, "What do you want me to do? I'm not mailing these postcards to myself!"

"Well, whoever's doing it, they better stop," he replied.

I told him, "Well, I can't stop them."

Then I asked, "Have you looked at these postcards?" I used to insult the guards when I thought I could get away with it. I said, "Maybe you should read them, maybe you'll learn something, you know? Why don't you go online and you can learn something from these people. This is an educational event." And they backed off. It turned out that I didn't receive about five hundred that had been sent, but that's okay, because I got the point and certainly they got the point, too. I have to tell you, it utterly turned my mood around.

At that time, I was starting to count down the days to release. I could have been released four months earlier. The Federal Bureau of Prisons decided not to allow me any halfway house time. That was punishment for my activism. At that point, whether I spent four months in a halfway house or four months in prison, it made no difference. But those postcards really kept my spirits up at a time when it was ten degrees below zero outside and we were confined to our cells or our housing units. There was nothing to look forward to. They really made me happy for the remainder of my time in prison.

Loneliness is probably the single worst thing in prison. Everybody feels lonely and forgotten. After all, you go to prison and people move on with their lives, and that's very depressing. But those cards showed me that people had not forgotten me—that people really did care about what happened to me—and that people cared about the issue of torture.

Since my incarceration, I've come to the conclusion that solitary confinement is a form of torture, because most people can't mentally or emotionally survive it. It makes you crazy, but we do it to everybody. There was a man named Albert Woodfox in Angola State Penitentiary in Louisiana who was kept in solitary confinement for nearly forty-four years. He did not speak to another human being who was not a prison guard for thirty years. How can you possibly maintain your sanity like that? You can't.

“Loneliness is probably the single worst thing in prison.”

I’ve also come to the conclusion that the tight and close protection of information leads to corruption. September 11 changed everything for our country. Reasonable people can agree to disagree on this, but I for one am willing to give up some of my safety and security in exchange for being able to keep my freedoms and my civil liberties. I don’t believe that the founding fathers wanted us to give up our constitutional freedoms. That’s what we’ve been fighting for the last two centuries—to keep those constitutional freedoms. Since September 11, Congress and the presidents (plural) have wanted us to give these freedoms up without debate and without complaint. And I’m not willing to do that. When it comes to freedom of information, I have seen how secrets corrupt the system. I have seen how secrets can lead to torture, for example. And I don’t think we can ever go back there. Information has to be free and available to the public. Americans have a right to know what their government is doing in their name.

About four months after I went to prison, I was shocked one day when I read a statement by Edward Snowden in the *New York Times* saying that former NSA executive Tom Drake and I had inspired him to go public with his revelations. I’m very proud of that. The point that Ed Snowden made in that interview is that you can’t keep the information secret. You can’t keep it bottled up. And for every whistle-blower that’s prosecuted, two more whistle-blowers are going to come forward.

If I could deliver a message to Ai Weiwei, it would be this: This was the worst experience of my life. What has happened to me since 2007, I wouldn’t wish on my worst enemy, but some of us decide to take this tough road. The only thing that we should be concerned about is that our children understand what we did, and why we did it, and that they respect us for it. What Ai Weiwei has done, although it has been hard, has cemented his legacy as a hero. His children are going to be proud. His grandchildren are going to be proud. And he should rest easy knowing that he did the right thing.

And to the other prisoners of conscience around the world, I would like to say: I know how easy it is to fall into a depression and to think that the world has turned its back on you. It hasn’t. And you may be in a situation that does not allow you to receive messages of goodwill or support, but know that those messages of goodwill and support exist. They’re out there, even if you’re not seeing them. You’re not alone. You are not forgotten. And people around the world are with you.

Below: John Kiriakou, in a still from director James Spione's film *Silenced*, 2014.

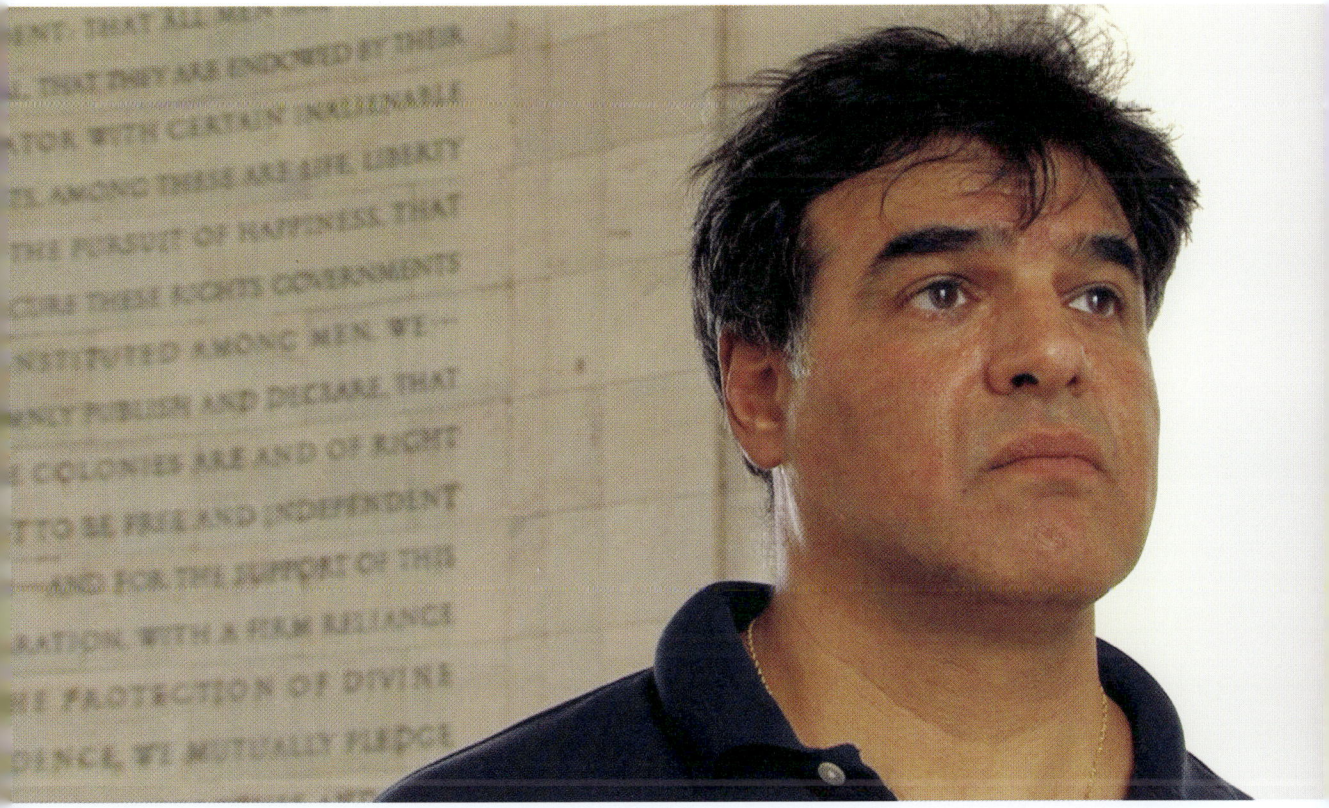

Following pages: A selection of *Yours Truly* postcards addressed to John Kiriakou

@LARGE
AI WEIWEI
ON ALCATRAZ

John,
Thank you for your struggle. Thank you for speaking out against waterboarding. We are all better because of your actions. Liz.

JOHN KIRIAKOU 79637-083
FEDERAL CORRECTIONAL
INSTITUTION, LORETTO
P.O. BOX 1000
LORETTO, PA 15940

United States · Bald Eagle

@LARGE
AI WEIWEI
ON ALCATRAZ

I am a former CIA employee who followed your case with interest and concern. Please know that there are many who admire your actions and sympathize with your plight.
Take care,
A friend

JOHN KIRIAKOU 79637-083
FEDERAL CORRECTIONAL
INSTITUTION, LORETTO
P.O. BOX 1000
LORETTO, PA 15940

United States · Bald Eagle

@LARGE
AI WEIWEI
ON ALCATRAZ

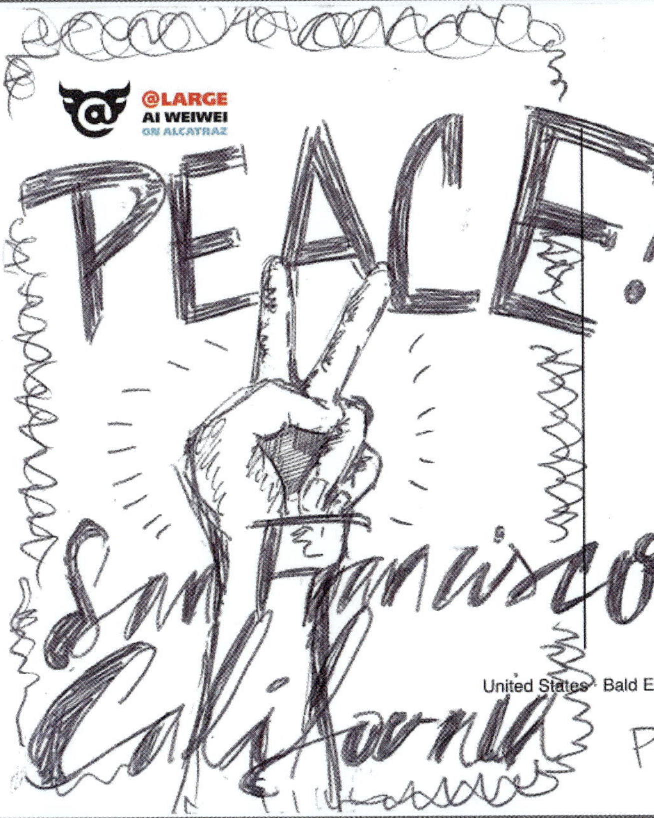

From
me

JOHN KIRIAKOU 79637-083
FEDERAL CORRECTIONAL
INSTITUTION, LORETTO
P.O. BOX 1000
LORETTO, PA 15940

U.K

United States · Bald Eagle

P.S. will follow your story

@LARGE
AI WEIWEI
ON ALCATRAZ

DEAR JOHN –
I ADMIRE YOUR COURAGE AND YOUR CONSCIENCE! YOUR SENTENCE IS SO UNJUST; IT SHOULD BE BUSH & CHENEY IN THERE, NOT YOU.
LA LUTTE CONTINUE...
PAMELA B,
BERKELEY, CA
NONE OF US IS FREE UNTIL YOU ARE.

JOHN KIRIAKOU 79637-083
FEDERAL CORRECTIONAL
INSTITUTION, LORETTO
P.O. BOX 1000
LORETTO, PA 15940

United States · Bald Eagle

@LARGE
AI WEIWEI
ON ALCATRAZ

Thank you for opening up dialogue about torture by Americans + forcing all of us to be more accountable.

PS Unfortunately, the Kardashians will prolly still be on TV when you are released... Best regards, Rick C

JOHN KIRIAKOU 79637-083
FEDERAL CORRECTIONAL
INSTITUTION, LORETTO
P.O. BOX 1000
LORETTO, PA 15940

United States · Bald Eagle

@LARGE
AI WEIWEI
ON ALCATRAZ

To John,

Nice move, but you do not want to mess with the government. Of course they are in the wrong but you are like a lone ranger against an army. No chance of victory.

From
Daniel (Age 10)

JOHN KIRIAKOU 79637-083
FEDERAL CORRECTIONAL
INSTITUTION, LORETTO
P.O. BOX 1000
LORETTO, PA 15940

United States · Bald Eagle

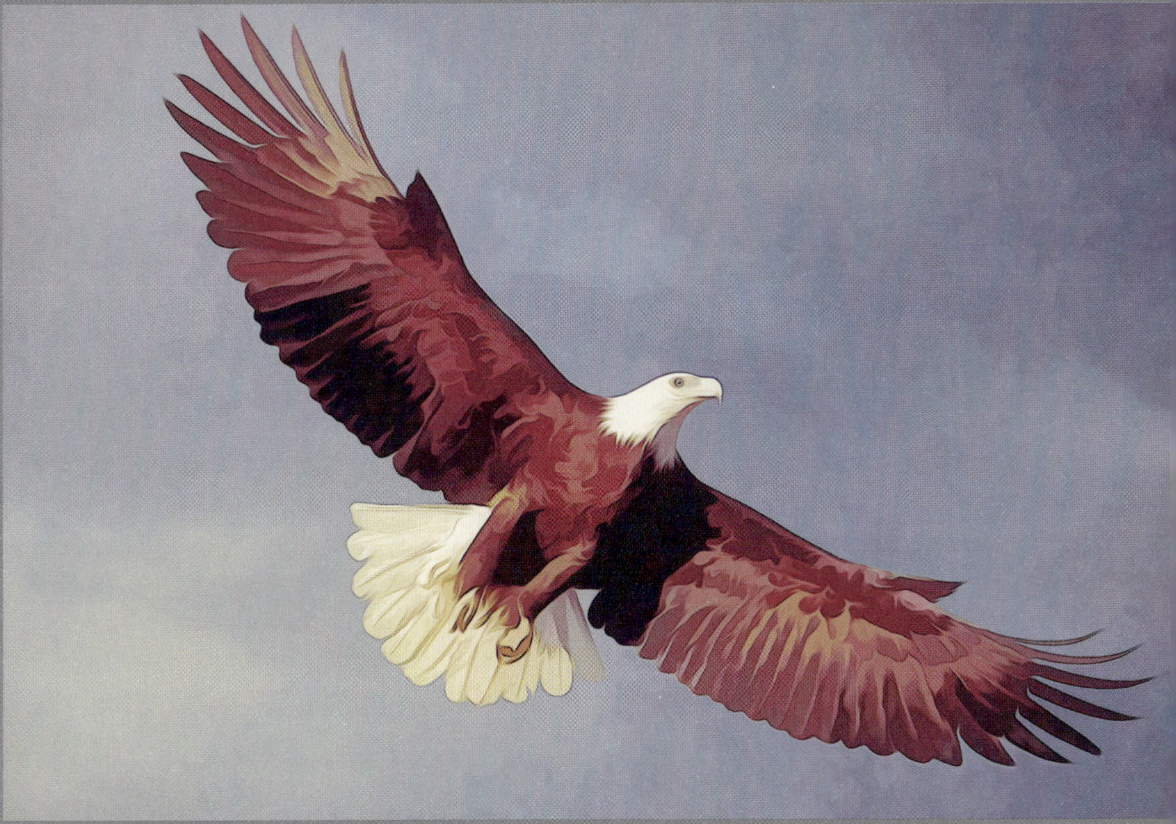

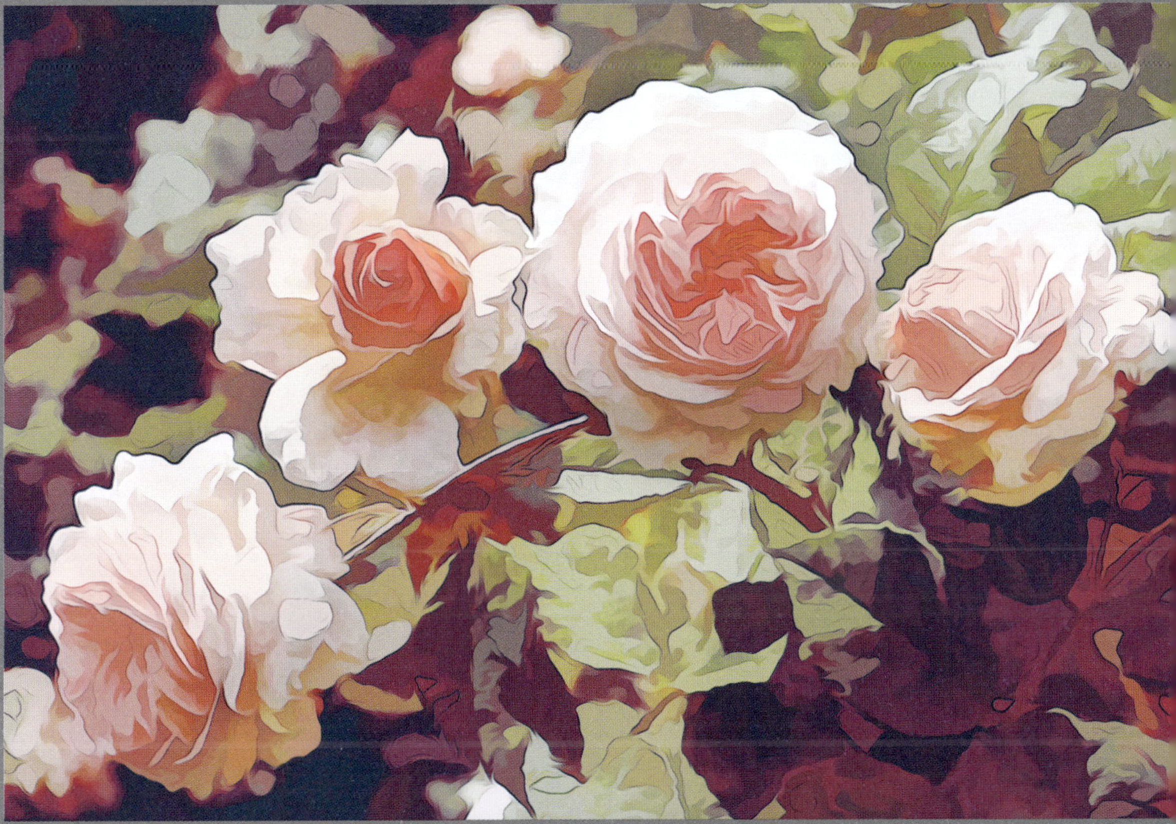

AHMED MAHER

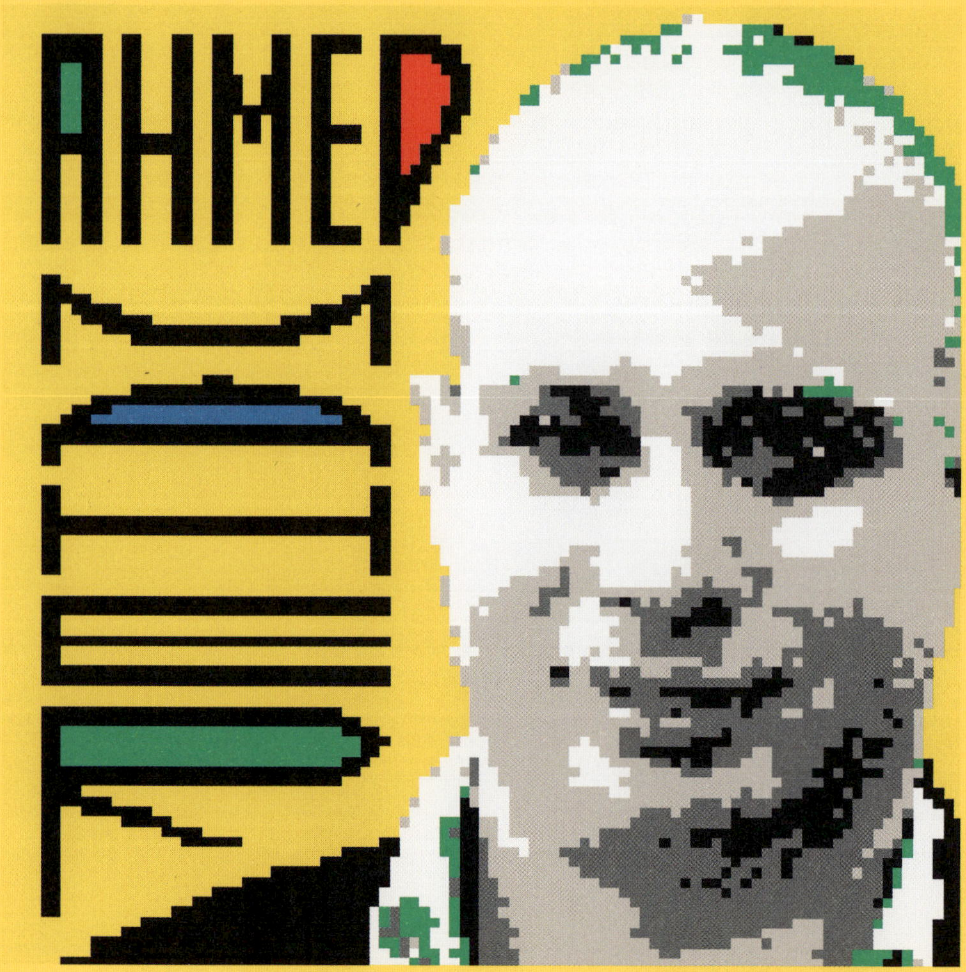

Activist Ahmed Maher is a cofounder of Egypt's April 6 Youth Movement, which spearheaded the demonstrations that ultimately led to the deposition of President Mubarak in February 2011. Maher is a civil engineer who has worked for construction firms in New Cairo. He earned a 2011 Nobel Peace Prize nomination for his work toward democratic reform.

A longtime activist in the fight for human rights, Maher was first arrested in 2006, during a sit-in protesting state interference with the judiciary. Two years later, Maher and fellow activist Esraa Abdel Fattah launched a Facebook group to promote a day of civil disobedience, calling for textile workers to stay home on April 6, 2008, to protest low wages and soaring food prices. The group quickly grew to more than seventy thousand members, evolving into what would become known as the April 6 Youth Movement. Following the protest, Maher began planning another demonstration, targeting the date May 4, 2008—President Mubarak's 80th birthday. In retaliation for his involvement in organizing these demonstrations, Maher was arrested on May 7, 2008, in New Cairo, where he was stripped and beaten while detained. Maher was again arrested and released in late July after speaking to local and international media about his detention and torture at the hands of state security. In June 2010, Maher helped organize a protest after Khaled Said, a young resident of Alexandria, was killed by Egyptian police.

In November 2013, Egypt adopted a new "Protest Law" designed to severely restrict freedom of assembly. Along with activists Ahmed Douma and Mohamed Adel, Maher was among the first to be charged with breaching the law in a protest against it. On December 22, 2013, together with Douma and Adel, Maher was sentenced to three years in prison and fined fifty thousand Egyptian pounds. A statement issued on behalf of the UN Secretary-General Ban Ki-moon characterized the international reaction to the Egyptian crackdown: "Under the controversial new law regulating protests, three prominent democracy and human rights activists were sentenced to three years in prison on Sunday . . . The Secretary-General views these actions, in restricting Egyptians' political space, as contrary to the spirit of Egypt's revolution nearly three years ago, when calls for freedom and democracy motivated Egyptians to take to the streets so courageously and decisively."

On January 4, 2017, after enduring unusually harsh prison conditions, Maher was freed, having completed his three-year sentence. However, under the terms of his release, for the next three years he is required to spend half of each day—from 6 P.M. to 6 A.M.—in lockdown at the local police station, a form of probation aimed at creating a precarious sense of freedom and stifling future activism.

When it became clear that Maher could not receive the hundreds of *Yours Truly* postcards intended for him, visitors to *@Large* were invited to record audio messages instead, which were played for Maher during his incarceration.

The first of the following two texts was written by Ahmed Maher during his imprisonment in Torah Prison in 2014, and it documents the profound sense of powerlessness he felt at the hands of his jailers. The second, produced by Maher shortly after his 2017 release, is a brief but complex reflection on the hopes that spawned the April 6 Youth Movement, the personal toll of his activism, and the strength that the messages from *Yours Truly* inspired.

Opposite: LEGO portrait of Ahmed Maher by Ai Weiwei.

Letter from Torah Prison

"These are the orders." This is a statement that I hear excessively on a daily basis, until it has become as common as "good morning" or "good night."

I spend twenty-two hours a day looking at the ceiling of the cell. And when I try to make a change to break the boredom in these twenty-two hours, I look at the metal ceiling of the two-level bunk bed or I stare at the power outlets. Alternatively, I might listen to the sound of water dripping all night, and sometimes I fall asleep.

A bunk bed. It is true that this is the first time I have slept on a bed with a mattress in prison, for the six times I have been arrested before—from 2005 to 2013—I was in prisons of lesser means. In the past, I slept on the floor; now, I sleep on a bed with a mattress and even a pillow, but I am alone twenty hours of the day.

AlTareed is the time that the inmates go out to play sports, walk, or talk to people, whether inmates, staff, or officers. Throughout my first two weeks here, all twenty-four hours were spent in solitary confinement. I would ask "Am I not going to go out for *AlTareed*!?" They would reply "No, not until eleven days have passed, and because you left and returned under different charges, they will be counted from the beginning."

I would ask, "Well, why can I not go after the first fifteen days? Why not now?" He would look at me, disregarding my question, and reply, "These are the orders." That was the answer!!!

The first fifteen days passed extremely slowly. Magazines, books, and writing were prohibited, and of course there was no television or radio. I sat alone for twenty-four hours a day in the prison cell, staring at its boundaries, the paint, the ground, the door, the windows, the socket outlets, the tap . . . until I had memorized them.

Finally, the solitary cell was opened. I greeted Alaa Abdel Fattah, and teased Ahmed Douma, who was still serving his eleven days of solitary confinement. Two hours later, they told us *AlTareed* time was over.

"Why is it over? Only two hours? Why is it only two hours?"

"These are the orders!"

"We used to have *AlTareed* time until sunset. Whatever happened to that? In Torah Prison in 2006, in Borg al-Arab Prison in 2008, and in al-Arab prison in 2013 . . . "

"That was a long time ago, when President Morsi was around."

"That was President Mubarak's time, before Morsi—and they can both go to hell. Why only two hours??!!"

"These are the orders!"

That is always the answer.

"The prison policy says all day. Also, we want televisions and radios and MP3s. We want to send letters."

"There is none of that here!"

"Why??!!"

"These are the orders."

"We had all of those things when we were detained before. Where are they?"

"Listen, Ahmed. The circumstances are different. We are in different times now, and this prison is not like other prisons."

"What do you mean? Other prisons have these things!"

"You are not in just any prison. Times and circumstances are different. You must understand this. Besides, this prison is cleaner than any other prison. You are in a clean place and you have your own mattress, blanket, pillow, and toilet, and all is well."

"I know that this place is cleaner than other prisons, and there are no insects in the cells. I have tried other prisons and I know. But over there, there were also televisions and radios, and I would walk around all day and see people and speak to them. And at the same time, the other inmates also had these things."

"Listen Ahmed, these are the orders. The circumstances are different, and you and your friends are not like other inmates."

The days pass slowly, and the hours pass slowly. I spend the twenty-two hours looking at the ceiling, the door, the windows, and the boundaries of the cell. I listen to the water dripping at night, and sometimes I sleep.

It is true that there are not the thousands of cockroaches, insects, and rats, as there were in Torah Prison in 2006. But there is nothing—no people, no sound, no television, no radio—nothing. Even the insects, cockroaches, and rats used to be some form of entertainment. You could keep yourself entertained trying to catch them.

And the phrase "these are the orders" repeats without justification, followed by intense arguments. *May God forgive me . . . God damn the orders. For the last time, I am not from the [Muslim] Brotherhood. I want to shave my beard. I have the right to shave my beard.*

And after long hours of arguments, finally they agree to allow shaving blades.

"Alright then, now let us have television or radio or MP3s. We want to listen to the news."

"No."

"Why not?"

"These are the orders."

Opposite: Egyptian protesters in Tahrir Square during a mass rally marking the first anniversary of the uprising, Cairo, January 25, 2012.

The usual reply. Damn the orders!!

There are no rules that prevent them; these minor things are common in any other prison. It is the right of an inmate to be out all day and see people and speak to them. There is nothing that prohibits television or radio or MP3s.

While I was alone in solitary confinement, I heard the music of the singers Umm Kulthum and Fairuz. I listened closely and enjoyed it. Wow! Who is the lucky son of a gun who has a radio? After days of struggling and arguing, they finally allowed Ahmed Douma to bring in a radio, but only AM. FM is prohibited. Only one frequency.

"Is the radio working for you, Douma?"

"No, it isn't picking up anything."

"Sir, we want FM radio. We want to listen to the news. It is our right."

"Prohibited."

"Why?"

"These are the orders."

"These strange orders of yours. The AM radio isn't picking up anything, only noise. Just to say that you allowed us some form of radio?"

Struggles and arguments lasting days over things that should be basic rights (books, letters, meetings, seeing the other inmates all day). Alright, let us be together instead of in solitary confinement. Television, radio, MP3s—these things were normal in the days of Mubarak and of Morsi.

What a boring detention!! So not only do I get [sentenced to] three years, but I am also deprived, kept in solitary confinement, barely able to see anyone, no way to follow the news!! All of this!! All of this because I opposed the Protest Law??

Damn the orders and whoever gave the orders. No one knows who gave the orders anyway, or why they want to deprive us further in our three years of prison??!!!!

Ahmed Maher
January 19, 2014

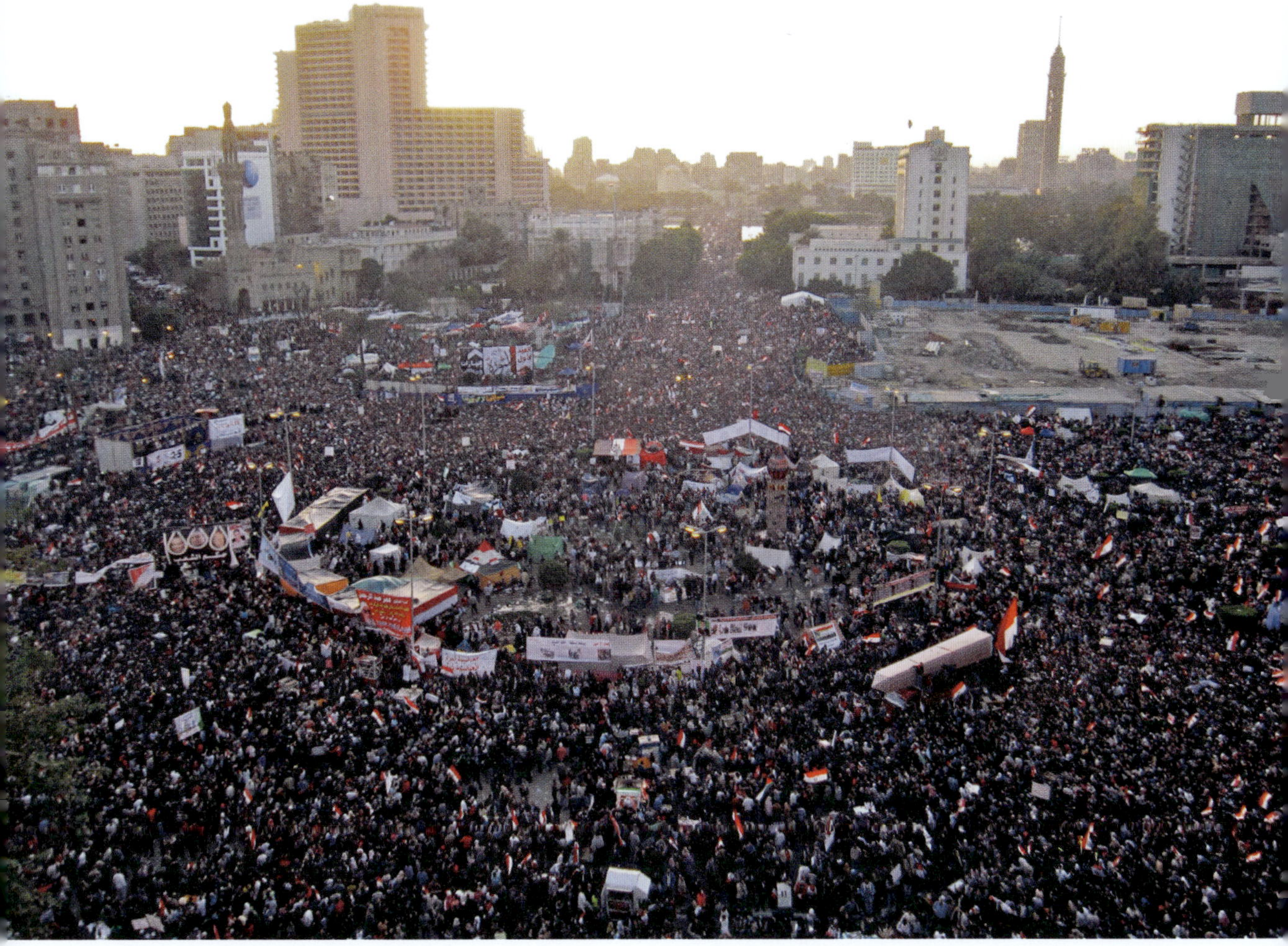

Reflections on Freedom

In 2008, we [the founders of what came to be known as the April 6 Youth Movement] were inspired by many models of social change, such as the revolutions and social movements in South America and Eastern Europe—those that had taken place in Chile, the Czech Republic, Serbia, Ukraine, Georgia, and especially Poland. We followed all these movements, reading and learning a lot about the various revolutions.

At that time, revolution was not our main goal. Our goal was to make a change, to create a better life for people, to foster democracy under a new regime that would respect human rights. We considered revolutionary action to be a tool, rather than a goal, so we started by encouraging people to join us, to say no to the government, and to be more active.

We used Facebook as a platform for the Youth Movement in order to attract new people to our group and to mobilize them with our messages. It was still a somewhat new website at that time. Social media was an important tool, but again, it was just a tool. The more important thing is the message you are trying to share, and how and when this message is spread. I think one difference between the success of that time and the failure [of today's activists] is that now the ruling regime understands the game and can do the same thing. They have a lot of electronic groups to defend any activity of the president. Now they are using social media against us.

Before this movement, I was arrested and spent three months in the prison, so I expected violence. But the police followed us a lot—me more than anyone else—before the revolution. It has not been easy for me and my colleagues in the

Youth Movement to have any rights inside of prison. From the beginning, the security forces used torture against us, as well as smearing our reputations. The conditions for any political prisoner are very bad—worse than those of a prisoner who is being held on criminal charges. But because they considered me to be the head of this movement, they put me under constant monitoring, searching my cell and destroying everything, violating my rights. They prevented me from having letters, books, or newspapers, which was within my rights. They were watching all the time, and it was difficult to visit the doctor or have any medical care inside the prison.

On a personal level, my activism has made my life unstable. I have been arrested many times and have spent three years in prison, so I don't have a stable life like an ordinary person. And my children's lives are also unstable. There have been a lot of rumors about me that are untrue, a lot of fake stories and conspiracy theories. My activism has also affected my mother and father, my wife, and my job. Everything is difficult after this kind of activism.

Now, with the conditions of my release, I am under surveillance and need to stay twelve hours of every day in the police station, in a cell like those in a prison. I'm not allowed to stay in my home in the evening, not allowed to travel outside of Cairo, not allowed to attend evening lectures at a university, not allowed to use the internet in the evening, and I experience a lot of monitoring. I heard about the surveillance Ai Weiwei was under following his release from detention—that his freedom was not complete freedom. Now, the conditions of my release are somewhat similar, and I can imagine that he felt like I do now.

In this time after prison, I cannot determine what I have gained, but we tried. We tried, and we will be continually trying. One thing that helps me to stay and continue my activism is that there are a lot of people who respect my efforts, and there are a lot of people who have tried to help. There is a lot backing up the regime, but people will always try to find a solution. They have the same dream, and I cannot betray them. I cannot betray my supporters, my friends, or my followers. I cannot betray my brothers, or my family, or the people who have trusted me. I need to keep up my efforts and keep my faith. Yes, it's not easy—especially after prison, under surveillance—but I am trying to recover and continue again.

Ai Weiwei's efforts have helped me a lot. When I first heard of Ai Weiwei's project *@Large*, I didn't know all the details. When I began to understand the story from inside prison—when I heard what he had done for my friends and I—it was a good feeling. I was surprised that someone in another country very far from me cared about my situation and supported me. It's given me a lot of support and it helped me to stay alone in solitary confinement. It's a very important question: How we can continue to try to help other prisoners of conscience who are enduring the same

Below: Ahmed Maher participating in a discussion at the official launch of United Nations Human Rights Day at the Ford Foundation, New York, December 10, 2012.

conditions in other countries? How can we give strength to other prisoners around the world, to help them face torture and corruption? The situation can be depressing for prisoners, so it's something we must continue to think about.

To be in solitary confinement is very bad. There is no one to talk to, no one to complain to, no one who can listen to you, no one who can say, "I am sorry for you." During my time at Torah Prison, the authorities didn't allow any postcards for the prisoners, so I didn't get the cards from *Yours Truly*. But voice messages, recorded by the visitors to *@Large*, were smuggled to me, and I was able to secretly listen to them inside the prison. I heard many of these messages, and they gave me a lot of support and helped me a lot. It was amazing that, when I was in solitary confinement, living alone for three years, I heard voice messages from people—I didn't know them, but they were supporting me. They had heard about me through *@Large*, and they encouraged my efforts, saying to me, "Keep on pushing, and keep your faith. Continue your efforts. It's very important." I received these messages during a very bad time of punishment in the prison, so when I heard them, it gave me a lot of support. When I knew that there were people around the world who knew about me and were supporting me, I thought, "I can stand, and I can be stronger."

Can you imagine that when the authorities visited me after midnight, following an illegal search and illegal punishment inside my cell, they said to me, "No one remembers you. No one cares about you, so you need to obey." Then, two or three days after that, I received these audio messages from *Yours Truly*. These voice messages from people outside Egypt, they saved me.

How can I do that for another prisoner? I think about that now.

Ahmed Maher
April 2017

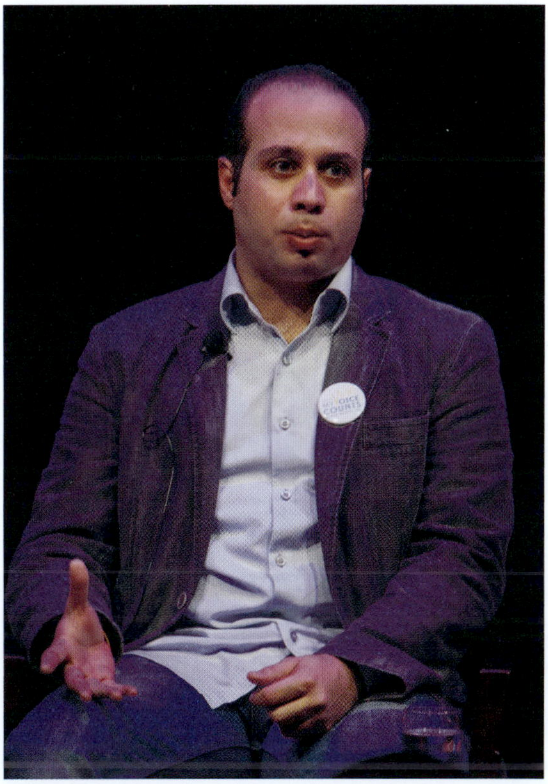

Following pages: A selection of *Yours Truly* postcards addressed to Ahmed Maher

@LARGE
AI WEIWEI
ON ALCATRAZ

Hello Ahmed,

I hope this letter finds you well, despite your current state of affairs. I strongly believe that you should not be in prison, but sometimes progress has a cost. I think you are awesome.

- Roy, 14

Egypt · Golden Eagle

AHMED MAHER
TORA (TURA) PRISON
TORA PRISON DISTRICT
SOUTH CAIRO
EGYPT

@LARGE
AI WEIWEI
ON ALCATRAZ

Dear Ahmed,

I'm writing on behalf of my brother, Ramesh Srinivasan, who I think you may have once met in Egypt and who told me tales of your bravery and courage. We all stand in solidarity with the Egyptian people in the face of the totalitarian injustice to which they are exposed. Please know that we stand with you! With love and peace, Mahesh, San Francisco, CA

Egypt · Golden Eagle

AHMED MAHER
TORA (TURA) PRISON
TORA PRISON DISTRICT
SOUTH CAIRO
EGYPT

@LARGE
AI WEIWEI
ON ALCATRAZ

You're a hero.

Never quit.
We support you.
You'll change the world, Mr. Maher.

- Benjamin S

AHMED MAHER
TORA (TURA) PRISON
TORA PRISON DISTRICT
SOUTH CAIRO
EGYPT

Egypt · Golden Eagle

@LARGE
AI WEIWEI
ON ALCATRAZ

[redacted] I'm Black. I'm a woman.
I'm gay. I'm an artist
My name is Leila
I want to thank you,
without protests and
"freedom of speech" in
Amenca I wouldn't
be able to connect
with you today.
WITH LOVE & GRATITUDE

AHMED MAHER
TORA (TURA) PRISON
TORA PRISON DISTRICT
SOUTH CAIRO
EGYPT

Egypt · Golden Eagle

@LARGE
AI WEIWEI
ON ALCATRAZ

Ahmed — I am a fellow Muslim born in the US. Both my parents are from Peshwar in Pakistan. I have always lived in the US but have visited Peshwar often. It was once a beautiful city that is now in decay. The Intercontinental Hotel where I spent my summers was blown up several years ago. I fear my parents home will become someplace where I can never take my children because Peshwar lacks leaders like you. I hope that you will continue to fight for Egypt after your incarceration ends.
I pray that there are men like you who can do the same in Pakistan.

—Sangeen

AHMED MAHER
TORA (TURA) PRISON
TORA PRISON DISTRICT
SOUTH CAIRO
EGYPT

Egypt · Golden Eagle

@LARGE
AI WEIWEI
ON ALCATRAZ

Hello Mr. Maher,

Your situation is unfortunate, and I hope freedom greets you soon. I am amazed and humbled by your courageous stand against the suppression of your natural ability to freely express your ideas. Here in the USA, we are witnessing massive protests in response to police brutality and murder. Protesters here in the land of the free have been assaulted, framed and arrested. However, the environment in the USA is so different from that of Egypt. Here, we have surely taken our constitutional right of peaceful assembly for granted—or, at least I have. I am unsure of how to respond or what to write. I will try to learn more of your struggle and to have (this will probably be small comfort for you) gratitude for the deeply flawed yet relatively permissive environment I live in. PEACE

[illegible]

AHMED MAHER
TORA (TURA) PRISON
TORA PRISON DISTRICT
SOUTH CAIRO
EGYPT

Egypt · Golden Eagle

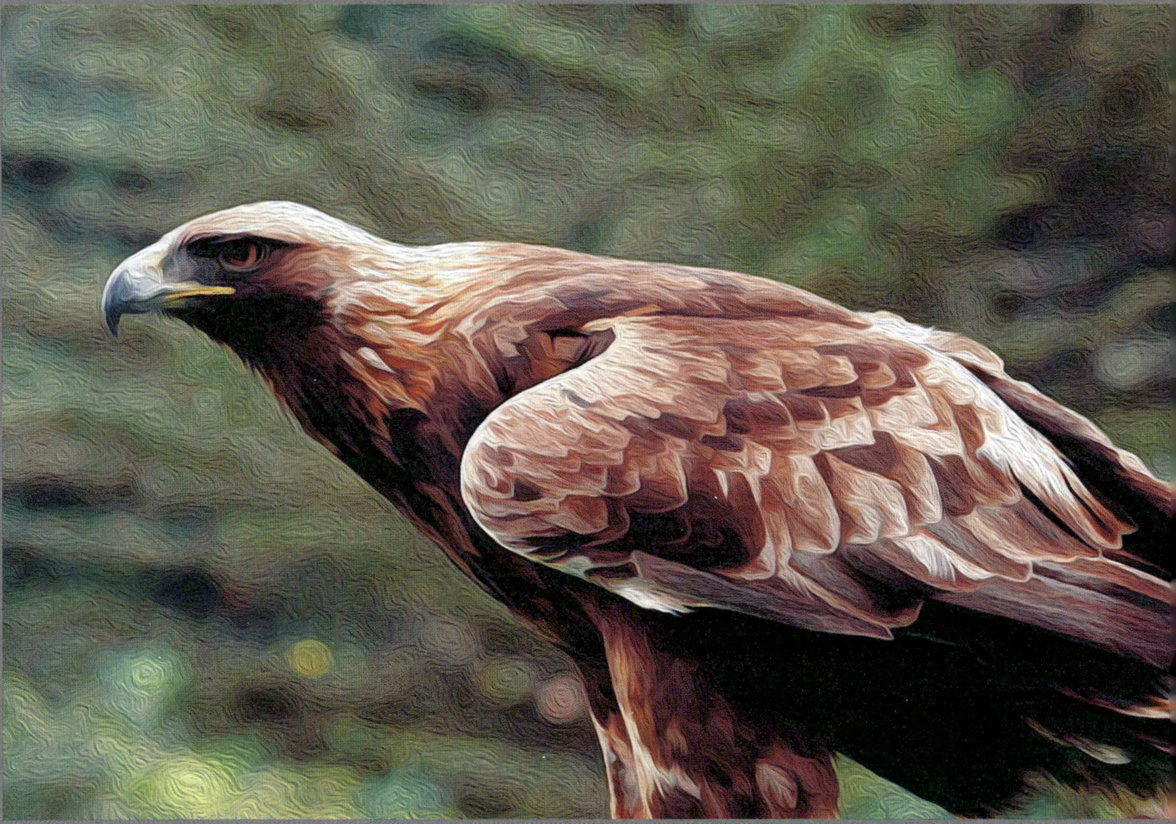

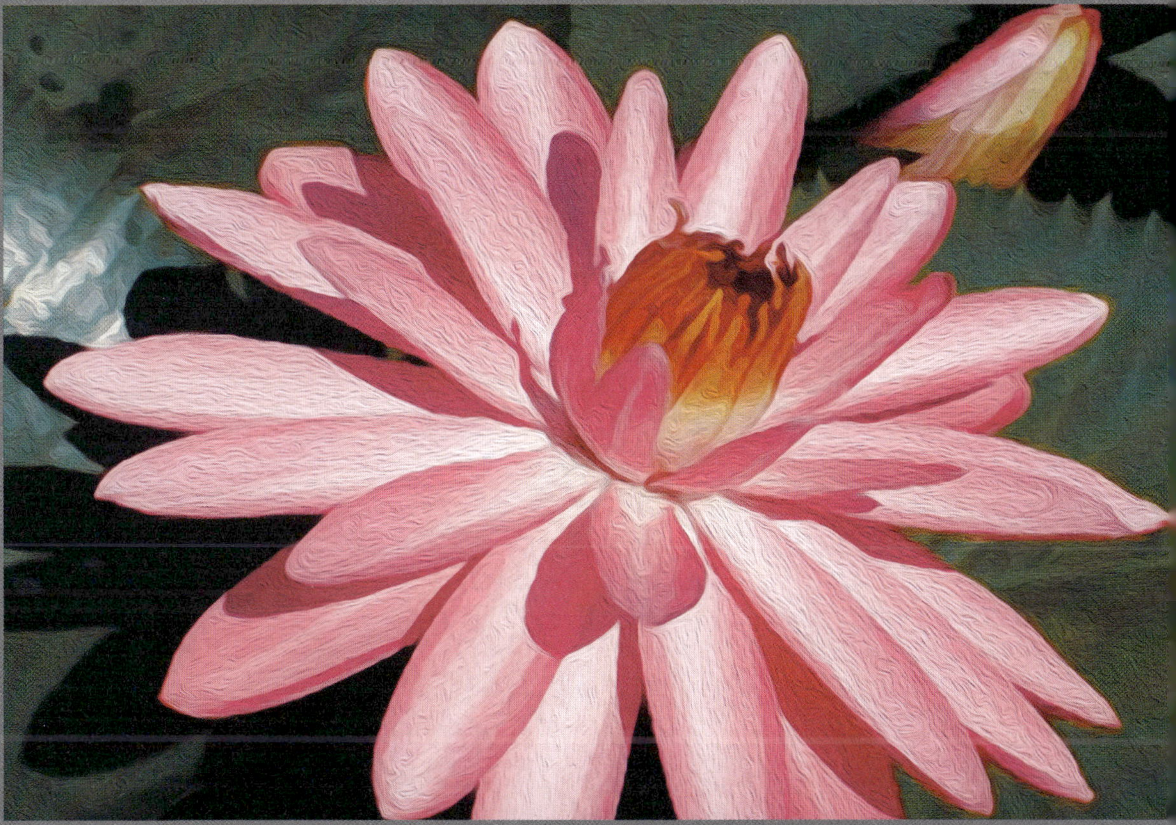

CHELSEA MANNING

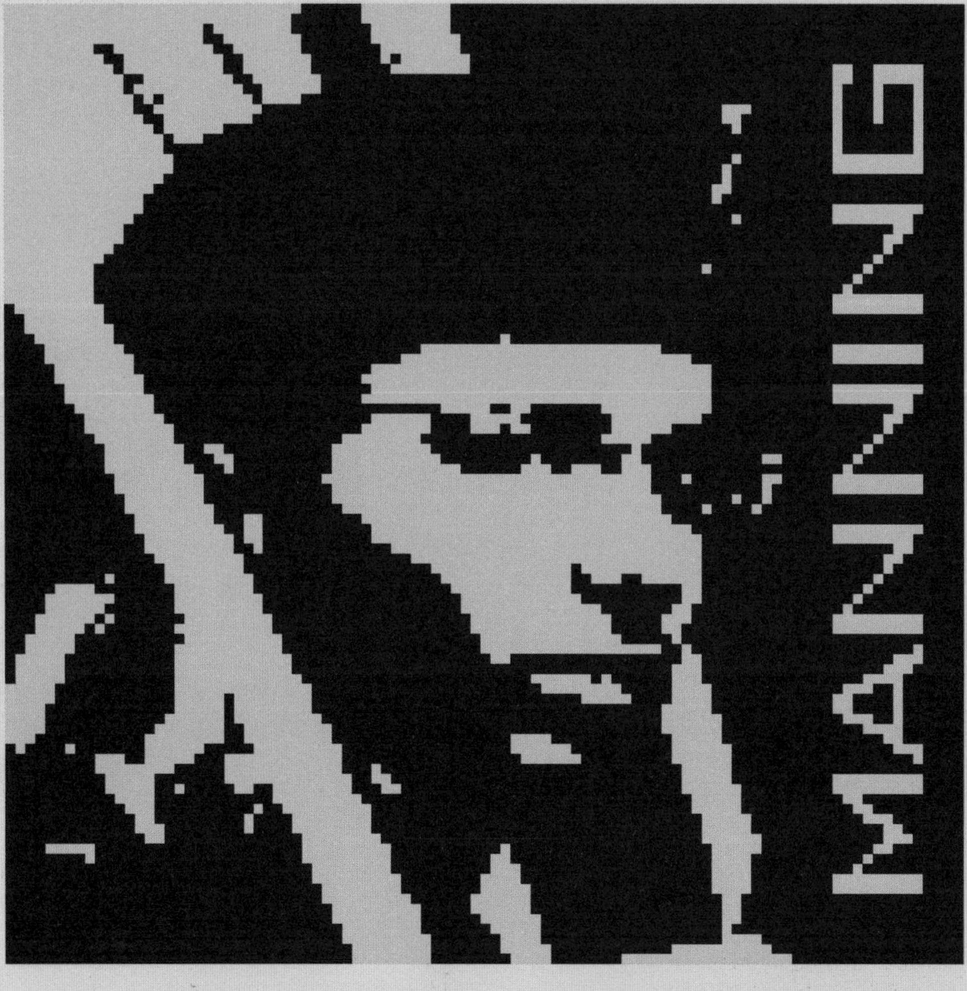

In 2009, then–US Army intelligence officer Chelsea Manning was stationed at Forward Operating Base Hammer in Iraq, an isolated site near the Iranian border. (Manning, who is transgender, was still known as Bradley Manning during this time.) Her duties as an intelligence analyst there gave her access to a great deal of classified information. Some of this information—including videos that showed unarmed civilians being shot at and killed—horrified Manning.

Manning reportedly made her first contact with Julian Assange's WikiLeaks in November 2009, after having made attempts to contact the *New York Times* and the *Washington Post*. While at work in Iraq, she amassed information that included war logs about the Iraq and Afghanistan conflicts, private cables from the State Department, and assessments of prisoners at the Guantanamo Bay detention camp. In February 2010, while on leave in Rockville, Maryland, she passed this information—which amounted to hundreds of thousands of documents, many of them classified—to WikiLeaks. In April, the organization released a video that showed a helicopter crew shooting at civilians after having confused a telephoto lens with weaponry. Additional releases of information continued throughout the year.

In June 2010, Manning was charged with leaking classified information. In March 2011, additional charges were added. These included the accusation of aiding the enemy, as the information Manning had leaked had been accessible to al-Qaeda.

Manning was first imprisoned in Kuwait, where she became suicidal. After returning to the United States, she was moved to a Marine base in Quantico, Virginia. Manning was kept in solitary confinement for most of her time there and was unable to leave her small, windowless cell for twenty-three hours each day. Deemed a suicide risk, she was watched over constantly, sometimes kept naked in her cell, and not permitted to have a pillow or sheets.

Opposite: LEGO portrait of Chelsea Manning by Ai Weiwei.

Even when a psychiatrist said that Manning was no longer a danger to herself, the conditions of her imprisonment did not improve. When word of these conditions spread, there was an international outcry. Manning was transferred to Fort Leavenworth, Kansas, in 2011, where she was allowed to have personal effects in a windowed cell. In January 2013, the judge in Manning's case ruled that her imprisonment had been unduly harsh and gave her a sentencing credit.

In February 2013, Manning pleaded guilty to storing and leaking military information. She explained that her actions had been intended to encourage debate, not harm the United States. She continued to plead not guilty to several other charges while her court martial proceeded. On July 30, Manning was found guilty of twenty counts, including espionage, theft, and computer fraud. However, the judge ruled she was not guilty of aiding the enemy, the most serious charge Manning had faced.

On August 21, 2013, Manning was sentenced to thirty-five years in prison, dishonorably discharged, reduced in rank, and forced to forfeit all pay. In May 2016, Manning's attorneys filed an appeal of her conviction and thirty-five-year sentence, stating, "No whistleblower in American history has been sentenced this harshly," and describing the sentence as "perhaps the most unjust sentence in the history of the military justice system."

Support for Manning's release grew and, in the final days of Barack Obama's presidency, 117,000 people signed a petition asking him to commute her sentence. On January 17, 2017, Obama did just that, cutting short Manning's remaining prison sentence. Manning was freed on May 17, 2017. "Whatever is ahead of me is far more important than the past," she said at the time of her release. Manning remains a vocal advocate for increased government transparency.

The following interview with Chelsea Manning was conducted via email by the editor of this book, David Spalding, with the assistance of her legal team during her incarceration at Fort Leavenworth, in August 2015.

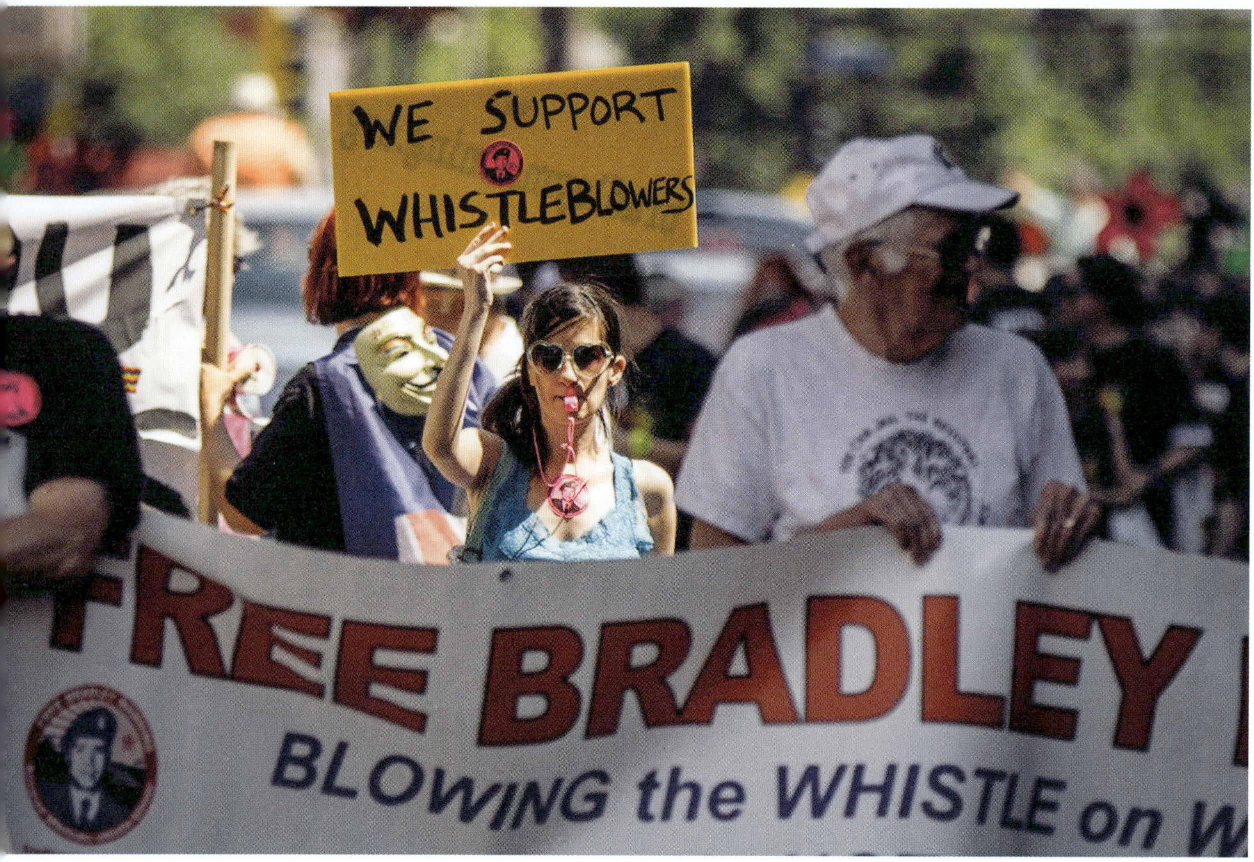

David Spalding: This publication addresses the moments when one's convictions compel one to act, even when that means sacrificing one's personal freedom. In your work as an analyst in Iraq, was there a particular event or incident that finally motivated you to take action?

Chelsea Manning: You know, there isn't a single moment that I can point to. I worked with so many documents in Iraq. But it eventually became clear that these documents were particularly important because they were the most detailed and proximate record of the wars that were available in a single place. They represented two separate, but related, counterinsurgency conflicts in real time from on the ground. Humanity has never had this complete and detailed a record of what modern warfare looks like—let alone what other forms of warfare in general actually look like.

DS: Were you surprised by the consequences of your actions?

CM: Back in 2010, I was a lot younger, so the consequences felt very vague to me at the time. But, when the prosecution of my case began, it was very interesting to see the logistics involved: the stacks of money spent; the gallons of fuel burned; the reams of paper printed; the length of the rolls of security personal, lawyers, and experts. It's hard not to be surprised by all of it.

DS: In your May 6, 2015, op-ed piece for the *Guardian*, you address what you call a "crack-down" in the United States, designed to prevent the circulation of information and to limit government transparency. What is at stake here?

CM: I wrote about how, in the past decade or so, we have seen an increasing number of clashes—both in public and behind the scenes—between the US government, the news media, and those in the public who are working for fair access to records that pertain to the implementation of national policies.

Opposite: Marchers in the Twin Cities Pride Parade carrying signs in support of Chelsea Manning, Minneapolis, Minnesota, 2014.

The most significant parts of this battle have been fought in the courts, whether it's been prosecutions in federal and military courts under the Espionage Act of 1917, the Computer Fraud and Abuse Act, or Freedom of Information Act lawsuits by news media organizations and civil liberties advocates. Though other parts have been more nuanced—with different interpretation of rules, minor changes in policies and regulations, or lobbying by the US government to prevent better transparency laws from passing.

What's at stake here is simple—but very, very important. When freedom of information and transparency are stifled, we've seen throughout history that bad decisions are made and heartbreaking tragedies occur as a result. Too often, these happen on a breathtaking scale that can leave all of us wondering: How did this happen? Just think about the recent debates we've had on torture, assassination by unmanned aircraft, secret warrants and detentions, intelligence and surveillance courts, military commissions, immigration detention centers, or the conduct of modern warfare. These are huge policies that indirectly and directly affect millions of people around the world every day. These are real people that can be affected at any time—our families, friends, coworkers, clergy, and even career politicians are not immune.

DS: Please describe the bill you've recently authored, entitled the National Integrity of Free Speech Protection Act.

CM: I wrote this bill after looking around for ways that we could ensure meaningful changes in the way government works to protect transparency. My search was very disappointing. I saw legislation proposals that were not being pushed very hard through the US Congress at all. To make matters worse, these proposals were so watered down as to make them too easy for the government to subvert. In the end, I decided to pull up my sleeves and write my own proposal.

My bill is the result of years of research and experience in fighting for transparency and [against] secrecy. It has a few simple tenets: a media "shield" law with teeth and substance that creates a federal privilege for communications between journalists and their sources; changes to the murky and awkward military offense of "aiding the enemy" to replace it with more traditional "treason" and "misprision of treason" offenses for those who openly wage war and attempt to overthrow the US government; a plethora of changes to the Freedom of Information Act that were nearly passed in the FOIA Improvement Act of 2014, which nearly passed in the US Congress in 2014 before being lobbied against by the government; and lastly, amendments to the Espionage Act and the Computer Fraud and Abuse Act that require the government to prove a clear intent to harm the government or anyone else, and to make the motive of the accused relevant at trial.

> **"Communication with the world is more important than I ever could have imagined previously."**

I believe that these changes, if implemented in the manner I wrote them, would go far—but certainly not all the way—toward ensuring that citizens can continue to be able to question and criticize their government without fear of being publicly humiliated by their own government.

DS: Describe the conditions you experienced in Quantico, Virginia, while awaiting trial. What was the most difficult part? What helped you to endure?

CM: When I arrived at Quantico in late summer 2010, I was basically brought into a tiny eight-by-six-foot cell—roughly two-and-a-half by two meters—to live alone in a row of cells that were all empty. I was not allowed to talk to anyone else—even though there wasn't anybody near me. There were at least two Marines who watched me from behind a one-way glass window at all times. I could see myself in the reflection of the window all day and night long. It was like a mirror right outside my cell.

I wasn't allowed to have anything in the cell that I wasn't actively using. I would hand most of my clothes to the Marines every night. If I wanted to use the toilet, I had to ask for toilet paper, and I would have to return it when I was done. The same was true for toothbrushes, books, and on a few occasions even my glasses. I was not allowed to lie down or sleep during the "duty day" from 5 A.M. to 7 P.M. I was only allowed to sit up straight on my bed and literally stare at the wall for hours on end. I was sometimes allowed to watch television during the evening, but I had no control over what was on. The Marines controlled what I was watching, and would change the channel when anything like news or current events shows would come on.

The entire experience was such a surreal nightmare—it just seemed comical to me after a while. I mean, here's this incredibly crazy experience happening to me, and all of these scenarios seem to require a sense of humor to cope with the painful emotional aspects of these complicated situations.

I tried to talk to the junior Marine Corps guards in as human a way as possible, as much as possible in their heavily scripted movements. Despite their sometimes very robotic manner of speech, most would start to show more openness and humanity. This certainly helped me endure.

DS: Had you heard about Ai Weiwei and his work before the *@Large* exhibition? Do you have any thoughts you'd like to share about the artist or the project on Alcatraz?

CM: Yes! I had heard about Ai Weiwei and his work before *@Large*. I have found his work to be pretty amazing and very meaningful symbolically. And I can only applaud him for not allowing anyone—whether an art critic or a despotic government—to stop him from speaking his mind and expressing himself.

My understanding is that he was subjected to very similar conditions while in confinement

Below: Chelsea Manning and Ai Weiwei, Washington, D.C., June 27, 2017.

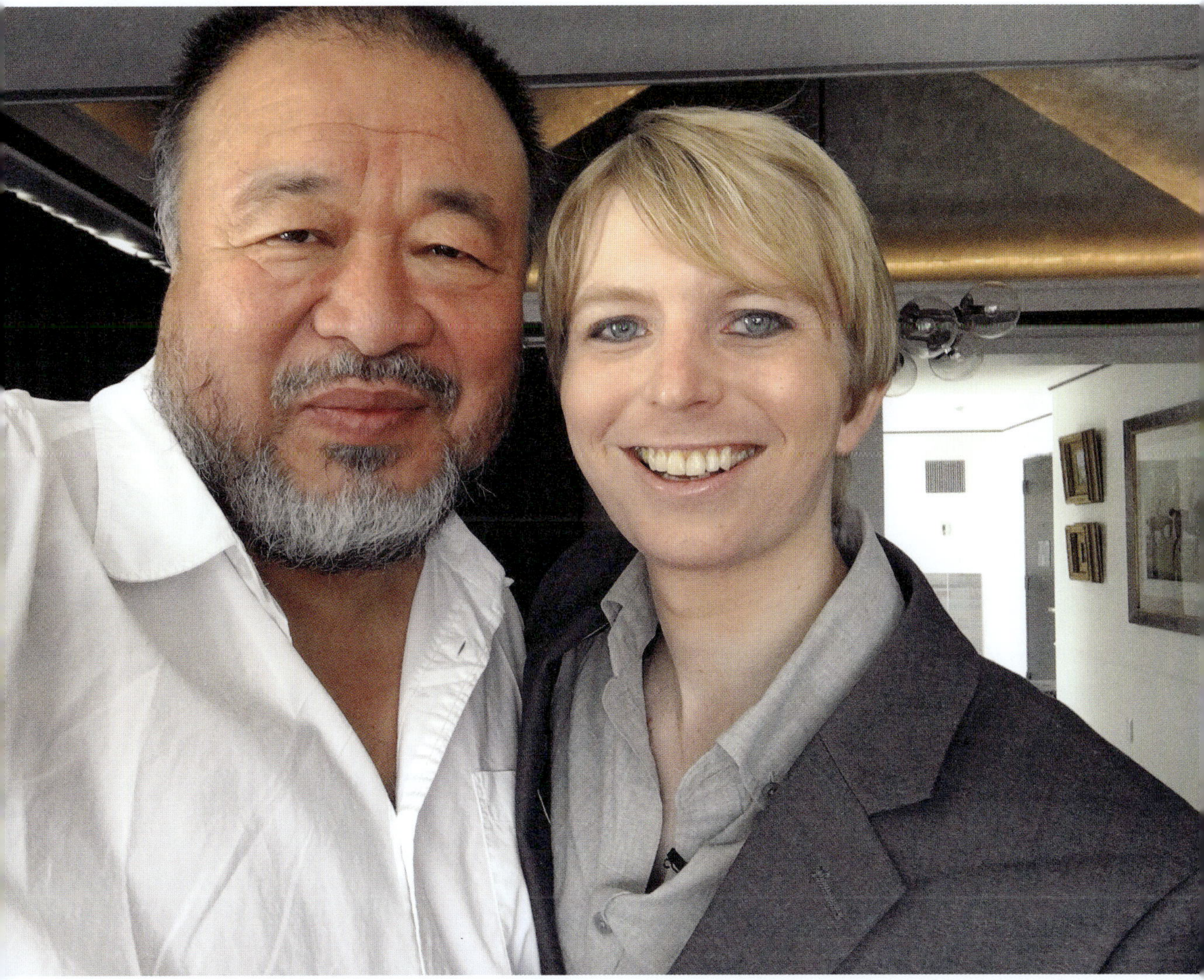

Right: Graffiti calling for Chelsea Manning's release, Vienna, Austria, 2014.

Far right: Still image from classified video footage leaked by Chelsea Manning showing Reuters employee Saneed Chmagh being killed by American military forces during an airstrike in Baghdad, Iraq, July 12, 2017.

himself, so I can definitely relate to him in that regard. I'd like to know if he had similar thoughts and feelings on life and our humanity as I did during my experience.

DS: During the exhibition, visitors to Alcatraz wrote more postcards to you than to anyone else in the *Yours Truly* project. Why do you think that people identify so strongly with your story?

CM: I don't have an answer to this question. I don't think I'm special or particularly different from anyone else, so it's actually kind of intimidating at times. I certainly don't feel like I can live up to the expectations of being a "heroine" or anything like that. I don't have any special powers or abilities like a comic book superhero. I feel like I'm a lot more vulnerable than that. I'm actually very, very vulnerable. I just try to be myself—and that's all I've aspired to be. If people can relate to that, then perhaps we have some kind of answer?

DS: Can you describe the experience of first receiving the *@Large* postcards while in prison? Were there any specific postcards that were particularly moving or memorable to you?

CM: Yes. The first batch of postcards came in some time around the end of 2014, I think. I was called to the prison mail window—typically this is to pick up or ship a package or legal documents. When I got there, one of the mail clerks handed me this massive stack of postcards—hundreds and hundreds of them—bundled together with this big rubber band. I was floored by it. I had read about the exhibit in the newspaper, and saw a brief segment on television about it, but I had no idea that I was featured in the exhibit, let alone that so many people would write to me.

There are so many of these postcards that I felt were very moving and memorable. I took the time to read every single one before I sent them to a friend to store them. There were ones from children with their parents or on school trips, there were ones from other trans people, and

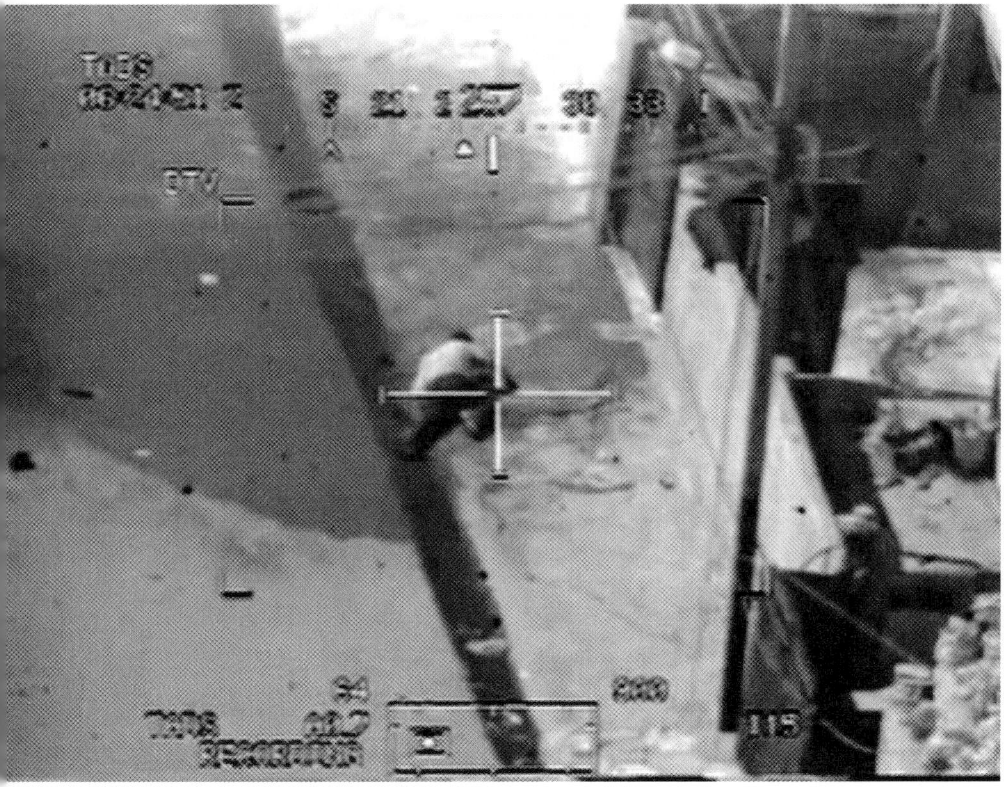

there was even one from the person to whom I was sending the cards to put into storage. We laughed about the funny circle it was making, from her all the way to me, and back to her again. I even got a few from Ai Weiwei himself.

The card that he sent to me that is most memorable to me is one that explained some of his thoughts and encouraged me to "Keep strong and hold on to your idea." I keep a photocopy of his words on the desk in my cell.

DS: You are now tweeting from prison and regularly receiving letters from people who wish to offer their support. Since your incarceration, how important has outside communication been to you?

CM: Communication with the world is more important than I ever could have imagined previously. Unfortunately, it seems that you only appreciate something so vital and important to life when such a lifeline has been threatened or severed completely. I feel that it's important for me to keep writing, and to keep coming up with new ideas so I can stay connected to the world. I've been in prison for a while now—likely with a longer time ahead, so it's very important that I keep in touch with my family, my friends, my supporters, and everyone else.

DS: If you could send a postcard to another prisoner of conscience from the past or present, to whom would you write, and what would you say?

CM: I hate to sound cliché here, but I really would like to send a postcard to Dr. Martin Luther King, Jr., during the time he wrote his "Letter from a Birmingham Jail." I mean, it's just amazing to me how he could come up with such a powerful message with so few resources and in such a short period of time. I now know from my own experience how difficult it would have been, emotionally as well as with the physical jail restrictions and lack of paper—and yet he did it, and it still resonates with people, even over half a century later.

Following pages: A selection of *Yours Truly* postcards addressed to Chelsea Manning

SEPT 27. 2014

@LARGE
AI WEIWEI
ON ALCATRAZ

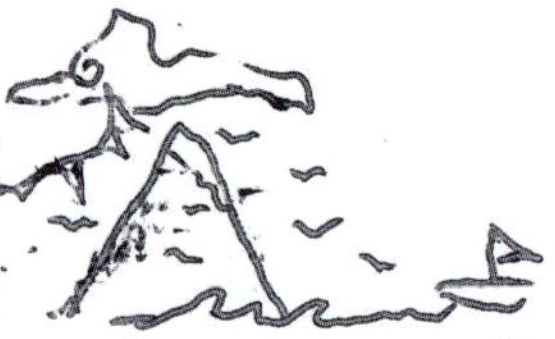

CHELSEA *
TEARS COME TO MY EYES AS I WRITE THESE WORDS. MY HEART IS FULL KNOWING YOUR STRENGTH EXISTS. PLEASE REMAIN STRONG & BALANCE WITH SOFTNESS WHERE YOU CAN. I SEND MY DEEPEST RESPECT FOR YOU. YOU ARE LOVE. YOU ARE ME...
THANK YOU.
♡ JASMINE IN OAKLAND, CA.

CHELSEA E. MANNING 89289
1300 NORTH WAREHOUSE RD.
FORT LEAVENWORTH,
KS 66027-2304

United States · Rose

@LARGE
AI WEIWEI
ON ALCATRAZ

DEAR CHELSEA,
I AM FROM THE CZECH REPUBLIC, A COUNTRY THAT WASN'T FREE JUST 25 YEARS AGO. I KNOW THAT I AM FREE BECAUSE OF PEOPLE LIKE YOU. I WOULD LIKE TO THANK YOU FOR WHAT YOU ACHIEVED - I BELIEVE THAT BECAUSE OF YOU, THERE WILL BE NO NEED FOR EXHIBITIONS LIKE THESE IN THE FUTURE.
I HOPE YOU WILL BE FREE SOON.
BEST WISHES, ADAM
BERKELEY, CA

CHELSEA E. MANNING 89289
1300 NORTH WAREHOUSE RD.
FORT LEAVENWORTH,
KS 66027-2304

United States · Rose

@LARGE
AI WEIWEI
ON ALCATRAZ

I REMEMBER MAIL CALL BEING EITHER ONE OF THE BEST OR WORSE PARTS OF THE DAY WHEN I WAS IN PRISON. IT'S NOT MUCH, BUT HERE'S HOPING THIS NOTE BRINGS A LITTLE JOY TO YOU.

CHERYLL
DALY CITY, CA

CHELSEA E. MANNING 89289
1300 NORTH WAREHOUSE RD.
FORT LEAVENWORTH,
KS 66027-2304

United States · Rose

@LARGE
AI WEIWEI
ON ALCATRAZ

i'm a trans person from brooklyn ny. thank you. for being so fucking brave. for showing up for yourself and for folks so deeply impacted by your actions in such positive ways. you are a brilliant human and i am so grateful you exist in this world. thank you. ♥ ♥

CHELSEA E. MANNING 89289
1300 NORTH WAREHOUSE RD.
FORT LEAVENWORTH,
KS 66027-2304

United States · Rose

Sat, Nov 6, 2014

@LARGE
AI WEIWEI
ON ALCATRAZ

Ms. Manning—
I commend your bravery and patriotism in revealing to the public the true workings of our government. I also appreciate your courage to adopt your true sex. You are a role model for me. Thank you,
Charles

United States · Rose

CHELSEA E. MANNING 89289
1300 NORTH WAREHOUSE RD.
FORT LEAVENWORTH,
KS 66027-2304

@LARGE
AI WEIWEI
ON ALCATRAZ

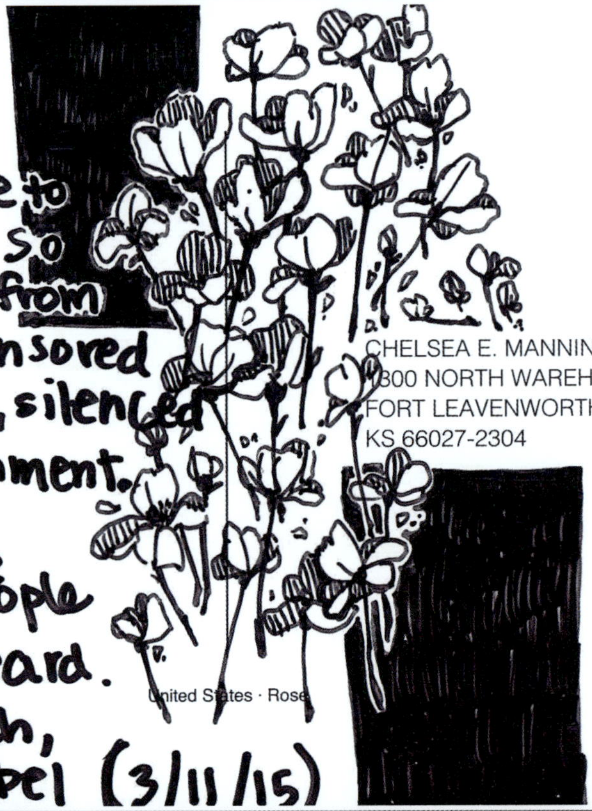

please continue to fight for us. So much is kept from the public, censored by the media, silenced by the government. Things need to be known, the people need to be heard.
thanks much,
Isabel (3/11/15)

United States · Rose

CHELSEA E. MANNING 89289
1300 NORTH WAREHOUSE RD.
FORT LEAVENWORTH,
KS 66027-2304

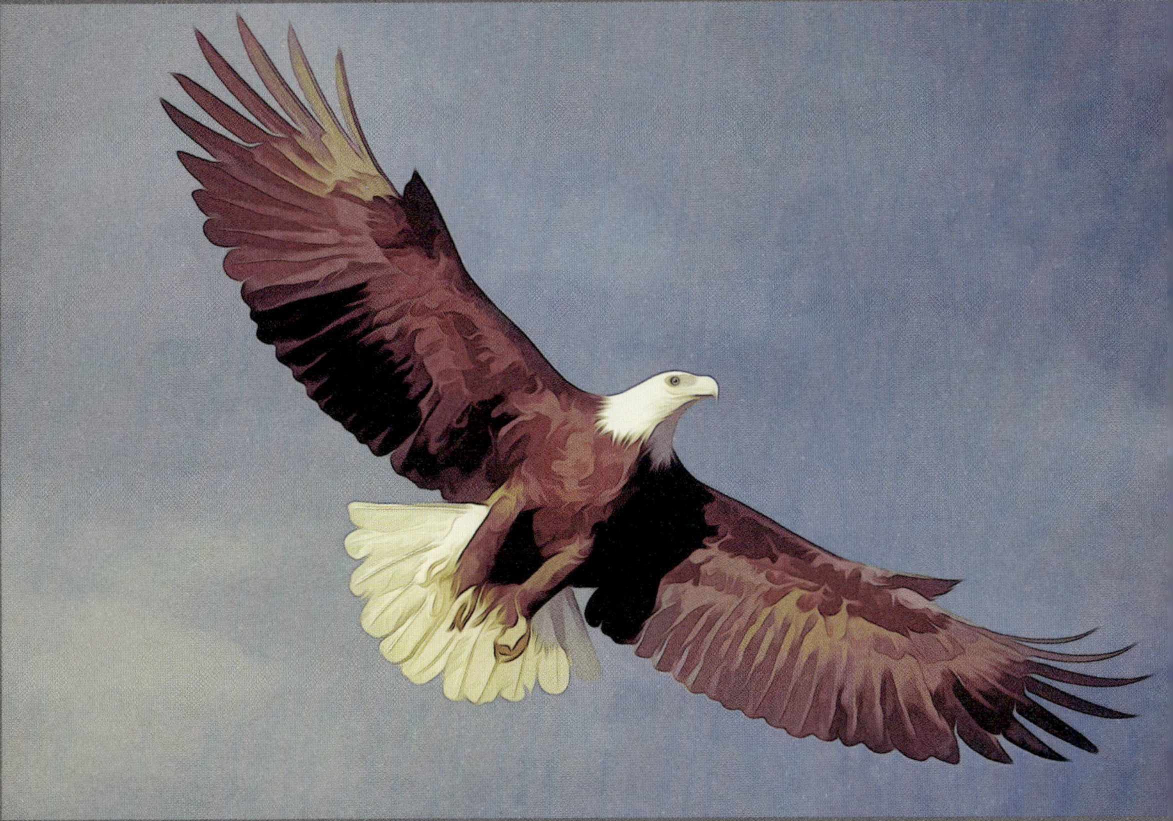

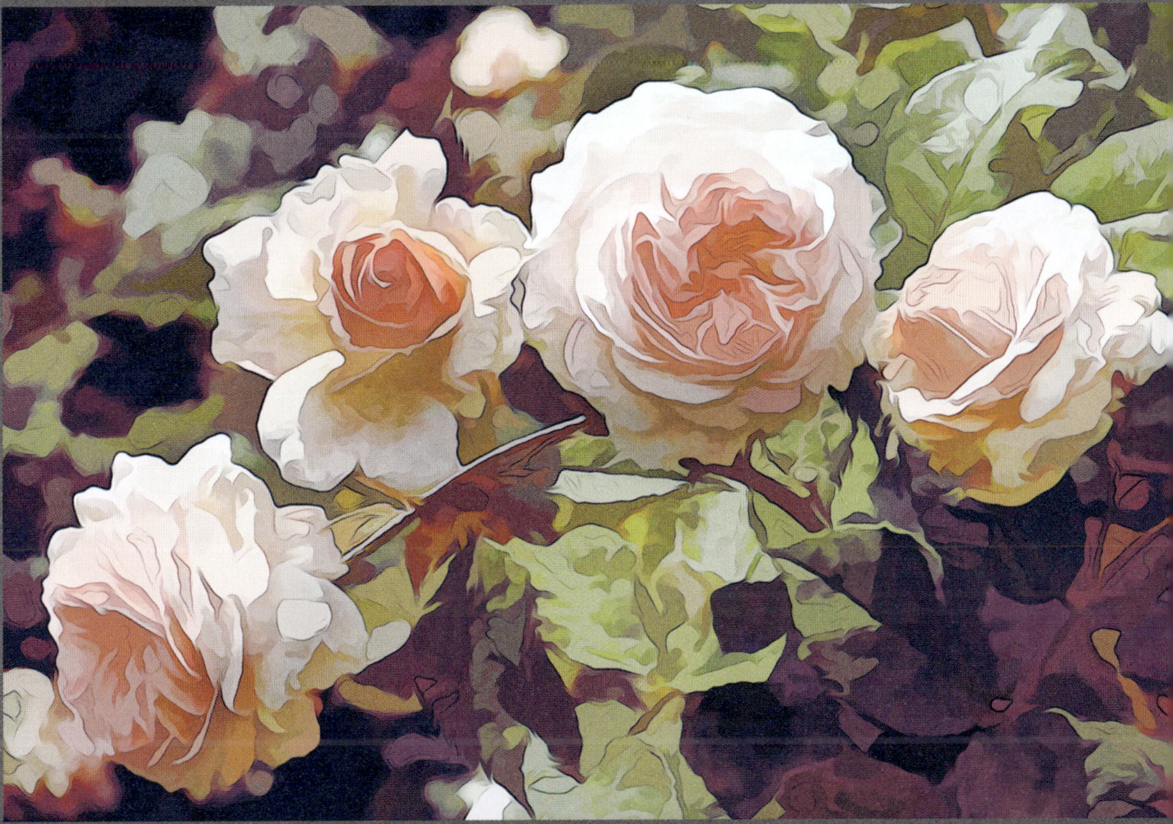

EBRAHIM SHARIF
AL SAYED

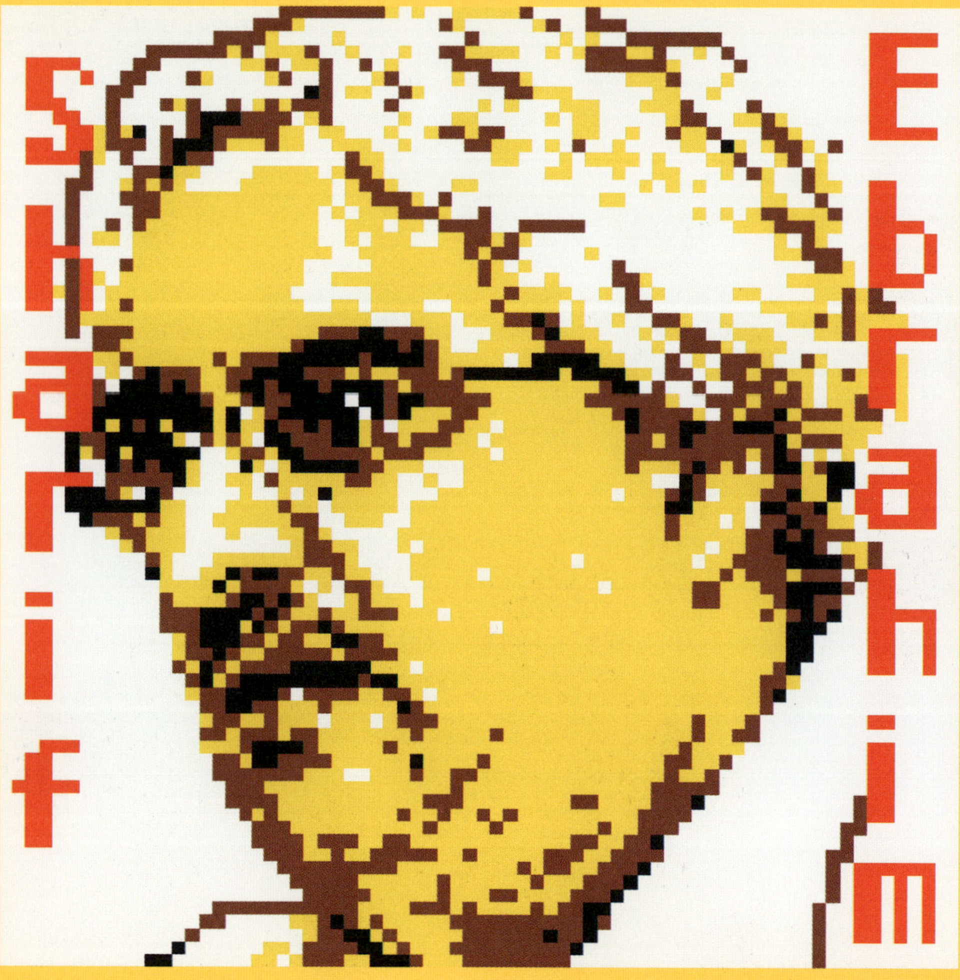

Ebrahim Sharif Al Sayed is a Bahraini politician, businessman, husband, and father. He served for a long time as the secretary-general of the National Democratic Action Society (also known as Wa'ad), a secular, moderate, and peaceful political opposition group in Bahrain. Sharif's work for governmental reform has addressed a wide range of issues, from political corruption in land dealings to the improvement of social welfare systems of Bahrain. Throughout his advocacy, Sharif has roundly rejected all forms of violence and intimidation by all parties, pushing instead for peaceful and moderate reforms.

From March 2011 to June 2015, Sharif was a political prisoner in Bahrain's Jaw Prison, after the Bahraini government charged him with "incitement to overthrow the regime" following a speech he gave that called on the government to make commitments to political reform. An appeals court upheld his sentence, despite determining that the evidence used against him was extracted through torture.

Sharif's arrest occurred amid a massive, military-backed security crackdown against pro-democracy protests that began in February 2011, during the Arab Spring protests in Bahrain's capital city, Manama. He was one of hundreds of pro-democracy activists and protesters who were incarcerated in Bahrain without access to their families or lawyers.

Released by royal pardon on June 19, 2015, Sharif was rearrested only a few weeks later, after giving a peaceful speech at a yearly event commemorating the murder of Hussam al-Haddad, a sixteen-year-old boy beaten to death by Bahraini riot police in 2012. Sharif ultimately served another year in prison for "incitement to hatred and contempt of the regime."

Opposite: LEGO portrait of Ebrahim Sharif Al Sayed by Ai Weiwei.

The political persecution of Ebrahim Sharif Al Sayed and his family continues. On March 20, 2017, Sharif was again charged with "inciting hatred against the regime" and against "factions of society" for messages he wrote on social media. The tweets included Amnesty International campaign materials on Bahraini prisoners of conscience. If convicted of these charges, Sharif faces up to three more years in prison.

On April 21, 2017, the authorities summoned both Sharif and his wife, the political activist Farida Ghulam, to appear for interrogation, where they were accused of participating in an "illegal gathering" in the Bahraini village of Diraz and subjected to a travel ban. Neither Sharif nor Ghulam have visited the village in years. At the time of writing, the freedom of both Sharif and Ghulam remains tenuous, and the outcome of these latest charges unknown.

Ghulam is an advocate for freedom of speech, human rights, and democratic reform in Bahrain. In the following accounts, Ghulam and two of the couple's children, Sharif Al Sayed and Aseel Al Sayed, discuss the profound impact that Sharif's repeated incarcerations have had on their family, as well as their visit to the *@Large* exhibition.

Among the countless stories of suffering that the Bahraini people have endured is the story of my own family: one of hardship, sacrifice, and pure injustice. My husband was arrested, incarcerated for four-and-a-half years, released for three weeks, and promptly rearrested.

Those three weeks were beautiful and magical. They were surreal. It's like what Ebrahim said when his daughter landed in Bahrain and woke him up the morning after his release. He asked her: "It's like a dream, isn't it?" Those three weeks passed by so quickly that they don't seem real; we've now plunged back into our old routines of monitored visits, monitored and limited phone calls, court hearings, and the anxiety inherent in facing a long dark tunnel with very little light ahead.

My husband and I, along with our political party, the National Democratic Action Society (also known as Wa'ad), have been advocating for democracy, fighting corruption, and highlighting social injustice in the Kingdom of Bahrain for a long time now. My husband, Ebrahim Sharif Al Sayed, is the former secretary-general of Wa'ad, and has run twice for a seat in Bahrain's parliament. During his campaign, he was able to gain traction with the people of Bahrain by raising awareness of social and economic corruption, as well as stressing shortcomings of the current political system and proposing needed reforms to build a true democracy. His campaign focused on the people being the source of any government's power, a statement that is ironically featured in Bahrain's constitution. He challenged the government in many economic and political domains, using his skills in finance and economics to easily prove the existence of corruption and discrimination.

The courage Ebrahim showed by exposing the government in such public ways understandably threatened the establishment, especially considering that he is a Sunni man, the same religious sect as Bahrain's ruling elites, which made him difficult to discredit along sectarian lines. Ebrahim's point of view, along with the points of view of other prominent opposition figures in Bahrain, was never addressed by the ruling powers, although these views were supported by the majority of Bahrain's people. The only responses that addressed these views were smear campaigns placed in pro-regime newspapers and TV networks.

After witnessing developments in Tunisia and Egypt during the Arab Spring of 2011, the Bahraini people took to the streets in peaceful demonstrations against the government. They set up a home base around the Pearl Roundabout in central Manama. It happened quickly and naturally, with no prior planning by opposition groups, which joined the mass movement a few days later by attending and giving speeches focused on peacefulness as a strategy in expressing the political demands addressed to the government. My husband was one of these opposition leaders. He spoke about what a true constitutional monarchy means and reiterated the views of his parliamentary campaign, which promised to put power in the people's hands by raising awareness and insisting on nonviolent measures to obtain the necessary changes for democratic advancement.

The government responded to this movement by cracking down a month later, sending in GCC (Gulf Cooperation Council) troops, tanks, tear gas, and weapons. Many people were killed in the ensuing chaos, and arrests of political leaders occurred over the following days. The roundabout was demolished by the government in an attempt to quickly erase the movement from people's memories and history. They exploited their declaration of martial law as an excuse to regain control and quell the protests entirely.

My husband's first arrest was an exercise in torment—solitary confinement, torture in the form of mass beatings by masked police, sleep deprivation, being forced to sleep on cold-water-soaked mattresses in incredibly cold, air conditioned rooms, constantly barking dogs, sexual harassment and threats, whipping with plastic pipes, insulting his family's honor, and standing for long hours with his hands held vertically in the air. At one point, he was beaten and then threatened—told that if he issued a complaint to the military prosecution he would be beaten again. Ebrahim filed the complaint; the man indeed kept his promise and Ebrahim was beaten again. To add to that, on the day that the military judge issued the verdict of guilty, all of the political leaders were taken to a back room in the courthouse and beaten because they had chanted the words "peacefulness, peacefulness" in response to the judge's verdict and sentences.

We have been telling our story over and over again since 2011. Ebrahim was sentenced to five years in prison, while the other political figures, part of the "Bahrain Thirteen," a group of political leaders that the Bahraini government alleges Ebrahim is a member of, received longer sentences ranging from ten years to life imprisonment. In June 2015, Ebrahim was released on a royal pardon, only to be rearrested a mere three weeks later on July 12 due to a speech he gave commemorating the death of a sixteen-year-old martyr who was barbarically shot at close range by police in 2012 and who received no justice.

As a family, we've decided that it is important for us to write about the hardships we have personally endured on an individual and family level as a direct consequence of the punishment handed down by the government, which fears the pure and peaceful expression of speech. The right to freedom of speech is recognized worldwide by an endless array of organizations, and while Bahrain claims to respect the International Declaration of Human Rights, it is abundantly clear that it does not. While the Kingdom of Bahrain is a signatory of the International Covenant on Civil and Political Rights and the International Covenant on Economic, Social, and Cultural Rights, what has happened to Ebrahim and other Bahrainis opposing the injustice and discrimination in the country proves the kingdom does not hold these covenants in high regard.

Farida Ghulam
October 2015

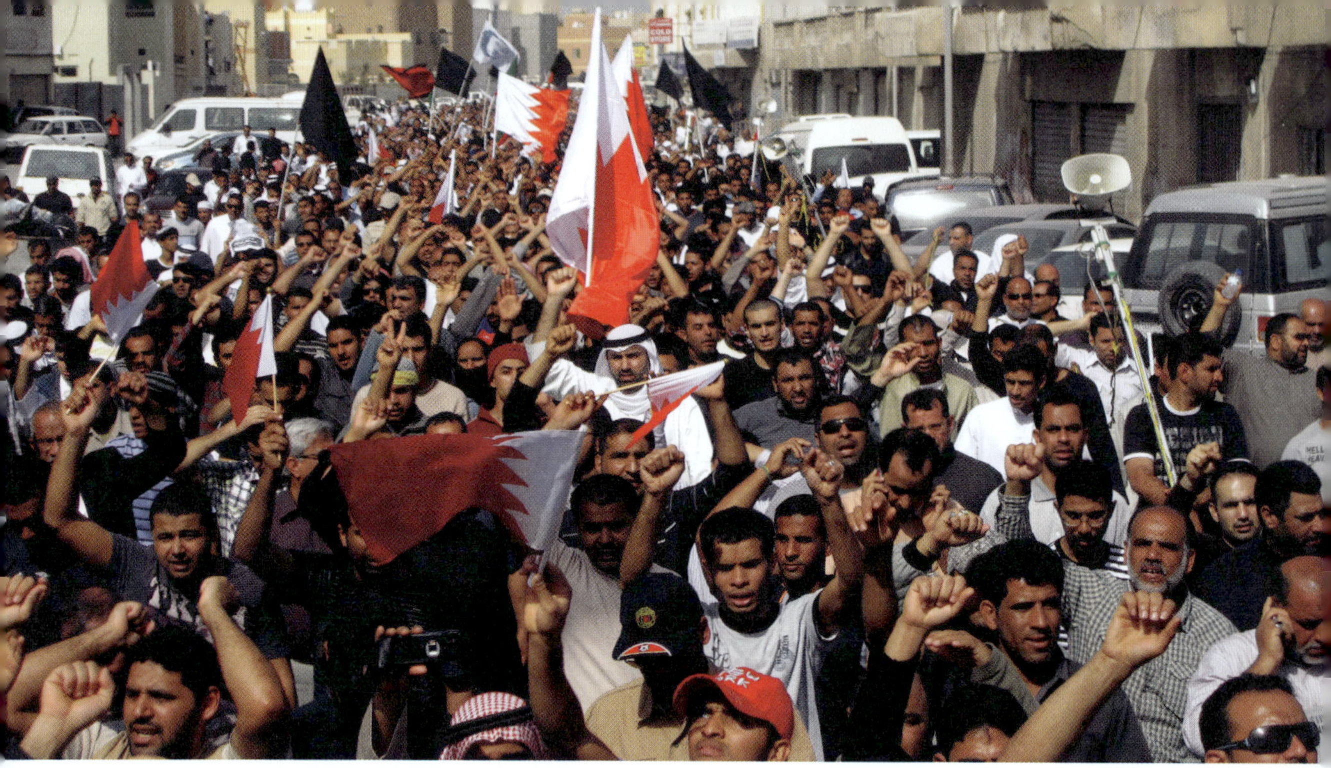

I heard about Ai Weiwei's *@Large* exhibition from a friend who visited the exhibition and recognized my father from all my Facebook posts. He immediately messaged me with photos of my father's LEGO portrait and the *Yours Truly* postcards, and asked, "Hey, is this your dad?" I was so touched and surprised that I quickly organized a trip over to the United States. My family was also excited to join. I started doing some research and responded to a tweet on the FOR-SITE Foundation's Twitter account featuring my father's portrait, saying that I looked forward to visiting in person. A representative from FOR-SITE was quick to ask me about my travel plans and was so supportive, offering us a tour on the last day of the exhibit and arranging a meeting with the executive director of Amnesty International USA, Steven Hawkins.

My family and I were truly humbled to be able to see Ai Weiwei's work and his solidarity with human rights and political activists around the world. The experience was overwhelming and touching. We wrote postcards to our father and to Ai Weiwei, thanking him for featuring the Bahraini prisoners of conscience in the show. We also received scanned postcards directed towards the Bahraini prisoners of conscience, and it was touching to read all the thoughtful messages from strangers who feel a connection to you and your family. I have a newfound appreciation for the arts after my visit and will never forget how this experience made me feel—a feeling that we are not alone in this struggle, and that many stand by us in solidarity.

Aseel Al Sayed
Daughter of Farida Ghulam and Ebrahim Sharif Al Sayed
March 2017

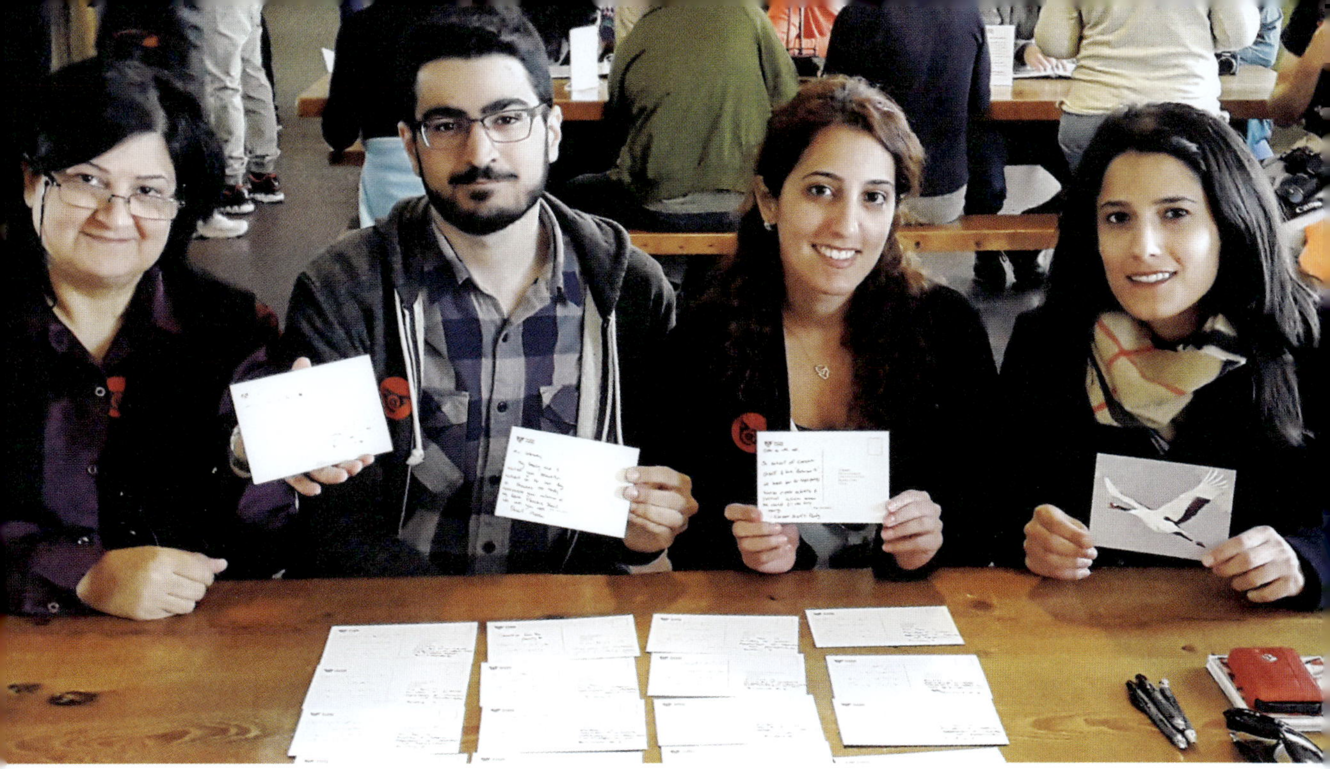

Above: The family of Ebrahim Sharif Al Sayed poses with their completed *Yours Truly* postcards during their visit to *@Large: Ai Weiwei on Alcatraz*, April 26, 2015. From left to right: Farida Ghulam, Sharif Al Sayed, Yara Al Sayed, and Aseel Al Sayed.

Opposite: Protesters seeking democratic reforms in Sitra, Bahrain, February 18, 2011.

No one should ever wake up to a call in the middle of the night to hear that something terrible has happened to a loved one, but that's exactly what I went through in my sophomore year of college, when my father was arrested in Bahrain for daring to speak his mind.

A friend of mine at the University of Michigan woke me up with his call and sounded a little tense and upset as he asked me if I had heard the news and if I was OK. I had no idea what he was talking about. That's when he told me my father had been arrested and that no one knew where he was. I couldn't believe what I was hearing. I felt like the walls were closing in on me, I couldn't breathe, and my heart was racing as I sat there in my dark dorm room, thousands of miles away from home, completely powerless to help.

My family was kept in the dark about my dad's whereabouts for quite a while afterward. Occasionally, there would be rumors that he had been spotted at some hospital or other receiving treatment, but that was all we had to go on. The feeling that my life was crashing down around me was with me every day, made worse by the fact that I still had lectures to attend, tests to take, projects to work on. I had to go about my life while my dad was missing. It was a soul-crushing experience, having to force myself to put aside my fears and my worries and my sadness and work on that next calculus set or programming assignment. Over time, we got more details as to my dad's whereabouts, and eventually he was allowed to call us. Just hearing his voice was an incredible relief because it meant that he was alive.

“No one should ever wake up to a call in the middle of the night to hear that something terrible has happened to a loved one.”

My dad has been forced to miss the entirety of my adult life. I'm a very different person now than I was when I got that call all those years ago, and I've had to go through the process of becoming an adult with only infrequent windows of contact with him, usually lasting no more than ten minutes every other week at most. He couldn't even attend my graduation. With every major life event I went through I had to wait a week or more before I could tell him about it. Even when we did get to talk, I had to condense topics and prioritize because there just wasn't enough time. Even then we were censored, as there were topics we weren't allowed to discuss over the phone, especially politics. Until his temporary release that lasted all of three weeks, the extent of my interactions with my dad as an adult were all through these little ten-minute windows, and occasionally longer visits when I was back home, where everything we said was being monitored. Not being allowed to even have a private conversation is insidiously oppressing—everything I say has to pass through a filter: “Can I say this? Will the monitors cut the call off? Am I OK with the Bahraini government knowing this?”

I am glad at the very least that my dad got to see my sisters and I as we are now, without any surveillance or prison walls separating us, for those three weeks that he was free. I want my dad back more than anything, and I am hopeful that he will be a full part of our lives again soon.

Sharif Al Sayed
Son of Farida Ghulam and Ebrahim Sharif Al Sayed
November 2015

Below: Ebrahim Sharif Al Sayed giving a speech.

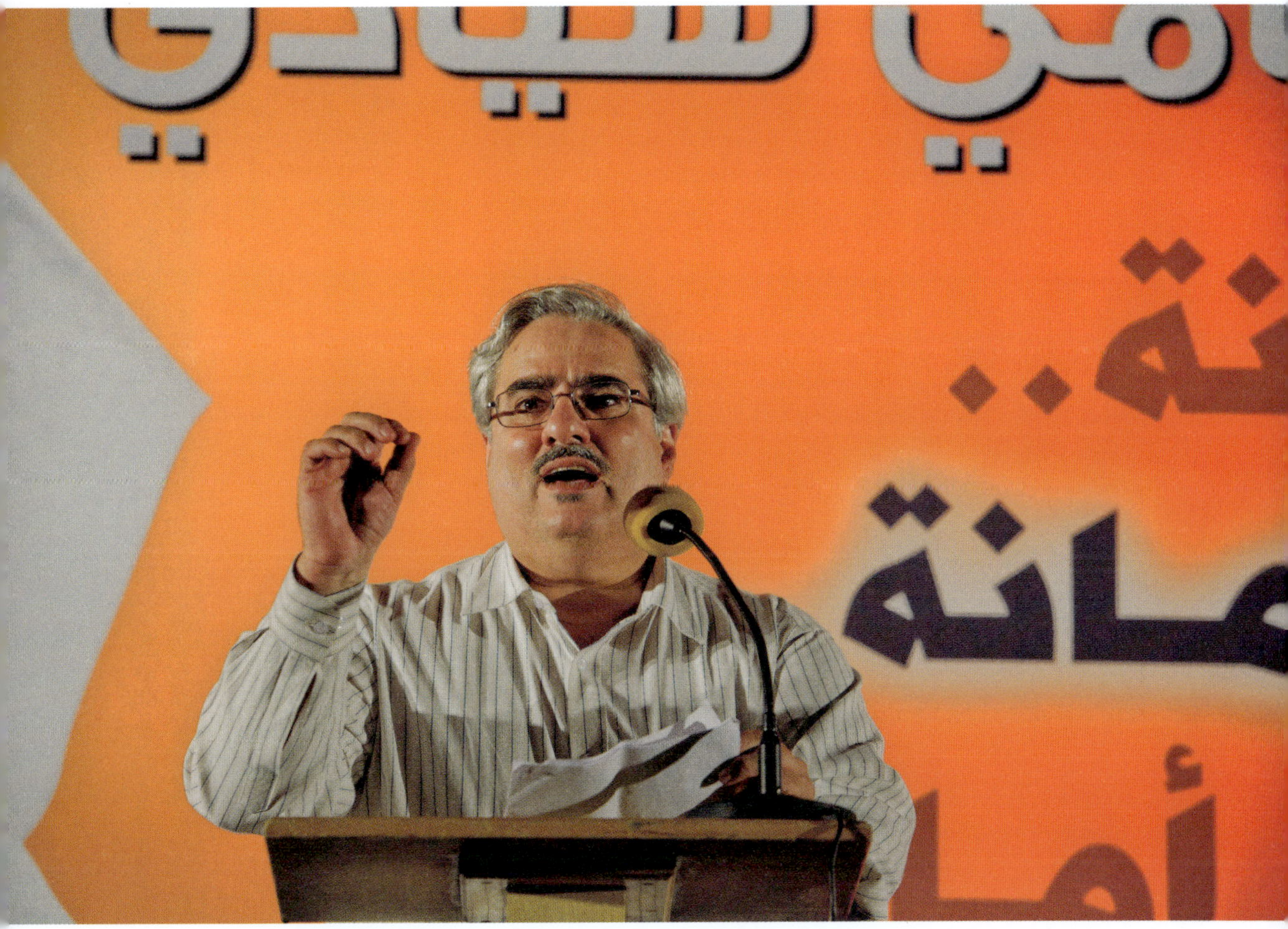

Following pages: A selection of *Yours Truly* postcards addressed to Ebrahim Sharif Al Sayed

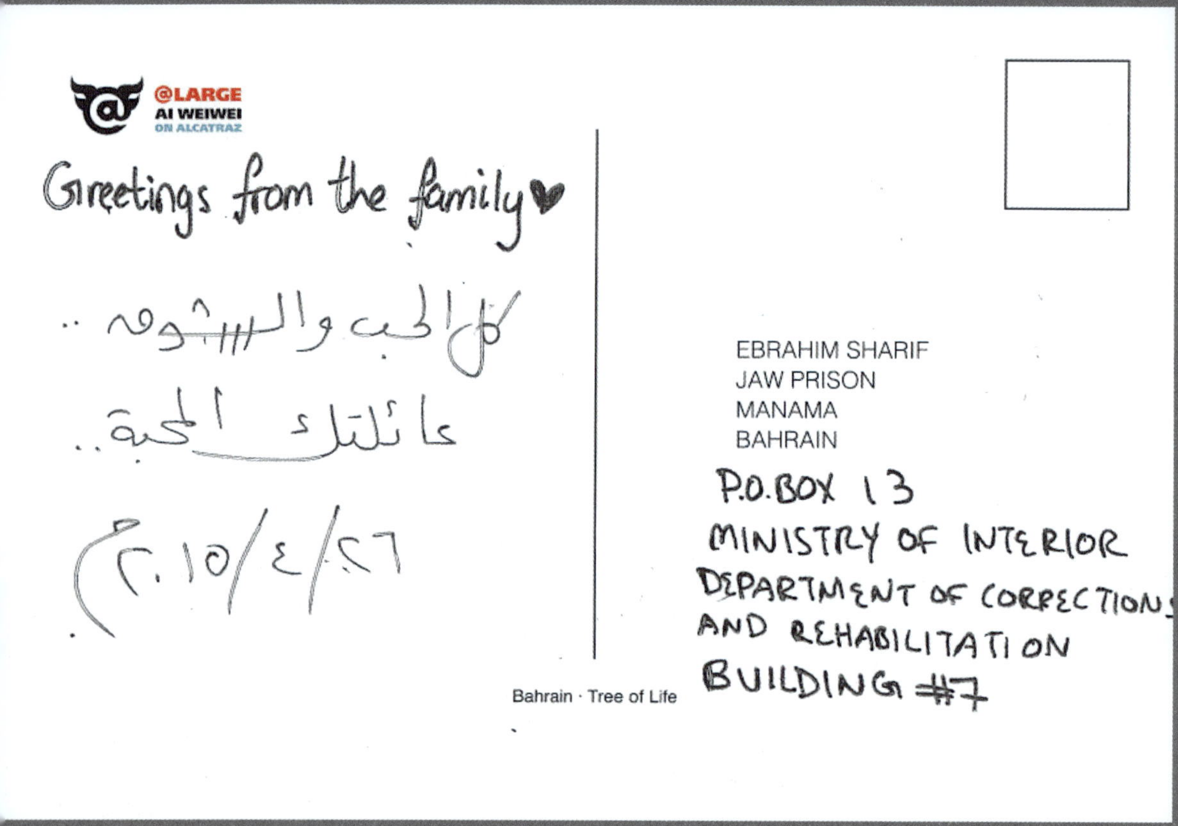

@LARGE
AI WEIWEI
ON ALCATRAZ

Greetings from the family ♥

كل الحب والشوق..
عائلتك المحبة..
٢٦/٤/٢٠١٥م

EBRAHIM SHARIF
JAW PRISON
MANAMA
BAHRAIN

P.O. BOX 13
MINISTRY OF INTERIOR
DEPARTMENT OF CORRECTIONS
AND REHABILITATION
BUILDING #7

Bahrain · Tree of Life

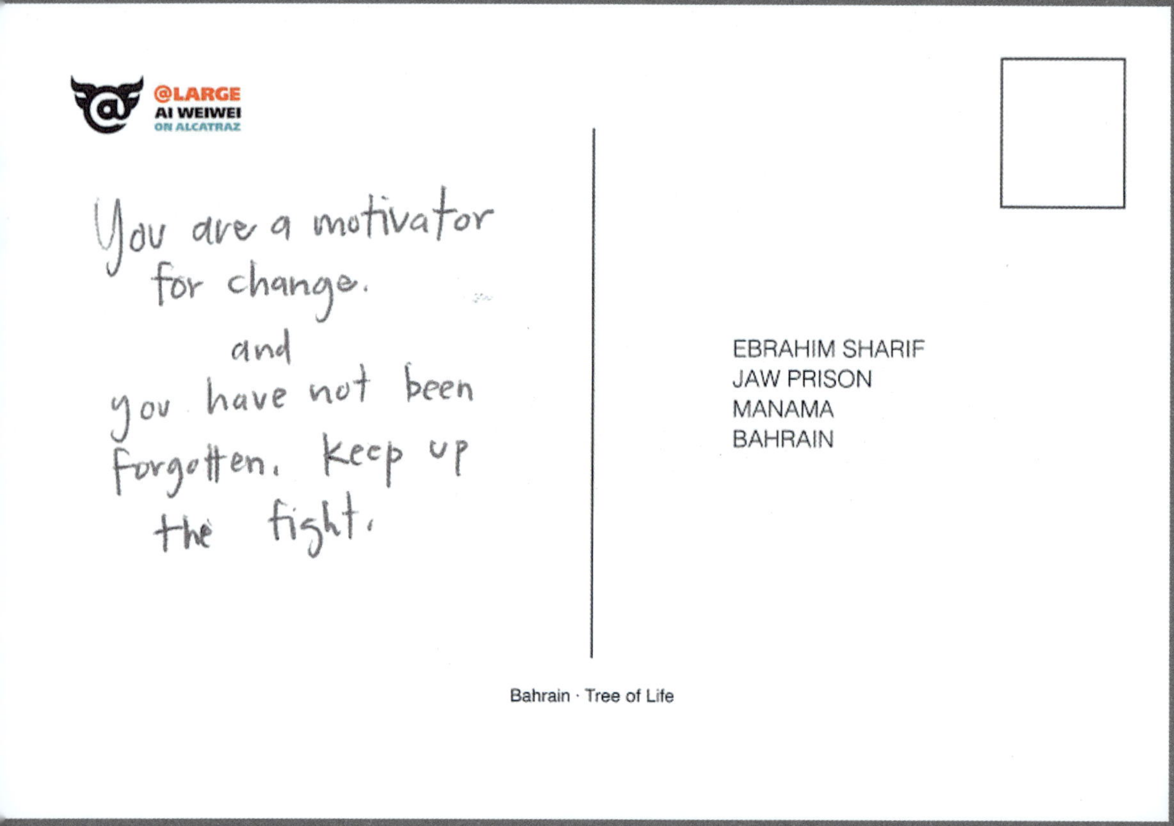

@LARGE
AI WEIWEI
ON ALCATRAZ

You are a motivator
for change.
and
you have not been
forgotten. Keep up
the fight.

EBRAHIM SHARIF
JAW PRISON
MANAMA
BAHRAIN

Bahrain · Tree of Life

@LARGE
AI WEIWEI
ON ALCATRAZ

You may not know artist Ai Weiwei, but your story (and many others) are included in his exhibit. I learned about you here. Many more will discover this situation and I hope we all will change things for you. You should be free. I will not forget you.

L

EBRAHIM SHARIF
JAW PRISON
MANAMA
BAHRAIN

Bahrain · Tree of Life

@LARGE
AI WEIWEI
ON ALCATRAZ

You're a person I'll never meet, but the human idea of working for freedom & liberation from oppression links us as People, living & breathing on this planet. Thank you.

From someone you've never met,

Jacquie, from Winnipeg, Manitoba, CANADA

EBRAHIM SHARIF
JAW PRISON
MANAMA
BAHRAIN

Bahrain · Tree of Life

@LARGE
AI WEIWEI
ON ALCATRAZ

Thank you for your courage and pursuit of justice despite the overwhelming resistance.

Change —

-Paola

CHICAGO, IL USA

Bahrain · Tree of Life

EBRAHIM SHARIF
JAW PRISON
MANAMA
BAHRAIN

@LARGE
AI WEIWEI
ON ALCATRAZ

Many feel compelled to follow the dictates of conscience, to expose the excesses of those in power, to protect others and the world we share.
We stand with you and condemn punishment of those who make their voices heard.

Bahrain · Tree of Life

EBRAHIM SHARIF
JAW PRISON
MANAMA
BAHRAIN

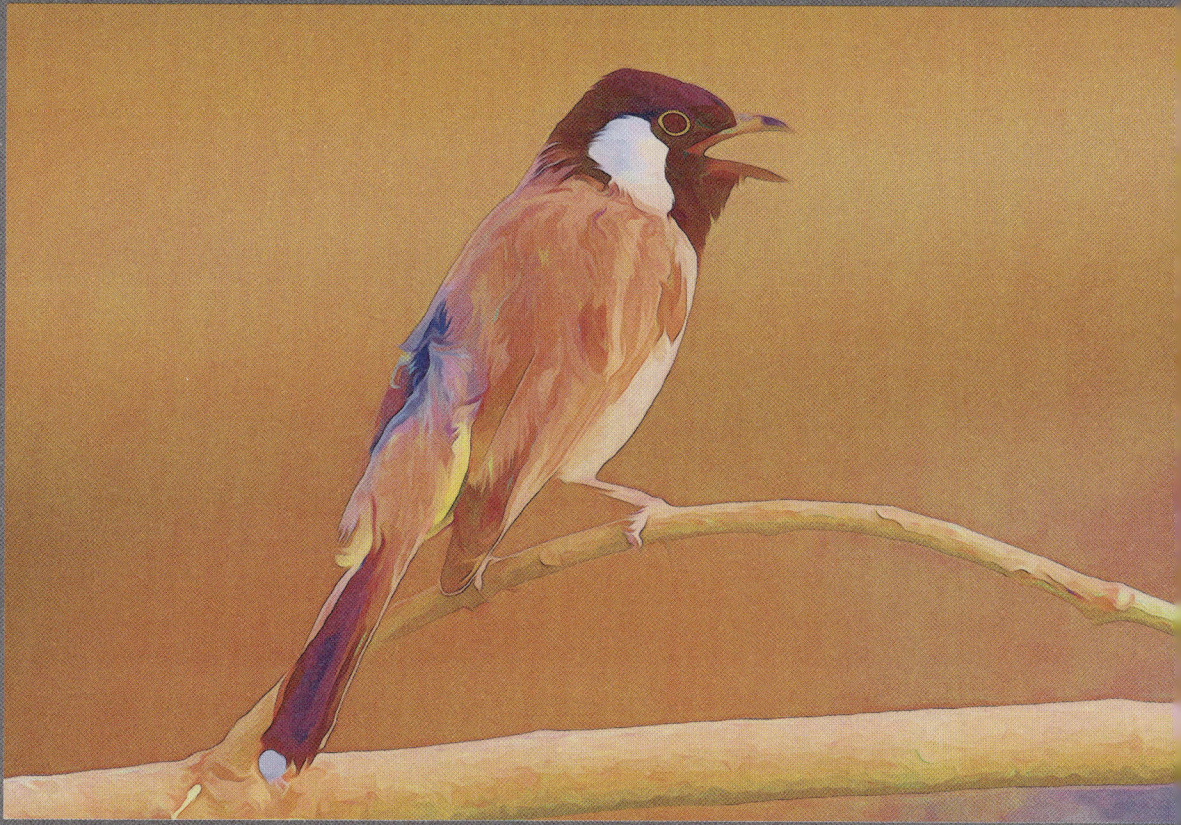

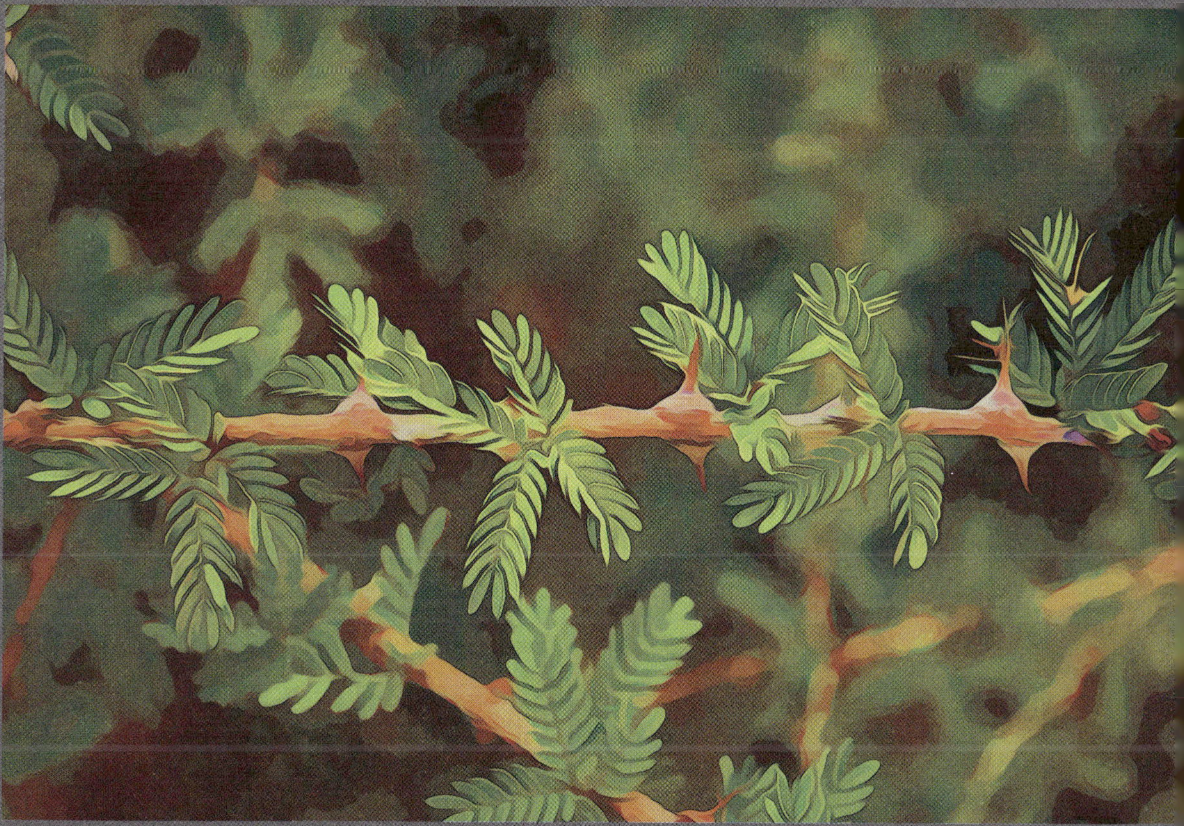

IROM SHARMILA CHANU

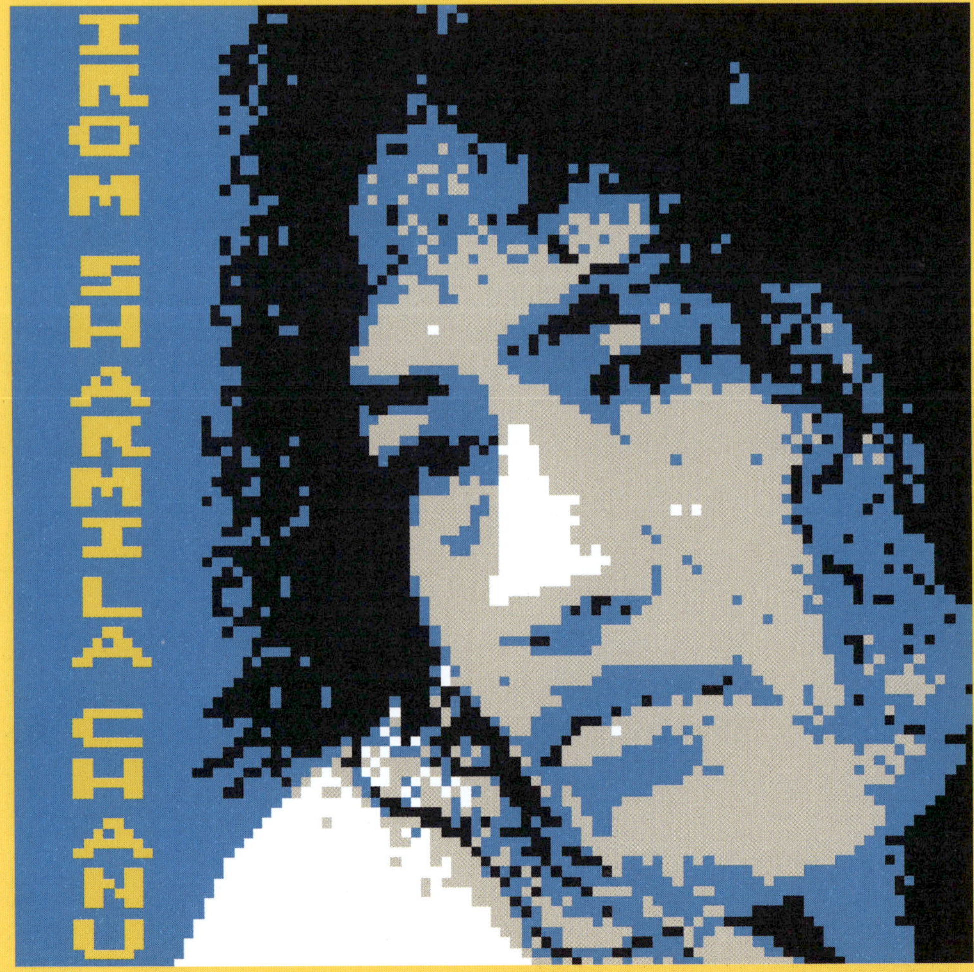

Irom Sharmila Chanu is one of India's most prominent civil rights activists, having withstood a sixteen-year hunger strike in protest against a controversial security law in her home state of Manipur in northeastern India. An international symbol of perseverance, hers was one of the longest-running hunger strikes on record, according to Human Rights Watch and Amnesty International. For much of her protest, Sharmila was detained in a hospital in Imphal, the capital of Manipur, where she was force-fed through a tube in her nose under a law that prohibits suicide.

Prompted by the death of ten civilians who were shot by the military while waiting at a bus stop in Manipur, Sharmila began her indefinite fast against a law called the Armed Forces (Special Powers) Act, or AFSPA, on November 5, 2000. The AFSPA was enacted by the Indian Parliament in 1958 to stem secessionist insurgency movements in seven northeastern states, including Manipur. The law gives security officials special enforcement powers and protects them against civilian prosecution. According to Amnesty International and other human rights groups, the AFSPA in Manipur has provided impunity for perpetrators of grave human rights violations, including extrajudicial executions, enforced disappearances, rape, torture and other ill treatment, and excessive use of force. International bodies, including the United Nations, have argued for a repeal of the law on human rights grounds. A three-member panel appointed by India's Supreme Court said in a 2013 report that security forces acting under the law were committing human rights violations. "What I am doing is just an intervention as a concerned citizen of my contemporary democratic society," Sharmila explained.

Abhirr VP, senior campaigner with Amnesty International India, said, "Irom Sharmila's hunger strike over the last sixteen years has been a testament to her passion for human rights, and her belief that a draconian law like the AFSPA has no place in any society. The government arrested her, confined her to a hospital room, and force-fed her for sixteen years, seemingly to break her will. There was zero dialogue. A peaceful protest was criminalized."

On August 9, 2016, Sharmila ended her fast and was subsequently released. She has used her newfound freedom to run in the state elections in Manipur as an independent candidate. "The only way to bring change is the electoral process," she has said. Repealing AFSPA remains her single issue. Eager to enjoy her freedom, she has recently announced plans to marry.

The following interview was conducted by New Delhi–based journalist Krishna Pokharel at the hospital where Irom Sharmila Chanu was incarcerated for much of her historic hunger strike, in the year prior to her release. It is followed by a short excerpt from one of Sharmila's letters, where she expresses gratitude for the postcards she received from *Yours Truly*.

Opposite: LEGO portrait of Irom Sharmila Chanu by Ai Weiwei.

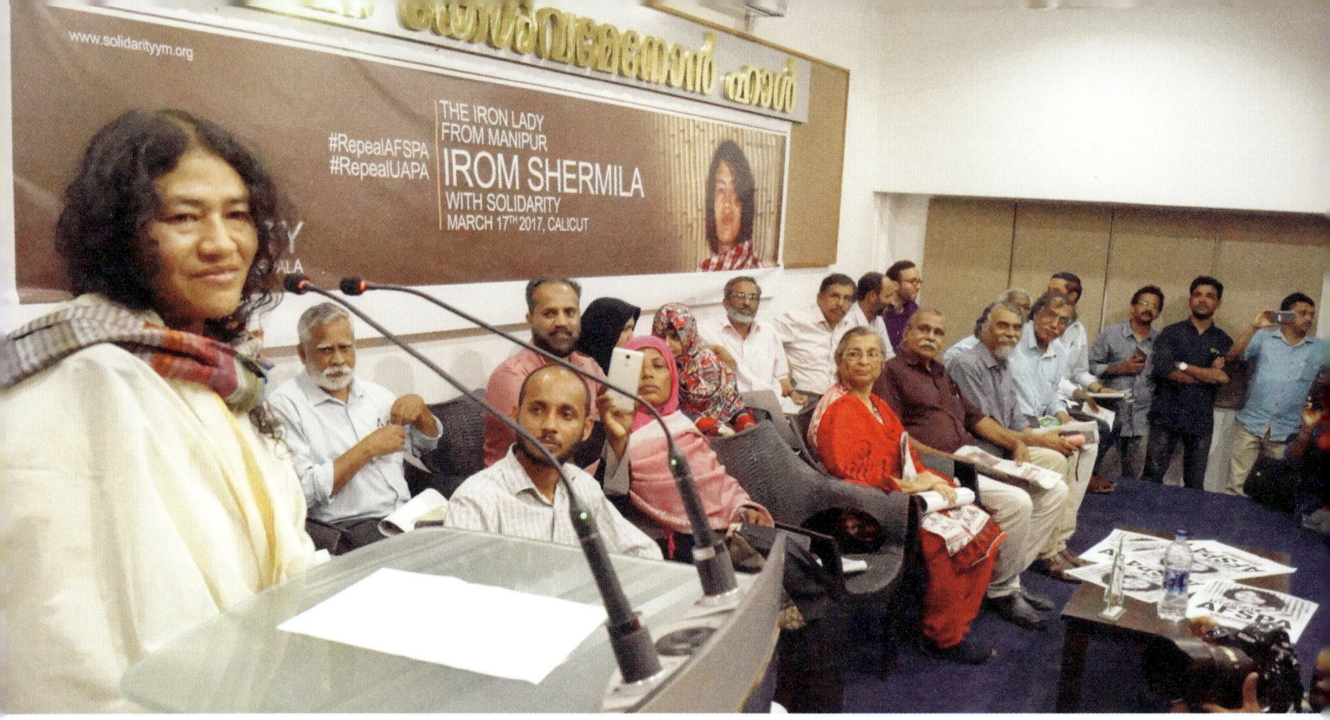

Krishna Pokharel: What motivated you to protest the Armed Forces (Special Powers) Act (AFSPA)?

Irom Sharmila Chanu: After the shootings on November 2, 2000, by paramilitary forces in which ten civilians died in Imphal, a curfew was imposed for two days in the city. I saw the bloodied pictures of the civilians in the newspapers the next day, the scene of the shock and empty roads and streets—a scene of devastation. I felt it was unusual, unnatural, and man made, and that we should intervene to not let it happen again.

I felt people needed to know about the Armed Forces (Special Powers) Act under which the security forces were operating. Why and how was it imposed? From children to adults, everybody needs to know about it. We need some realization about the real situation of our society, our condition, our predicament. Then I resolved to fast.

PK: What is your main concern about the AFSPA?

ISC: Under the imposition of this Act, innocent people are harassed daily, continually—the raping of women, the disappearances of students due to the mere suspicion of their being revolutionaries by the armies. People are killed in fake encounters [extra-judicial killings]. There are thousands of victims here in Manipur affected by the Armed Forces (Special Powers) Act. In short, what I am doing is just against wrong governance: an intervention as a concerned citizen of my contemporary democratic society.

PK: Do you want other people to join your movement?

ISC: Why not? I am a social being. I don't like living alone, isolated as if in a jungle. But people remain just analyzing what I am doing and they want me to stand on a pedestal without a voice, making a statue of me. But I am against it because I have bad sides and good sides. Why should they worship me after my passing away from this Earth, like a goddess or saint or nun? Instead, I want them to support me physically. I need their support.

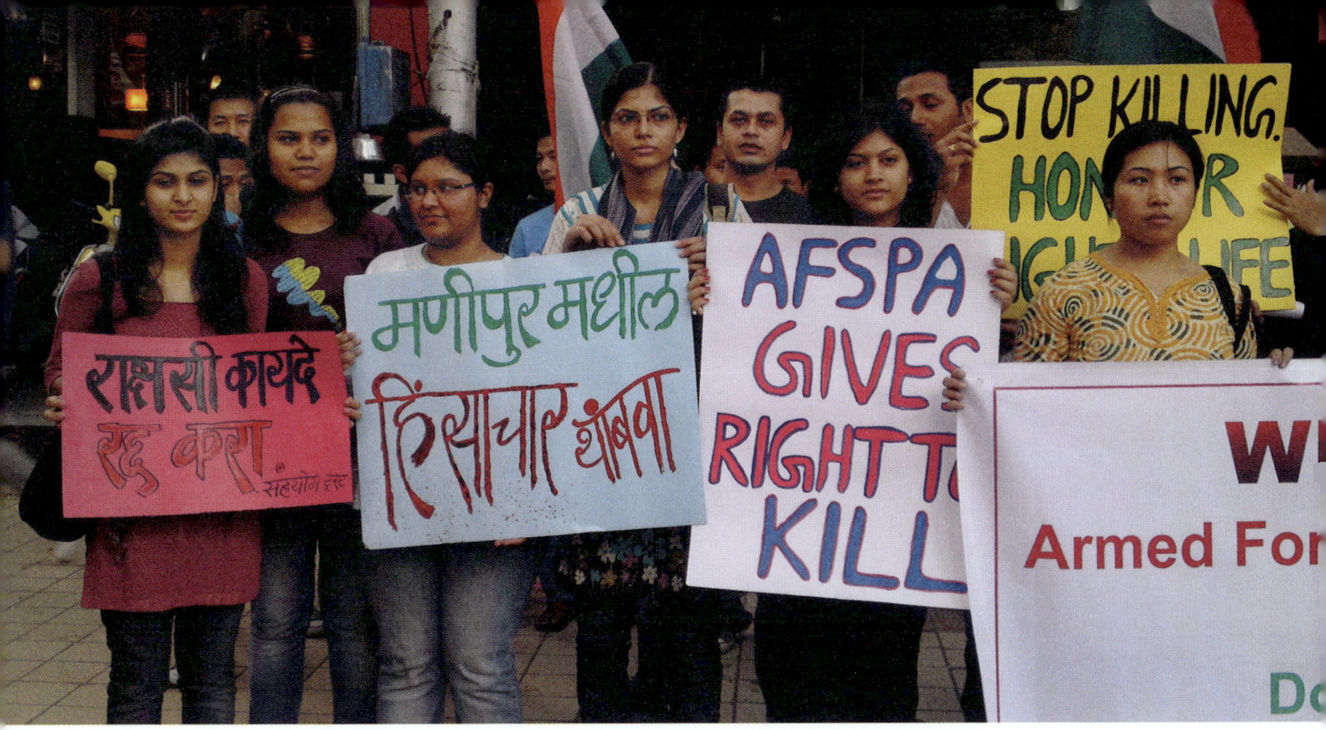

Above: Protesters take to the streets to advocate for the repealing of the Armed Forces (Special Powers) Act, Manipur, India, 2017.

Opposite: A reception given for Irom Sharmila Chanu by the Solidarity Youth Movement, Kozhikode, India, March 26, 2017.

PK: Would you encourage others to go on hunger strike against the law?

ISC: No, no. I just want them awakened. I want to influence them, but I don't want them to follow me in my tactics. I want to remind them that we, as rational beings, as social beings, as democratic citizens, need to question if the law that is meant to serve us is turned against us, to harass us, to torture us, to kill us. I want them to raise their voices against this law. I want them to join my struggle. I just demand their full moral support.

PK: What message do you have for the armed insurgents and the Indian government?

ISC: I want them not to use arms. But in a society, we need revolutions for betterment, to be uplifted. But revolutions without arms. We need a revolution with love and kindness.

Recently (on November 30, 2016), the prime minister of India, Mr. Narendra Modi, came to Manipur for the closing ceremony of Sangai festival [a local tourism festival]. I did not expect his visit to me, but it was a dream that he would. I want to press the prime minister: If you repeal that very repressive law from the northeast region, the revolutionaries who are all against your visit will change their mindset. I want to convince him.

The mentality of armed revolutionaries is very contradictory to [that of] we the normal, innocent people. They want to see us as equal to the people of mainland India and they know that we are exploited and face racism elsewhere in the country because our features are different. But they are exploiting that fact to serve their cause.

There are Indian parliamentarians who are totally against the removal of the Armed Forces (Special Powers) Act. They say we are rebellious, anti-nationalist people. They think that to govern India, for India's integration, we need this act, because once it is removed, we will press for liberation from India. It will just lead to India's disintegration, they fear. They are scared. They are just waiting to weaken me, which is impossible, because my protest is based on my

"We need a revolution of love and kindness."

conscience, my philosophy as a rational being. Without others' persuasion or instigation, I just entered into such a drastic step.

PK: What's your plan for your life if the Armed Forces (Special Powers) Act is repealed?

ISC: I want to enter my normal life—as part of a couple—because I want to taste motherhood. I want to taste all stages of life. I don't want to be a nun or a saint or a goddess or a public figure or a politician or anything. I just want to live as a successful person. Like a harbinger of peace, love, truth—like an angel.

Jawaharlal Nehru Institute of Medical Sciences
Manipur, India
January 7, 2015

A dissident artist from China whose name is Ai Weiwei has already influenced all the continents of the world about me and my cause with his creative art by installing a great exhibition based on prisoners of conscience from across the world, with the aim of spreading awareness of our forced imprisonment and the repression of voices of truth throughout world. I gathered all this information only after I read through all the postcards—around 2,500 in number. I received the first batch February 5, 2015, in two big boxes enclosing ten bundles; the second batch arrived on February 21, which held around four hundred cards. I was so pleased upon receiving such a great number of letters at one time. It has broadened my view toward my struggle. I felt indebted to all those well-wishers from across the world. I felt the impact of their daily prayers for my freedom with victory.

Irom Sharmila Chanu
March 18, 2015

Below: Irom Sharmila Chanu runs for office in Manipur, India, 2017.

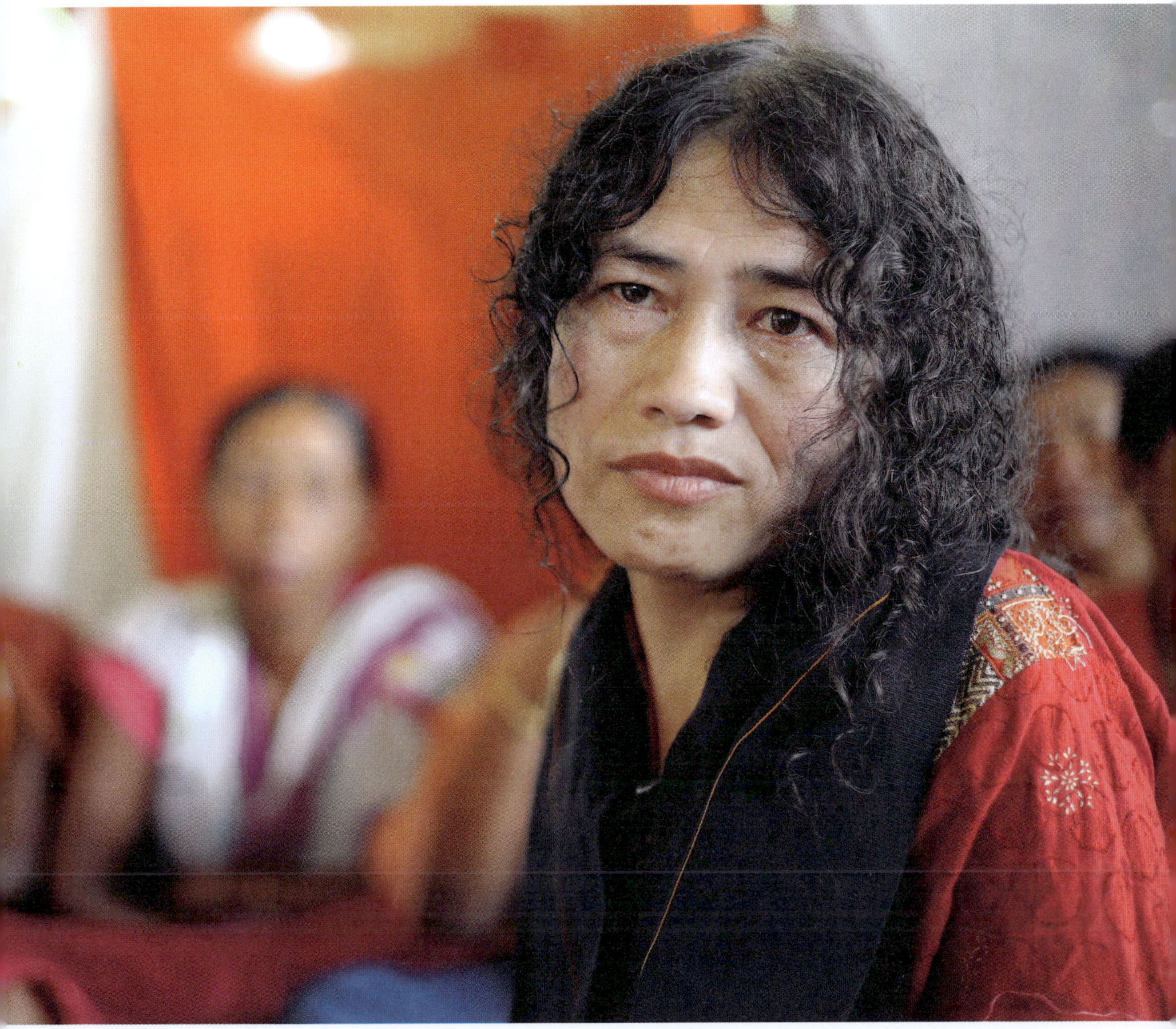

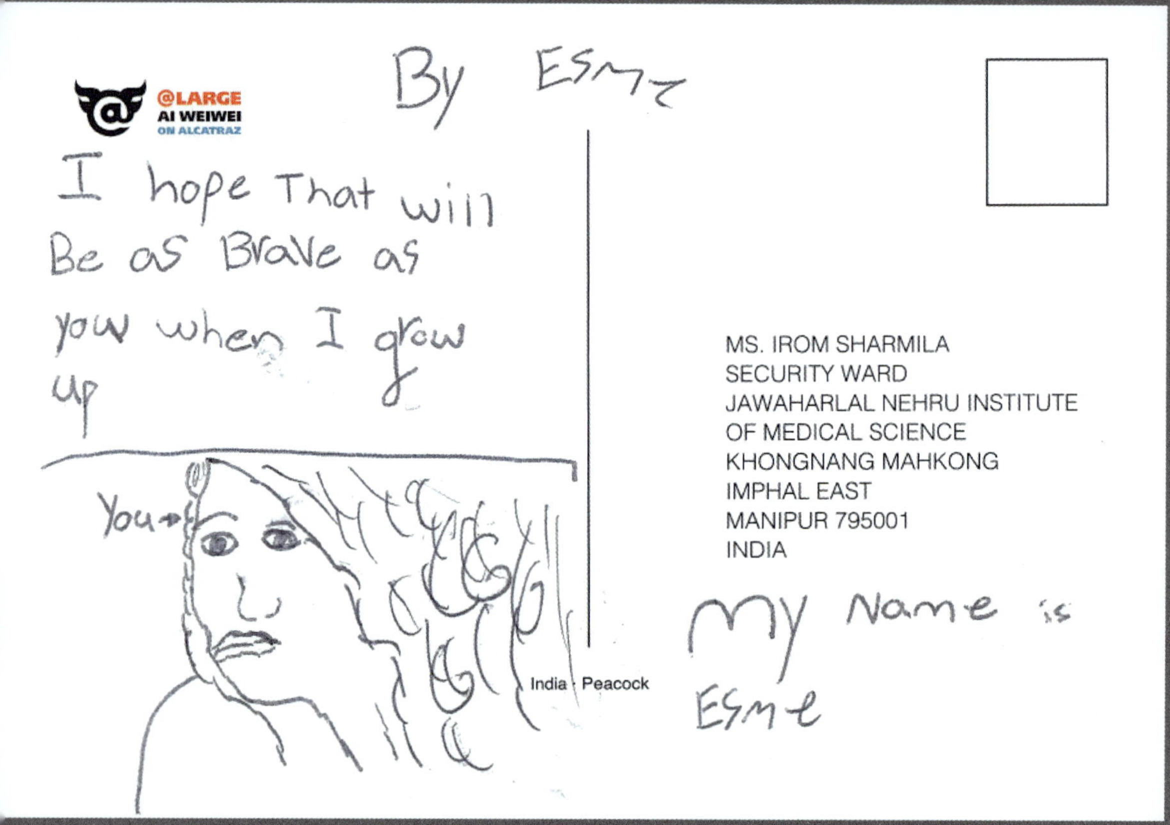
@LARGE
AI WEIWEI
ON ALCATRAZ
By Esme
I hope That will Be as Brave as you when I grow up
You→
MS. IROM SHARMILA
SECURITY WARD
JAWAHARLAL NEHRU INSTITUTE
OF MEDICAL SCIENCE
KHONGNANG MAHKONG
IMPHAL EAST
MANIPUR 795001
INDIA
India · Peacock
My Name is Esme

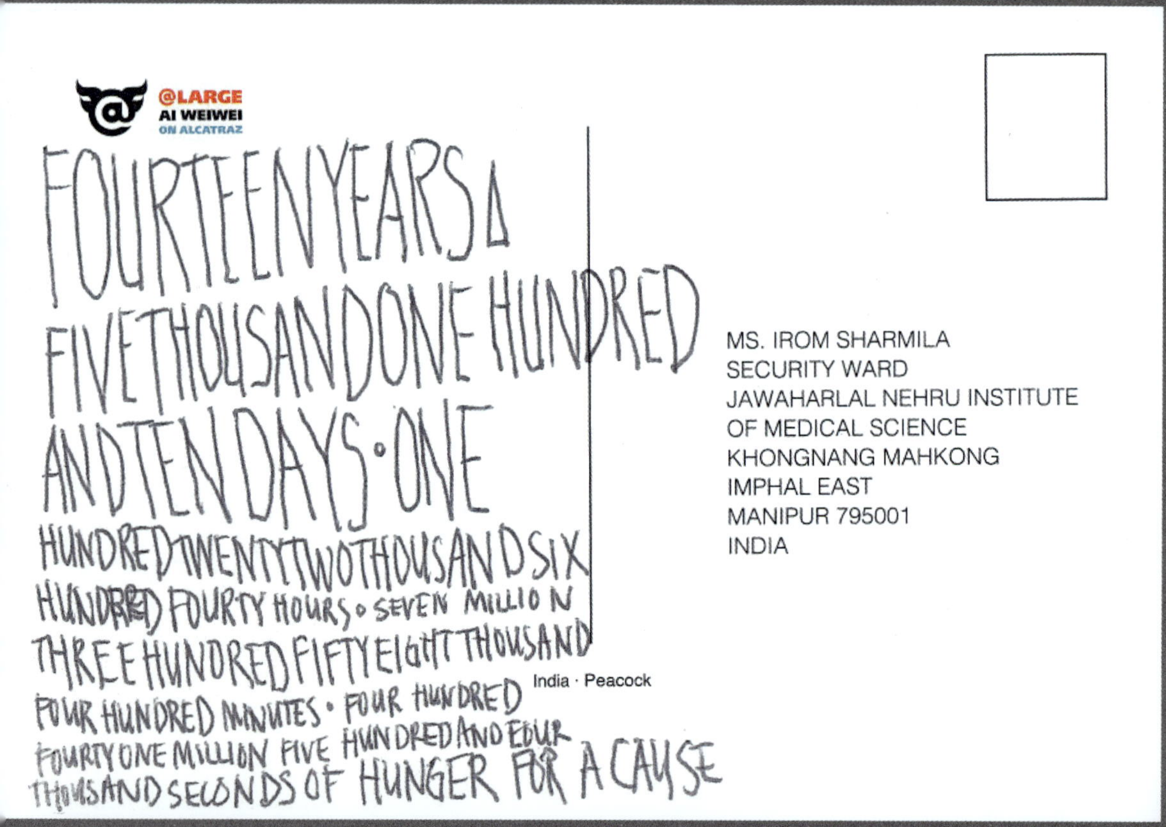
@LARGE
AI WEIWEI
ON ALCATRAZ
FOURTEEN YEARS Δ FIVE THOUSAND ONE HUNDRED AND TEN DAYS • ONE HUNDRED TWENTY TWO THOUSAND SIX HUNDRED FOURTY HOURS • SEVEN MILLION THREE HUNDRED FIFTY EIGHT THOUSAND FOUR HUNDRED MINUTES • FOUR HUNDRED FOURTY ONE MILLION FIVE HUNDRED AND FOUR THOUSAND SECONDS OF HUNGER FOR A CAUSE
MS. IROM SHARMILA
SECURITY WARD
JAWAHARLAL NEHRU INSTITUTE
OF MEDICAL SCIENCE
KHONGNANG MAHKONG
IMPHAL EAST
MANIPUR 795001
INDIA
India · Peacock

@LARGE
AI WEIWEI
ON ALCATRAZ

Funny.
They make you eat, yet they can't seem to swallow the truth.

MS. IROM SHARMILA
SECURITY WARD
JAWAHARLAL NEHRU INSTITUTE
OF MEDICAL SCIENCE
KHONGNANG MAHKONG
IMPHAL EAST
MANIPUR 795001
INDIA

India · Indian Lotus

@LARGE
AI WEIWEI
ON ALCATRAZ

Dear Ms. Irom Sharmila,
We recently visited Kashmir and Ladakh, and were horrified by the level of militarization and the daily harassment that the population is subject to. Thank you for your courage and commitment!

Lisa & Samia

MS. IROM SHARMILA
SECURITY WARD
JAWAHARLAL NEHRU INSTITUTE
OF MEDICAL SCIENCE
KHONGNANG MAHKONG
IMPHAL EAST
MANIPUR 795001
INDIA

India · Indian Lotus

@LARGE
AI WEIWEI
ON ALCATRAZ

You are not alone. You are not unheard. You are a light even if you are currently experiencing darkness. Thank you for being so brave in standing up for what you believe in. The civilians who died can rest in peace with your dedication of love.

—Georgia

MS. IROM SHARMILA
SECURITY WARD
JAWAHARLAL NEHRU INSTITUTE
OF MEDICAL SCIENCE
KHONGNANG MAHKONG
IMPHAL EAST
MANIPUR 795001
INDIA

India · Indian Lotus

@LARGE
AI WEIWEI
ON ALCATRAZ

Dear Irom Sharmila,

"The life you live is the lesson you teach" — no words can sing more true to the person you have chosen to be. Your being comprised of your choices and actions means something — it has inspired countless people to embrace who they are and stand up strongly for what they believe in. Thank you for your courage, conscience, and resilience — I wish you continued strength & fortitude!

Smiles, Angela — San Francisco, California

MS. IROM SHARMILA
SECURITY WARD
JAWAHARLAL NEHRU INSTITUTE
OF MEDICAL SCIENCE
KHONGNANG MAHKONG
IMPHAL EAST
MANIPUR 795001
INDIA

India · Peacock

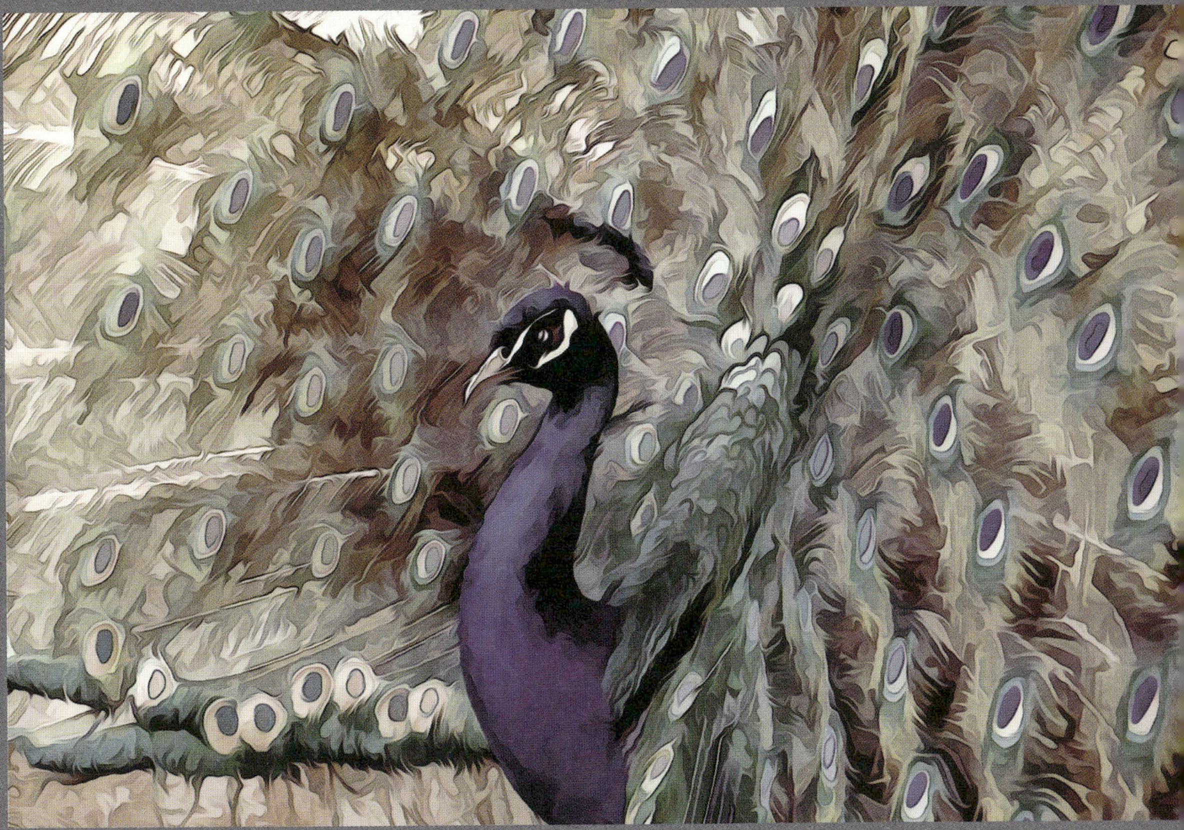

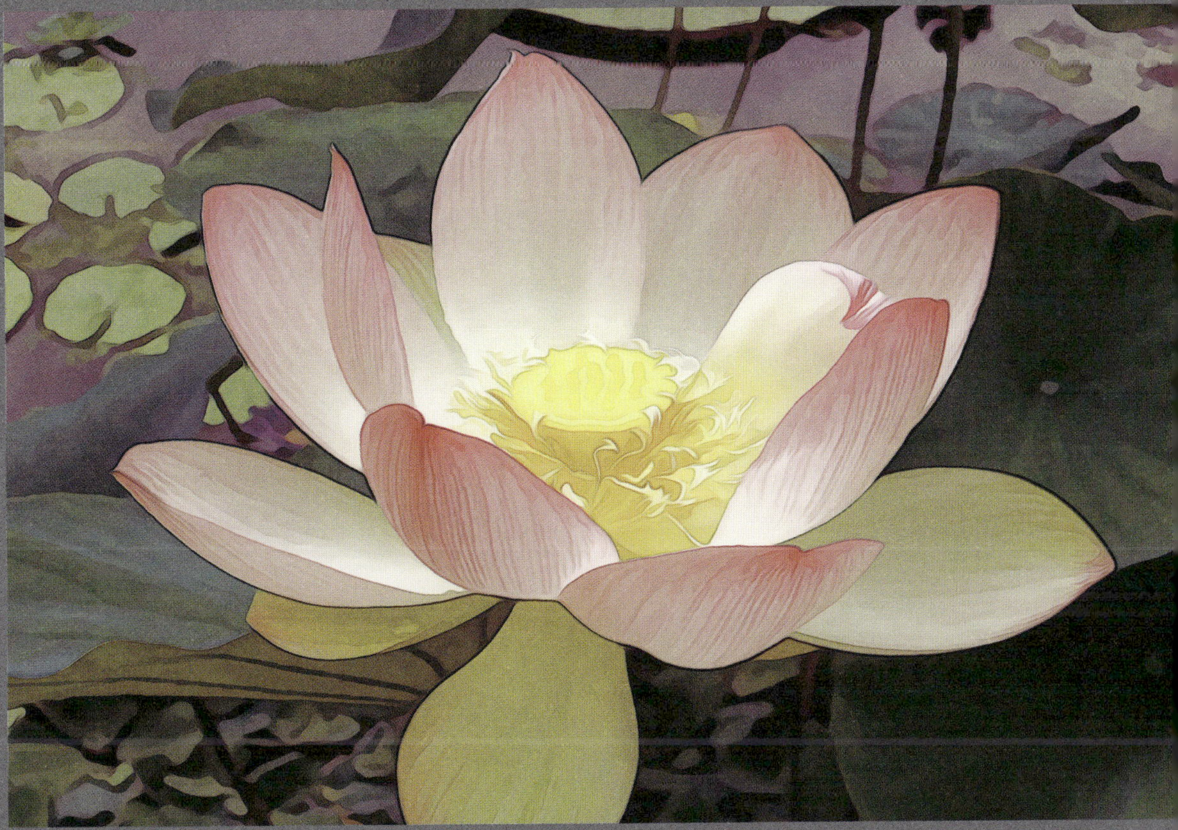

Image Credits

The photographs in this book come from a variety of sources and are either copyrighted or subject to other use restrictions. Please contact the individual or archive cited with use-related questions.

Page 6: Alcatraz Island seen from the San Francisco Bay. Image by Ben Fash, courtesy of Golden Gate National Recreation Area.

Page 8: Main cell house, Alcatraz Island. Image by Jan Stürmann, courtesy of the FOR-SITE Foundation.

Page 10: Ai Weiwei, *Yours Truly*, 2014 (detail); interactive installation: custom-designed postcards, racks, and furniture; part of *@Large: Ai Weiwei on Alcatraz*, Alcatraz Island, 2014–2015. Image by Robert Divers Herrick, courtesy of the artist and the FOR-SITE Foundation.

Page 12: Ai Weiwei, *Yours Truly*, 2014 (detail); interactive installation: custom-designed postcards, racks, and furniture; part of *@Large: Ai Weiwei on Alcatraz*, Alcatraz Island, 2014–2015. Image by Eric Gregory Powell, courtesy of the artist and the FOR-SITE Foundation.

Page 14: Ai Weiwei, *Trace*, 2014; installation: LEGO plastic bricks; part of *@Large: Ai Weiwei on Alcatraz*, Alcatraz Island, 2014–2015. Image by Robert Divers Herrick, courtesy of the artist and the FOR-SITE Foundation.

Page 16: Ai Weiwei, *Refraction*, 2014 (detail); installation: Tibetan solar panels, steel; part of *@Large: Ai Weiwei on Alcatraz*, Alcatraz Island, 2014–2015. Image by Robert Divers Herrick, courtesy of the FOR-SITE Foundation.

Page 18: Ai Weiwei, *With Wind*, 2014 (detail); installation: handmade kites (paper, silk, and bamboo); part of *@Large: Ai Weiwei on Alcatraz*, Alcatraz Island, 2014–2015. Image by Robert Divers Herrick, courtesy of the FOR-SITE Foundation.

Page 20: Ai Weiwei, *Stay Tuned*, 2014 (detail); sound installation: custom-made furniture, audio files, speakers; part of *@Large: Ai Weiwei on Alcatraz*, Alcatraz Island, 2014–2015. Image by Jan Sturmann, courtesy of the FOR-SITE Foundation.

Page 22: Ai Weiwei, *Illumination*, 2014 (detail); sound installation: audio files, speakers; part of *@Large: Ai Weiwei on Alcatraz*, Alcatraz Island, 2014–2015. Image by Robert Divers Herrick, courtesy of the FOR-SITE Foundation.

Page 24: Ai Weiwei, *Blossom*, 2014 (detail); installation: porcelain, hospital fixtures (sinks, toilets, bathtubs); part of *@Large: Ai Weiwei on Alcatraz*, Alcatraz Island, 2014–2015. Image by Robert Divers Herrick, courtesy of the FOR-SITE Foundation.

Page 28: Former Iraqi-American prisoner of conscience Shakir Hamoodi with a stack of *Yours Truly* postcards he received during his incarceration, 2014. Image courtesy of the FOR-SITE Foundation.

Page 30: Bags of completed postcards were routinely collected from Alcatraz Island for processing. Image by Robert Divers Herrick, courtesy of the artist and the FOR-SITE Foundation.

Page 35: Ai Weiwei with FOR-SITE executive director Cheryl Haines at the artist's Beijing studio, spring 2014. Image by Jan Stürmann, courtesy of the FOR-SITE Foundation.

Page 38: Ai Weiwei, *S.A.C.R.E.D. (Accusers)*, 2011–2013; fiberglass and iron; overall dimensions: 148⅜ × 78 × 60⅕ inches. Image courtesy of Ai Weiwei Studio.

Page 40: Ai Weiwei in front of the door to his Beijing studio, 2014. Image by Jan Stürmann, courtesy of the FOR-SITE Foundation.

Page 44: Yorm Bopha raises her fists in defiance as she is placed in van and returned to Prey Sar Prison, Phnom Penh, Cambodia, March 27, 2013.

Page 47: Postcards pre-addressed to prisoners freed during the *@Large: Ai Weiwei on Alcatraz* exhibition. Image courtesy of the artist and the FOR-SITE Foundation.

Page 48: Completed *Yours Truly* postcards, sorted by country and prepared for mailing, 2014. Image by Tyler Reed, courtesy of the artist and the FOR-SITE Foundation.

Pages 50–55: Visitors to *@Large* completing postcards destined for prisoners of conscience. Images by Nina Dietzel, courtesy of the artist and the FOR-SITE Foundation.

Pages 56–57: A sampling of the thousands of *Yours Truly* postcards completed during *@Large: Ai Weiwei on Alcatraz*. Courtesy of the artist and the FOR-SITE Foundation.

Pages 58–59: Postcard art featured in *Yours Truly*. Courtesy of the artist and the FOR-SITE Foundation.

Page 63: Cellhouse bars on Alcatraz Island. Image by Alison Taggart-Barone, courtesy of Golden Gate National Recreation Area.

Page 64: Ai Weiwei, *Yours Truly*, 2014; interactive installation: custom-designed postcards, racks, and furniture; part of *@Large: Ai Weiwei on Alcatraz*, Alcatraz Island, 2014–2015. Image by Eric Gregory Powell, courtesy of the artist and the FOR-SITE Foundation.

Page 66: LEGO portrait of John Kiriakou by Ai Weiwei. Image courtesy of the artist and the FOR-SITE Foundation.

Page 70: Members of Witness Against Torture and Amnesty International dressed as Guantanamo detainees protesting in front of the US Supreme Court to mark the detention center's eleventh anniversary. Image by Justin Norman / Shrieking Tree.

Page 73: John Kiriakou, in a still from director James Spione's film *Silenced*, 2014. Image courtesy of James Spione / Morninglight Films.

Pages 74–77: A selection of *Yours Truly* postcards addressed to John Kiriakou. Courtesy of the artist and the FOR-SITE Foundation.

Page 78: LEGO portrait of Ahmed Maher by Ai Weiwei. Image courtesy of the artist and the FOR-SITE Foundation.

Page 83: Egyptian protesters in Tahrir Square during a mass rally marking the first anniversary of the uprising, Cairo, January 25, 2012. Image by Gigi Ibrhaim / Wikimedia Commons.

Page 85: Ahmed Maher participating in a discussion at the official launch of United Nations Human Rights Day at the Ford Foundation, New York, December 10, 2012. Image by John Gillespie / Wikimedia Commons.

Pages 86–89: A selection of *Yours Truly* postcards addressed to Ahmed Maher. Courtesy of the artist and the FOR-SITE Foundation.

Page 90: LEGO portrait of Chelsea Manning by Ai Weiwei. Image courtesy of the artist and the FOR-SITE Foundation.

Page 92: Marchers in the Twin Cities Pride parade carrying signs in support of Chelsea Manning, Minneapolis, Minnesota, 2014. Image by Tony Webster / Wikimedia Commons.

Page 95: Chelsea Manning and Ai Weiwei, Washington, D.C., June 27, 2017. Photo by Ai Weiwei, courtesy Ai Weiwei Studio.

Page 96: Graffiti calling for Chelsea Manning's release, Vienna, Austria, 2014. Image by Smuconlaw /Wikimedia Commons.

Page 97: Still image from classified video footage leaked by Chelsea Manning showing Reuters employee Saneed Chmagh being killed by American military forces during an airstrike in Baghdad, Iraq, July 12, 2017. Image courtesy of WikiLeaks.

Pages 98–101: A selection of *Yours Truly* postcards addressed to Chelsea Manning. Courtesy of the artist and the FOR-SITE Foundation.

Page 103: LEGO portrait of Ebrahim Sharif Al Sayed by Ai Weiwei. Image courtesy of the artist and the FOR-SITE Foundation.

Page 106: Protesters seeking democratic reforms in Sitra, Bahrain, February 18, 2011. Image by Al Jazeera English / Wikimedia Commons.

Page 107: The family of Ebrahim Sharif Al Sayed poses with their completed *Yours Truly* postcards during their visit to *@Large: Ai Weiwei on Alcatraz*, April 26, 2015. From left to right: Farida Ghulam, Sharif Al Sayed, Yara Al Sayed, and Aseel Al Sayed. Image courtesy of Aseel Al Sayad.

Page 109: Ebrahim Sharif Al Sayed giving a speech. Image courtesy of Wa'ad (National Democratic Action Society).

Pages 110–113: A selection of *Yours Truly* postcards addressed to Ebrahim Sharif Al Sayed. Courtesy of the artist and the FOR-SITE Foundation.

Page 114: LEGO portrait of Irom Sharmila Chanu by Ai Weiwei. Image courtesy of the artist and the FOR-SITE Foundation.

Page 116: A reception given for Irom Sharmila Chanu by the Solidarity Youth Movement, Kozhikode, India, March 26, 2017. Image by Zuhairali / Wikimedia Commons.

Page 117: Protesters take to the streets to advocate for the repealing of Armed Forces (Special Powers) Act, Manipur, India, 2012. Image courtesy of Kamayani Bali-Mahaba.

Page 119: Irom Sharmila Chanu runs for office in Manipur, India, 2017. Image by Akhil Kumar.

Pages 120–123: A selection of *Yours Truly* postcards addressed to Irom Charmila Chanu. Courtesy of the artist and the FOR-SITE Foundation.

Front and back flaps: Postcard art featured in *Yours Truly*. Courtesy of the artist and the FOR-SITE Foundation.

Front flap: LEGO portrait of Ilham Tohti by Ai Weiwei. Image courtesy of the artist and the FOR-SITE Foundation.

Front flap: LEGO portrait of Fomusoh Ivo Feh by Ai Weiwei. Image courtesy of the artist and the FOR-SITE Foundation.

Back flap: LEGO portrait of Andualem Arage by Ai Weiwei. Image courtesy of the artist and the FOR-SITE Foundation.

Back flap: LEGO portrait of Tran Huynh Duy Thuc by Ai Weiwei. Image courtesy of the artist and the FOR-SITE Foundation.

Text Credits

Pages 27, 67, 79, 91, 103, and 115: LEGO® is a trademark of the LEGO group of companies.

Page 27: Mandela, Nelson, *Long Walk to Freedom*, 1994

Page 27: Text by Margaret Mead used under license from the Mead Trust.

Page 104–108: Texts by Farida Ghulam and Sharif Al Sayed first appeared on the Index on Censorship website (http://www.indexoncensorship.org). Reprinted with permission from the authors.

Page 116–118: Interview with Irom Sharmila Chanu reprinted with permission of the *Wall Street Journal*. © 2015, Dow Jones & Company, Inc. All Rights Reserved Worldwide. License number 4118990193614.

Acknowledgments

The editor extends his deepest gratitude to the following people for their assistance in making this publication possible: Madison Donzis, Michelle McElroy, and Aseel Al Sayed, for their invaluable help in liaising with Chelsea Manning; Ahmed Maher, and the family of Ebrahim Sharif Al Sayed, respectively; Zeke Johnson, Senior Director of Programs, Amnesty International USA, and the Amnesty team worldwide, for their expert advice; Nina Dietzel, whose images of the visitors to Alcatraz Island are rendered with unparalleled empathy and grace; and the many other photographers who generously allowed their work to be reproduced here: Divya Adusumilli, Robert Divers Herrick, Justin Norman, Eric Gregory Powell, Adam Ramsey, Tyler Reed, James Spione, and Jan Stürmann; designer Jen Burke, for updating her indelible *@Large* logo for a second life within these pages; Jackie von Treskow and Alison Konecki from the FOR-SITE Foundation, whose collective good humor and tenacity moves mountains; Cheryl Haines, whose vision and passion fueled the creation of *@Large* and this publication; Ai Weiwei, an artist with an unwavering commitment to human rights; and those brave activists and prisoners of conscience around the world who continue to inspire us and to better our world.

Contributors

Ai Weiwei is among the world's most celebrated contemporary artists and an outspoken critic of injustice, both in China and abroad. His sculptures, photographs, installations, and public artworks often repurpose recognizable forms and materials—from ancient Chinese ceramics to life vests worn by Syrian refugees—to address today's most pressing contemporary social concerns. An ardent human rights activist, Ai was arrested by Chinese authorities on April 3, 2011, and held incommunicado for eighty-one days. For over four years following his release, he was prohibited from traveling abroad and subjected to ongoing government surveillance. Having relocated to Berlin, Ai continues to extend his practice across multiple disciplines, using exhibitions and social media to communicate with a global public. His latest project, *Human Flow*, is a documentary film addressing the plight of refugees worldwide.

Cheryl Haines is principal of Haines Gallery and founding executive director of the FOR-SITE Foundation, both organizations located in San Francisco. She was the curator of *@Large: Ai Weiwei on Alcatraz*. For over thirty years, Haines has developed exhibitions and site-specific public programs that have exposed new audiences to contemporary art and advanced the discourse on art about place. Haines's dynamic curatorial stance presents challenging and provocative exhibitions by artists who explore cultural and environmental issues through a wide range of media, as well as public, site-specific commissions on a national scale.

Jasmine Heiss has worked on criminal justice issues, including solitary confinement, mass incarceration, and police accountability, at the local, national, and global level. As the senior campaigner for the Individuals at Risk Program for Amnesty International USA, she helped to achieve victories including the passage of the U.S.'s first reparations package for police torture survivors. She also helped secure the release of two of the longest held prisoners in solitary confinement, Herman Wallace and Albert Woodfox of the Angola 3. A frequent commentator and writer, Heiss has been cited in publications including the Associated Press, CNN, the *New York Times*, and NPR. Heiss now serves as the director of coalitions and outreach at the Coalition for Public Safety.

David Spalding is an internationally recognized writer, curator, and editor based in San Francisco, where he serves as executive director of Haines Gallery and consulting editor for the FOR-SITE Foundation. Over the past decade, he has published more than one hundred texts on contemporary art, contributing regularly to monographs and periodicals such as *Artforum* and *Frieze*. His most recent books are *@Large: Ai Weiwei on Alcatraz*, *The King of Kowloon: The Art of Tsang Tsou-choi*, and *Doublethink: Kata Legrady and Wang Luyan*. Previously, Spalding was curator at the Ullens Center for Contemporary Art in Beijing.